1st Workshop on Tools and Resources to Empower People with REAding DIfficulties (READI 2020)

Marseille, France
11-16 May 2020

Editors:

Núria Gala
Rodrigo Wilkens

ISBN: 978-1-7138-1275-3

LREC 2020 Workshop
Language Resources and Evaluation Conference
11–16 May 2020

**1st Workshop on Tools and Resources to Empower People
with REAding DIfficulties (READI)**

PROCEEDINGS

Edited by
Núria Gala and Rodrigo Wilkens

Proceedings of the LREC 2020 first workshop on Tools and Resources to Empower People with REAding DIfficulties (READI)

Edited by: Núria Gala and Rodrigo Wilkens

For more information:
European Language Resources Association (ELRA)
9 rue des Cordelières
75013, Paris
France
http://www.elra.info
Email: lrec@elda.org

Preface

Recent studies show that the number of children and adults facing difficulties in reading and understanding written texts is steadily growing. Reading challenges can show up early on and may include reading accuracy, speed, or comprehension to the extent that the impairment interferes with academic achievement or activities of daily life. Various technologies (text customization, text simplification, text to speech devices, screening for readers through games and web applications, to name a few) have been developed to help poor readers to get better access to information as well as to support reading development. Among those technologies, text simplification is a powerful way to leverage document accessibility by using NLP techniques.

The "First Workshop on Tools and Resources to Empower People with REAding DIfficulties" (READI), collocated with the "International Conference on Language Resources and Evaluation" (LREC 2020), aims at presenting current state-of-the-art techniques and achievements for text simplification together with existing reading aids and resources for lifelong learning, addressing a variety of domains and languages, including natural language processing, linguistics, psycholinguistics, psychophysics of vision and education. A particular focus is put on methods, tools and resources obtained through automatic text adaptation, ultimately addressed to children struggling with difficulties in learning to read, to the community of teachers, to speech-language pathologists, to parents seeking solutions, and to those professionals involved with adults struggling with reading (e.g. illiterates, aphasic readers and low vision readers).

These proceedings comprise the papers of the workshop, initially foreseen for May 11, 2020, in Marseille (France), but postponed at the time of preparing these proceedings due to the COVID-19 situation around the world. 21 propositions have been submitted from 62 different authors from 12 different countries (France 5, UK 4, Italy 2, Spain 2, Sweden 2, Switzerland 2, Belgium 1, Brazil 1, Germany 1, Iceland 1, Netherlands 1, Pakistan 1). The total rate of accepted papers is 66% (14 papers), 5 of them chosen as oral presentations and 9 for the poster session. READI also features one invited speaker, Arne Jönsson from Linköping University.

We are thankful to the authors who submitted their work to this workshop, to our Program Committee members for their contributions, to the reviewers and the additional reviewers who did a thorough job reviewing submissions, to Arne Jönsson who kindly accepted to be our invited speaker, and to LREC committee for including this workshop into their program.

Núria Gala and Rodrigo Wilkens

Organizers:

Delphine Bernhard, Université de Strasbourg, France
Thomas François, Université catholique de Louvain, Belgium
Núria Gala, Aix Marseille Université, France
Daria Goriachun, Aix Marseille Université, France
Ludivine Javourey-Drevet, Aix Marseille Université, France
Anne Laure Ligozat, Université Paris Sud, France
Horacio Saggion, Université Pompeu Fabra, Catalonia, Spain
Amalia Todirascu, Université de Strasbourg, France
Rodrigo Wilkens, University of Essex, United Kingdom
Johannes Ziegler, Aix Marseille Université, France

Program Committee:

Delphine Bernhard, Université de Strasbourg, France
Dominique Brunato, ILC, Pisa, Italy
Eric Castet, Aix Marseille Université, France
Thomas François, Université catholique de Louvain, Belgium
Núria Gala, Aix Marseille Université, France
Arne Jönsson, Linköping University, Sweden
Ekaterina Kochmar, University of Cambridge, United Kingdom
Anne Laure Ligozat, Université Paris Sud, France
Detmar Meurers, Université de Tübingen, Germany
Ildiko Pilan, University of Oslo, Norway
Horacio Saggion, Université Pompeu Fabra, Catalonia, Spain
Sanja Stajner, Symanto Research, Germany
Anaïs Tack, Université catholique de Louvain, Belgium
Amalia Todirascu, Université de Strasbourg, France
Vincent Vandeghinste, Instituut voor de Nederlandse Taal, Netherlands
Giulia Venturi, ILC, Pisa, Italy
Aline Villavicencio, University of Sheffield, United Kingdom
Elena Volodina, University of Gotheburg, Sweden
Rodrigo Wilkens, University of Essex, United Kingdom
Johannes Ziegler, Aix Marseille Université, France

Additional Reviewers:

Carlos Ramisch, Aix Marseille Université, France
Leonardo Zilio, University of Surrey, United Kingdom
Michael Zock, Aix Marseille Université, France

Invited Speaker:

Arne Jönsson, Linköping University, Sweden

Table of Contents

1st Workshop on Tools and Resources to Empower People with REAding DIfficulties (READI2020), pages 1–5
Language Resources and Evaluation Conference (LREC 2020), Marseille, 11–16 May 2020
© European Language Resources Association (ELRA), licensed under CC-BY-NC

Disambiguating Confusion Sets as an Aid for Dyslexic Spelling

Steinunn Rut Friðriksdóttir, Anton Karl Ingason
Faculty of Icelandic and Comparative Cultural Studies
University of Iceland, Sæmundargata 2, 102 Reykjavík
srf2, antoni@hi.is

Abstract

Spell checkers and other proofreading software are crucial tools for people with dyslexia and other reading disabilities. Most spell checkers automatically detect spelling mistakes by looking up individual words and seeing if they exist in the vocabulary. However, one of the biggest challenges of automatic spelling correction is how to deal with real-word errors, i.e. spelling mistakes which lead to a real but unintended word, such as when *then* is written in place of *than*. These errors account for 20% of all spelling mistakes made by people with dyslexia. As both words exist in the vocabulary, a simple dictionary lookup will not detect the mistake. The only way to disambiguate which word was actually intended is to look at the context in which the word appears. This problem is particularly apparent in languages with rich morphology where there is often minimal orthographic difference between grammatical items. In this paper, we present our novel confusion set corpus for Icelandic and discuss how it could be used for context-sensitive spelling correction. We have collected word pairs from seven different categories, chosen for their homophonous properties, along with sentence examples and frequency information from said pairs. We present a small-scale machine learning experiment using a decision tree binary classification which results range from 73% to 86% average accuracy with 10-fold cross validation. While not intended as a finalized result, the method shows potential and will be improved in future research.

Keywords: homophones, dyslexia, reading disabilities, confusion sets, disambiguation, context dependency, Icelandic

1. Introduction

According to Mody and Silliman, dyslexia accounts for 80% of diagnosed learning disabilities. It causes problems with the mapping process between orthographic and phonological words and parts (Mody and Silliman, 2008). This means that dyslexic individuals might show difficulties in word segmenting as well as phoneme identification and manipulation. There are two main types of orthographic errors considered when evaluating effects of dyslexia on spelling. Phonetically accurate errors include, for example, adding an unnecessary double consonant or omitting a silent letter, resulting in plausible orthographic representations of the phonemes in question. Phonetically inaccurate errors include phoneme omissions, additions and substitutions which cannot be taken to represent the phonemes in the intended word (Bernstein, 2009).

One possible representation of phonetically accurate spelling mistakes is the substitution of homophones. Examples of this include when *then* is written in place of *than* or when *by* is written in place of *buy*. Since these mix-ups result in unintended but valid words, they often go undetected by spell checkers and other proofreading software which would otherwise pick up on an out-of-vocabulary spelling mistake. Bernstein also notes in his paper that these phonetically accurate, orthographic errors are the most prominent ones among spellers with no reading disabilities (Bernstein, 2009). They can therefore prove problematic for anyone relying on automatic spelling correction, regardless of learning disabilities. In this paper, we present a corpus of Icelandic homophones and a potential approach to a context sensitive spelling correction.

This paper is organized as follows: In Section 2, we discuss the task of context-sensitive spelling correction and the case of the morphologically rich Icelandic language. In Section 3, we present the compilation and contents of the Icelandic Confusion Set Corpus (ICoSC). In Section 4, we briefly discuss our machine learning experiments with the corpus. We conclude in Section 5.

2. Context sensitive spelling correction

The idea behind the majority of spell checkers and proofreading software commercially available is to look up an isolated word and to prompt an error message if the word doesn't exist in the vocabulary. While this method is very useful for detecting typos and non-words, mistakes that result in real but unintended words go undetected. As noted by Rello, Ballesteros and Bigham, nearly 20% of the errors that people with dyslexia make are real-word errors and therefore it's vital that the tools that they use can detect these spelling mistakes (Rello et al., 2015). To tackle the homophone substitution problem, another approach to spell checking is needed. Instead of looking at a word in isolation, it's crucial to look at its context to determine which word is most likely to have been intended, given the morphological and semantic aspects of the surrounding words (Golding and Roth, 1999).

2.1. Confusion sets and the case of Icelandic

In a highly inflected language such as Icelandic, the need to disambiguate homophone word pairs is particularly apparent. Due to the morphological richness of the language, there is often very little orthographic difference between grammatical genders or cases for example which can be a great nuisance, not least for dyslexic individuals and L2 learners. As an example, the difference between the nominative and the accusative form of a masculine noun can often be found in the number of *n*'s in its suffix, i.e. *morgunn* (*morning*, nom.) / *morgun* (*morning*, acc.). Another example is that the letter *y* often appears in the subjunctive past tense form of a verb, i.e. *bindi* ('bind', subjunctive, present tense) / *byndi* ('bind', subjunctive, past tense). As an attempt to solve this problem, a confusion set is defined consisting of word candidates that commonly get confused with one another. When a spell checker encounters these words, it tries to evaluate based on the context which candidate from the set is more likely to have been intended.

2.2. Previous work

The problem of automatically correcting real-word errors has been addressed by NLP specialists, particularly for high resource languages such as English. In their 2015 paper, Rello et al. presented a system called *Real Check*, which is based on a probabilistic language model, a statistical dependency parser and Google n-grams. They created confusion sets for Spanish using the Levenshtein Automaton dymamic algorithm in order to combat real-word errors. The results from their system is comparable to the state-of-the-art spell checkers (Rello et al., 2015). In the same year, Rokaya used a combination of the confusion set method and statistical methods to disambiguate semantic errors in Arabic (Rokaya, 2015) and Samani M.H., Rahimi Z. and Rahimi S. addressed real-word spelling mistakes in Persian using n-gram based context retrieval for confusion sets (Samani et al., 2015). Both experiments resulted in around 85-90% precision rate. In the case of Icelandic, Ingason et al. conducted a small-scale experiment in 2009 using feature extraction from the context of confusion set candidates. These features were then fed to the Naive Bayes and Winnow algorithms with promising results. We hope to expand this research in our experiments, using a much larger database than previously available.

3. The Icelandic Confusion Set Corpus

The focus of our research was gathering data for what has now become *The Icelandic Confusion Set Corpus* (hereinafter referred to as the ICoSC). It was compiled during the course of three months in the winter of 2019. This task was only made possible through the 2017 release of the *Icelandic Gigaword Corpus* (IGC) (Steingrímsson et al., 2018), which consists of about 1.3 billion running words of text, tagged morphologically using *IceStagger* (Loftsson and Östling, 2013). The IGC is divided into 6 text categories, including media text, official documents and the text collection of the Árni Magnússon Institute for Icelandic studies. In our project, we cross-referenced the IGC with the *Database of Icelandic Morphology* (Bjarnadóttir et al., 2019) in order to ensure that the dataset would cover as many word pairings as possible. We start by collecting words containing a chosen letter pair (i.e. *y/i*) from the DIM and then collect sentence examples and frequency information from the IGC about those pairs. The end result has been made available under a CC-BY licence on CLARIN-IS, the Icelandic repository for the European Research Infrastructure for Language Resources and Technology.

3.1. Content

The ICoSC consists of seven categories of confusion sets, selected for their linguistic properties as homophones, separated orthographically by a single letter. Each category includes a text file which contains the full list of words from

that category. It also contains a text file containing all sentences from the IGC which contain said word. The sentence examples are organized so that each word from the word list appears, preceded by two semicolons and followed by the appropriate sentence examples. Each line in the sentence examples contains a word and a PoS tag, separated by a tab. The confusion set categories are:

- 196 pairs containing y/i (*leyti 'extent' / leiti 'search'*): In modern Icelandic, there is no phonetic distinction between these sounds (both of which are pronounced as [ɪ]) and thus their distinction is purely historical. The use of y refers to a vowel mutation from another, related word, some of which are derived from Danish. Confusing words that differ only by these letters is therefore very common when writing Icelandic.

- 150 pairs containing ý/í (*sýn 'vision' / sín 'theirs (possessive reflexive)'*): The same goes for these sounds, which are both pronounced as [i]. The original rounding of y and ý started merging with the unrounded counterparts of these sounds in the 14th century and the sounds in question have remained merged since the 17th century (Gunnlaugsson, 1994).

- 1203 pairs containing nn/n (*forvitinn 'curious(masc.)' / forvitin 'curious (fem.)'*): The alveolar nasal [n] is not elongated and therefore there is no real distinction between these sounds in pronunciation (although the preceding vowel to a double n is often elongated). The distinction between them is often grammatical and refers to whether the word has a feminine or masculine grammatical gender. However, the rules on when to write each vary and have plenty of exceptions, many of which are taught as something to remember by heart. It is therefore common for both native and nonnative speakers to make spelling and/or grammar mistakes in these type of words.

- 8 pairs commonly confused by Icelandic speakers: These confusion sets could prove useful in grammar correction as their difference is in their morphological information rather than their orthography. These include for example *mig/mér* (*'me' (accusative) / 'me' (dative)*) which commonly get confused when followed by experiencer-subject verbs (Jónsson and Eythórsson, 2005; Ingason, 2010; Thráinsson, 2013; Nowenstein, 2017).

- 24 pairs containing hv/kv (*hvað 'what' / kvað 'chanted'*): Hv and kv in initial position are homophones for the majority of Icelandic speakers who pronounce both as [kʰv-]. Exceptions to this can be found in Southern Icelanders, where the initial phone is the fricative [x] (Rögnvaldsson, 2013).

- 42 pairs containing rð/ðr (*veðri 'weather' (dative) / verði 'will become'*): Included due to their potential confusability, though they are strictly speaking not homophones. These pairs are often used in tongue twisters.

Word form	Total	POS tags and their frequency	Word form	Total	POS tags and their frequency	Grammatically disjoint	Grammatically identical	Min freq
skyldi	1335	['svg3eþ', 1170, 'svg1eþ', 144, 's	skildi	775	['sfg3eþ', 518, 'sfg1eþ', 203, 's	FALSE	FALSE	775
skyldu	313	['svg3fþ', 173, 'nveo', 103, 'nv	skildu	149	['sfg3fþ', 138, 'svg3fþ', 6, 'sbg	FALSE	FALSE	149
leyst	129	['ssg', 79, 'sþghfn', 30, 'sþgher	leist	118	['sfm3eþ', 114, 'sfg2eþ', 3, 'sfi	TRUE	FALSE	118
breytt	267	['sþghen', 147, 'ssg', 105, 'lhe	breitt	113	['aa', 42, 'lhensf', 26, 'sþghen'	FALSE	FALSE	113
eytt	99	['ssg', 82, 'sþghen', 15, 'lhensf	eitt	3145	['tfheo', 1050, 'foheo', 683, 't	FALSE	FALSE	99
lyst	60	['nveo', 31, 'nveþ', 21, 'ssg', 6,	list	134	['nveo', 54, 'nveþ', 47, 'nven',	FALSE	FALSE	60
skyldum	98	['svg1fþ', 52, 'nvfþ', 28, 'sfg1f	skildum	60	['sfg1fþ', 58, 'nhfþ', 2]	TRUE	FALSE	60
leyti	1105	['nheþ', 866, 'nheo', 239]	leiti	44	['nheþ', 33, 'svg3fn', 4, 'nheþs	FALSE	FALSE	44
ynni	44	['svg3eþ', 37, 'svg1eþ', 7]	inni	1796	['aa', 1775, 'nheþ', 7, 'nkeþ', 4	TRUE	FALSE	44

Figure 1: Frequency table for category y/i

- 110 pairs containing rr/r (*klárri 'smart' (indef. fem. dative) / klári 'smart' (def. masc. nominative)*): Included due to their potential confusability, as the pronunciation difference is only in the preceding vowel, similar to the nn/n-pairs.

The ICoSC also includes CSV spreadsheets which contain all the confusion sets collected for each category and their frequencies. These files are organized in the following way: for each confusion set, each candidate appears with its total frequency in the IGC. The following column shows the frequency of each possible PoS tag for the candidate in question. In the seventh and eight column, binary values appear which refer to whether the confusion set is grammatically disjoint (the two candidates have no PoS tags in common) or grammatically identical (all PoS tags are identical for the two candidates). In the final column, the frequency of the less frequent candidate of the set is shown, which can be used to determine which sets are viable in an experiment. An example of a frequency table can be found in Figure 1. As the n/nn examples are by far the most frequent confusion sets, the corpus also includes a word list and sentence examples for the 55 most frequent sets from that category. All files have UTF-8 encoding.

3.2. Particular uses for dyslexia in Icelandic

According to Sigurmundsdóttir and Torfadóttir (2020), learning disabilities such as dyslexia cause problems in spelling that may be even harder to attack than similar problems in reading. As people with dyslexia have a weaker phonological awareness, the conversion of sounds to orthographic symbols is often problematic. They explain that the most common symptoms of dyslexia in spelling are:

- Omission of letters.

- Difficulties distinguishing between long and short vowels. This is particularly problematic when deciding whether or not there should be a double consonant in Icelandic words, i.e. *áttu (had) / átu* (ate).

- Difficulties distinguishing between voiced and unvoiced consonants, i.e. *magi (stomach) / maki (romantic partner)*.

- Difficulties distinguishing between phonetically similar letters, i.e. *dýr (animal) / dyr (door)*.

- Letter switching.

As at least three of these cases can easily lead to accidental homophone mix-ups in Icelandic, a confusion set classification method is vital for the creation of a context sensitive spelling correction suitable for people with reading disabilities.

3.3. Uses for L2 learners

Another group of people that could benefit in particular from a context-sensitive proofreading software are those who are learning Icelandic as a second language. The number of immigrants living in Iceland has been steadily growing in recent years. In her 2017 pilot study, Arnórsdóttir tried to shed light on which mistakes non-native speakers are most likely to make when speaking Icelandic (Arnórsdóttir, 2017). She compared the performance of Francophone and German speakers. Her results indicate that Francophones struggle more with grammatical genders and case agreement than Germans do, indicating that language transfer might be harder from the roman languages than from other germanic languages. In any case, this indicates that L2 learners could benefit significantly from a context-sensitive spell checker.

4. Machine learning approach

After the compilation of the ICoSC, we conducted a small scale machine learning experiment on the data, using three distinct categories of confusion sets. They are:

- Grammatically disjoint word pairs *(they/them)*: The PoS tags for each word never overlap with the other. This is very common for Icelandic. We tested 60 pairs from this category (42 taken from the *n/nn* category, 6 from the *y/i* category, 5 from the *ý/í* category and 7 from the *various* (grammatically separated) category);

- Grammatically identical word pairs *(principle/principal)*: Both words within the pair belong to the same distributional class and differ only by semantics. Somewhat surprisingly, this turned out to be the smallest category in our research where only seven word pairs had high enough frequency to be of value (3 are from the *y/i* category, 2 are from the *ý/í* category and 2 are from the *n/nn* category);

- Word pairs that fall under neither aforementioned category and thus the words within the pair can differ both in their semantic and syntactic properties, *(lose/loose)*. We tested 25 pairs from this category (8 from the *n/nn* category, 10 from the *y/i* category and 7 from the *ý/í* category).

The algorithm performs best on grammatically disjoint pairs, which suggest that the results could be significantly improved with a more careful consideration of the linguistic features of the context words, as they are less likely to overlap. On the other hand, the algorithm performs worst on grammatically identical pairs, where the difference between candidates is purely semantic. This could potentially be improved by looking at their semantic distance. It should be noted though that the number of grammatically identical sets is significantly lower than that of the other categories and may not be properly representative.

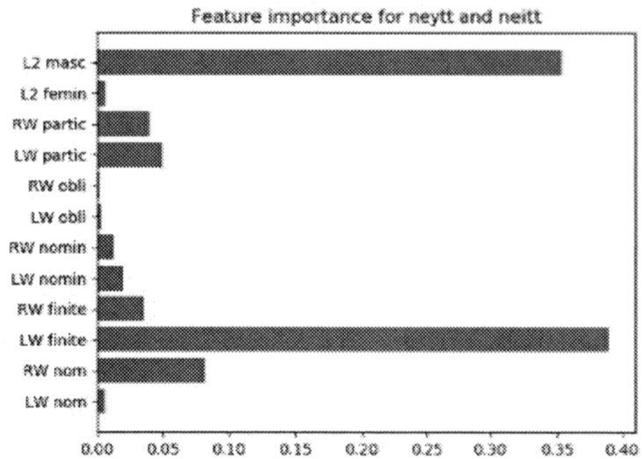

Figure 2: Feature importance for neytt 'consumed' / neitt 'anything'

In our experiment, first published in Friðriksdóttir and Ingason 2020, we used the decision tree algorithm from Scikit learn (Pedregosa et al., 2011) to create a binary classifier. We extracted linguistic features from the context of the confusion set candidates, taking into consideration the two closest words to the left of the candidate as well as the single closest word to the right of the candidate. As Icelandic grammar is quite regular, the presence of a finite verb for example can give a lot of important grammatical information of the neighbor word. We chose this narrow context for its simplicity, but adding the second word to the left is intended to capture the subject of the phrase (i.e. *"he is happy"* or *"the girl is running"*). The features were handpicked by the authors for their assumed generalizability and have binary values (true/false). The following were considered for both left and right context words: is nominal (words with grammatical case, such as nouns and pronouns); is finite (a verb that inflects for person agreement); is nominative; is oblique (has some grammatical case other than nominative); is a particle. For the word second to the left of the target word we consider if it is feminine or masculine. Example of the feature importance for a specific confusion set can be seen in Figure 2. The results were obtained using 10-fold cross validation on all the sentence examples in the data containing the two candidates. While our experiment should be considered as proof of concept rather than a finalized result, the average precision obtained for all categories ranged from 73-86% (see Table 1 which includes average for all word pairs taken from the two types of categories), indicating that results could be perfected with further research.

Type	Accuracy	Precision	Recall	F-score
Disjoint	0.78	0.77	0.76	0.75
Identical	0.73	0.68	0.66	0.64
Overlap	0.79	0.75	0.68	0.68
y/i	0.86	0.76	0.74	0.73
ý/í	0.79	0.82	0.79	0.78
nn/n	0.75	0.74	0.73	0.70
Various	0.75	0.71	0.66	0.66

Table 1: Average scores for categories.

5. Conclusion

In recent years, Icelandic primary schools have tested children for reading disabilities within their first three months of attendance in order to ensure early intervention and that every child gets appropriate support while learning to read (Sigurmundsdóttir and Torfadóttir, 2020). The resources available for dyslexic adults are nevertheless scarce and mostly focused on reading rather than writing. No open-source spell-checking tools exist for Icelandic when this is written. The three most commonly used are Púki Writing Error Protection, Skrambi, and an Icelandic version of the Hunspell-spell checker. None of them is actually context-sensitive, although Skrambi offers a very limited confusion set lookup (Nikulásdóttir et al., 2017). However, the number of Icelandic language technology resources has finally started to grow thanks to The Icelandic language technology programme 2018-2022. It is our hope that the compilation of the ICoSC will lead to further development in context-sensitive proofreading tools, suitable for the needs of people with dyslexia and other reading disabilities.

6. Bibliographical References

Arnórsdóttir, A. L. (2017). *Je parle très bien l'islandais, surtout à l'écrit: recherche sur les transferts du français vers l'islandais chez les apprenants francophones.* Unpublished BA-thesis, University of Iceland.

Bernstein, S. E. (2009). Phonology, decoding, and lexical compensation in vowel spelling errors made by children with dyslexia. *Reading and Writing*, 22(3):307–331.

Bjarnadóttir, K., Hlynsdóttir, K. I., and Steingrímsson, S. (2019). DIM: The Database of Icelandic Morphology. In *Proceedings of the 22nd Nordic Conference on Computational Linguistics*, NODALIDA 2019, Turku, Finland.

Friðriksdóttir, S. R. and Ingason, A. K. (2020). Disambiguating confusion sets in a language with rich morphology. In *The 12th International Conference on Agents and Artificial Intelligence (ICAART 2020)*, number 1, pages 446–451.

Golding, A. R. and Roth, D. (1999). A winnow-based approach to context-sensitive spelling correction. *Machine learning*, 34(1-3):107–130.

Gunnlaugsson, G. M. (1994). *Um afkringingu á/y, ý, ey/í íslensku.* Málvísindastofnun Háskóla Íslands.

Ingason, A. K. (2010). Productivity of non-default case. *Working papers in Scandinavian syntax*, 85:65–117.

Jónsson, J. G. and Eythórsson, T. (2005). Variation in subject case marking in Insular Scandinavian. *Nordic Journal of Linguistics*, 28.2:223–245.

Loftsson, H. and Östling, R. (2013). Tagging a morphologically complex language using an averaged perceptron tagger: The case of Icelandic. In *Proceedings of the 19th Nordic Conference of Computational Linguistics (NODALIDA 2013)*, pages 105–119, Oslo, Norway, May. Linköping University Electronic Press, Sweden.

Mody, M. and Silliman, E. R. (2008). *Brain, behavior, and learning in language and reading disorders*. Guilford Press.

Nikulásdóttir, A. B., Guðnason, J., and Steingrímsson, S. (2017). *Language Technology for Icelandic. Project Plan*. Icelandic Ministry of Science, Culture and Education.

Nowenstein, I. (2017). Determining the nature of intra-speaker subject case variation. In Caroline Heycock Hjalmar P. Petersen Thráinsson, Höskuldur et al., editors, *Syntactic Variation in Insular Scandinavian*, pages 91–112. John Benjamins.

Pedregosa, F., Varoquaux, G., Gramfort, A., Michel, V., Thirion, B., Grisel, O., Blondel, M., Prettenhofer, P., Weiss, R., Dubourg, V., Vanderplas, J., Passos, A., Cournapeau, D., Brucher, M., Perrot, M., and Duchesnay, E. (2011). Scikit-learn: Machine learning in Python. *Journal of Machine Learning Research*, 12:2825–2830.

Rello, L., Ballesteros, M., and Bigham, J. P. (2015). A spellchecker for dyslexia. In *Proceedings of the 17th International ACM SIGACCESS Conference on Computers & Accessibility*, pages 39–47.

Rögnvaldsson, E. (2013). Hljóðkerfi og orðhlutakerfi íslensku. *Reykjavík: Eiríkur Rögnvaldsson. Link: https://notendur. hi. is/eirikur/hoi. pdf*.

Rokaya, M. (2015). Arabic semantic spell checking based on power links. *International Information Institute (Tokyo). Information*, 18(11):4749–4770, 11.

Samani, M. H., Rahimi, Z., and Rahimi, S. (2015). A content-based method for persian real-word spell checking. In *2015 7th Conference on Information and Knowledge Technology (IKT)*, pages 1–5, May.

Sigurmundsdóttir, H. and Torfadóttir, S. (2020). Lesvefurinn um læsi og lestrarerfiðleika. Last accessed: February 7th 2020.

Steingrímsson, S., Helgadóttir, S., Rögnvaldsson, E., Barkarson, S., and Guðnason, J. (2018). Risamálheild: A Very Large Icelandic Text Corpus. In *Proceedings of the Eleventh International Conference on Language Resources and Evaluation*, LREC 2018, Miyazaki, Japan.

Thráinsson, H. (2013). Ideal speakers and other speakers. the case of dative and other cases. In Beatriz Fenández et al., editors, *Variation in Datives – A Micro-Comparative Perspective*, pages 161–188. Oxford University Press.

1st Workshop on Tools and Resources to Empower People with REAding DIfficulties (READI2020), pages 6–13
Language Resources and Evaluation Conference (LREC 2020), Marseille, 11–16 May 2020
© European Language Resources Association (ELRA), licensed under CC-BY-NC

Is it simpler? An Evaluation of an Aligned Corpus of Standard-Simple Sentences

Evelina Rennes

Department of Computer and Information Science, Linköping University
RISE, Research Institutes of Sweden
Linköping
`evelina.rennes@liu.se`

Abstract

Parallel monolingual resources are imperative for data-driven sentence simplification research. We present the work of aligning, at the sentence level, a corpus of all Swedish public authorities and municipalities web texts in standard and simple Swedish. We compare the performance of three alignment algorithms used for similar work in English (Average Alignment, Maximum Alignment, and Hungarian Alignment), and the best-performing algorithm is used to create a resource of 15,433 unique sentence pairs. We evaluate the resulting corpus using a set of features that has proven to predict text complexity of Swedish texts. The results show that the sentences of the simple sub-corpus are indeed less complex than the sentences of the standard part of the corpus, according to many of the text complexity measures.

Keywords: parallel corpus, monolingual alignment, automatic text simplification, text complexity

1. Introduction

Automatic Text Simplification (ATS) denotes the process of transforming a text, semantically, syntactically or lexically, in order to make it easier while preserving meaning and grammaticality. The simplification of text can have different purposes. Historically, it has been used as a preprocessing step to facilitate other natural language processing tasks, such as machine translation and text summarisation. The intuition was that a simpler syntactic structure of input texts would lead to less ambiguity, which would improve text processing performance.

Another purpose of ATS is to make texts available to a broader audience, for example by adapting texts for people with different kinds of reading difficulties (Saggion, 2017). Examples of target groups that have been accounted for within the field are people with dyslexia, people with aphasia, children, the deaf and hearing-impaired, second language learners, and the elderly.

Data-driven techniques have gained ground the last years within the field of natural language processing, and the simplification field is no exception. Recent approaches regard simplification as a task analogous to (monolingual) machine translation (Specia, 2010; Coster and Kauchak, 2011b; Coster and Kauchak, 2011a; Wubben et al., 2012; Xu et al., 2016; Nisioi et al., 2017; Zhang and Lapata, 2017; Zhang et al., 2017).

One well-recognised issue with data-driven techniques is that these techniques typically demand large-scale high-quality data resources, which can be problematic for less-resourced languages. A widely used resource in previous automatic text simplification research is Wikipedia and Simple English Wikipedia (Zhu et al., 2010; Coster and Kauchak, 2011b; Hwang et al., 2015; Kajiwara and Komachi, 2016), but its quality as a resource has been questioned (Xu et al., 2015). The collaborative and uncontrolled nature of Wikipedia makes it somewhat unreliable as a resource, and the authors pointed out that simple articles generally are not rewritten versions of the standard articles, which can be problematic when attempting to perform sentence alignment.

Another commonly used resource is the Newsela corpus[1]. Newsela contains 1,130 original news articles in English, manually simplified to 3–4 complexity levels by professional writers. The readability levels correspond to education grade levels, thus targeting children of different reading levels. Although there are many advantages of Newsela, such as the high quality of the texts, there is one disadvantage: researchers are not allowed to publicly release model output based on this corpus, which in turn hinders model comparison. The Newsela corpus has been used in some studies for text simplification (Zhang and Lapata, 2017; Alva-Manchego et al., 2017; Scarton et al., 2018).

The need for more and better resources for sentence simplification was highlighted by Alva-Manchego et al. (2020), and proposed as one of the key topics that should be addressed by the field.

In Sweden, most websites of public authorities and municipalities have versions adapted to people in need of simple text. These texts are often based on guidelines learned from the professional experience of expert writers and editors. The Swedish Agency for Accessible Media (MTM) describes some of these guidelines[2]:

- The text should be adapted to the type of reader that will read the text

- The text should have a common thread and capture the interest of the reader immediately

- The context should be clear, and the text should not demand any extensive prerequisites

---

[1] `https://newsela.com/data`
[2] `https://www.mtm.se/`
`produkter-och-tjanster/lattlast/`
`om-latta-texter/`

- The text should contain everyday words and the text rows should be short

- If a picture is presented next to a text, it should interplay with the text

- The language and presentation should be adapted to the specific demands and purposes of the specific type of media

These properties are, for obvious reasons, difficult to model in a concrete and unambiguous way to be fed into a system that automatically simplifies text.

Professionally written texts comprise, however, concrete examples of sentences that adhere to these guidelines. They can therefore be used for learning how experts write simple text. This motivated us to collect a corpus of web texts from Swedish public authorities and municipalities (Rennes and Jönsson, 2016).

The collected corpus contained a total of 1,629 pages in simple Swedish, and 136,501 pages in standard Swedish, with a total of 29.6 million tokens.

The corpus was aligned using three different alignment algorithms, broadly following Kajiwara and Komachi (2016). The alignment algorithms, originally proposed by Song and Roth (2015); Average Alignment (AA), Maximum Alignment (MA), and Hungarian Alignment (HA), align sentence pairs by calculating and combining the similarities of word embeddings to create a sentence similarity score.

The AA algorithm bases the sentence similarity on the average of the pairwise word similarities of all words of a pair of sentences. The MA algorithm considers the word pairs that maximise the word similarity of all words of a pair of sentences, and the sentence similarity score is given by the sum of the word similarity scores. The HA algorithm determines the sentence similarity by calculating the lowest cost (in our case, the highest cosine value) for every possible word pair, and the resulting sum is normalised by the length of the shortest sentence in the sentence pair.

Thus, for all algorithms, we could alter the *word similarity threshold* (the threshold of when a word pair is regarded similar enough) and *sentence similarity threshold* (the threshold of when a sentence pair is similar enough and should be aligned).

A few modifications of the Kajiwara and Komachi (2016) implementation were made. The language was changed to Swedish, and unknown words, so called Out-of-Vocabulary (OOV) words, were treated differently. Since Kajiwara and Komachi (2016) used word embeddings trained on a large-scale corpus, they disregarded the OOV words when calculating the sentence similarity scores. However, since we used a much smaller set of Swedish word embeddings, Swectors (Fallgren et al., 2016), ignoring OOV words was not a viable approach. Instead, we used Mimick (Pinter et al., 2017) to train a recurrent neural network at the character level, in order to predict OOV word vectors based on a word's spelling. Mimick works by generating approximated word embeddings for OOV words. The intuition behind this approach is that word embeddings that are generated based on the spelling of a word provide a better vector estimation than other common methods (such as creating a randomised word embedding) since they capture features related to the shape of a word.

In this article, we present detailed results on the nature of the different algorithms using a combination of evaluations. In Section 2.1., we investigate at what sentence similarity threshold humans perceive the aligned sentence pairs as semantically similar. In Section 2.2., we aim to find the algorithm and the best combination of parameters to maximise alignment performance. In Section 2.3., we investigate whether the sentences in the aligned sentence pairs differ in complexity. In Section 3., results and methodological considerations are discussed, and the conclusions are presented in Section 4..

The main contribution of this work is the provision and evaluation of a new text simplification corpus for Swedish.

2. Evaluations

A total of three evaluations were performed. The first two evaluations aimed to tune the values of the word and sentence similarity thresholds to maximise the performance of the algorithms. An aligned corpus was then created of sentence pairs using the best-performing threshold values.

The third evaluation aimed to investigate whether the aligned corpus consisted of sentence pairs that differed in complexity, i.e. if we really had a corpus of standard and simple Swedish. Since the sentences are extracted from corpora consisting of standard and simple documents, it is intuitive that the extracted sentences are good representatives of standard and simple text segments. However, given the way the corpus was created, we cannot know that the sentence pairs are true alignments, that is, that the simple sentence is a *simplified version of the standard sentence*. The third evaluation aims to investigate whether the sentences of the different parts of the corpus in fact differs in complexity.

2.1. Evaluation I: Human Evaluation

The quality of the sentence pairs generated by the alignment algorithms was evaluated in a human evaluation conducted through a web survey. The word threshold value was set to 0.49 following Kajiwara and Komachi (2016). The intuition behind this evaluation was to see at what sentence threshold humans perceive the aligned sentences as semantically similar.

2.1.1. Procedure

From the three corpora generated by the different algorithms, we randomly picked three sentence pairs per similarity interval (0.51–0.60, 0.61–0.70, 0.71–0.80, 0.81–0.90, 0.91–1.0). The number of sentence pairs aligned by the AA algorithm were, however, very few (<10). AA was therefore excluded from this evaluation. For MA and HA a total of 30 sentence pairs were extracted.

All extracted pairs from HA and MA were then included in a web survey, and participants were asked to grade the sentence pairs on a four-graded scale regarding similarity. The grading was based on categories previously used to create a manually annotated data set (Hwang et al., 2015). For this evaluation, the categories were translated into Swedish and slightly reformulated to suit non-experts. The reformulated categories were:

1. **Meningarna handlar om helt olika saker**
   The sentences treat completely different things

2. **Meningarna handlar om olika saker men delar en kortare fras**
   The sentences treat different things, but share a shorter phrase

3. **En menings innehåll täcks helt av den andra meningen, men innehåller även ytterligare information**
   The content of a sentence is completely covered by the second sentence, but also contains additional information

4. **Meningarnas innehåll matchar helt, möjligtvis med små undantag (t. ex. pronomen, datum eller nummer)**
   The content of the sentences matches completely, possibly with minor exceptions (such as pronouns, dates or numbers)

Convenience sampling was used to gather responses, and 61 participants submitted a response to the web survey.

2.1.2. Results

The results of the human evaluation are presented in Table 1, and further illustrated in Figure 1.

MA	0.51-0.60	0.61-0.70	0.71-0.80	0.81-0.90	0.91-1.0
Mean	0.363	1.282	2.451	1.989	2.522
Std.Dev.	0.646	0.918	0.774	0.796	0.652
HA					
Mean	0.344	0.300	1.464	0.645	1.539
Std.Dev.	0.624	0.504	0.848	0.874	1.314

Table 1: Results of the human evaluation of MA and HA. Good=3, Good Partial=2, Partial=1 and Bad=0.

The sentence pairs in the corpus using the MA algorithm were generally considered more similar, than the sentence pairs of the corpus aligned with the HA algorithm.

For the MA algorithm, a sentence threshold over 0.71 seemed to produce similar sentences. The HA algorithm did not reach an average value above 2.

The high standard deviation through all intervals shows that these results should be interpreted with caution.

2.2. Evaluation II: Gold Standard

The gold standard evaluation was performed to find the best parameter settings regarding word and sentence thresholds for all three alignment algorithms (AA, MA, HA).

2.2.1. Procedure

All alignment algorithms used a threshold for word alignment and a threshold for sentence alignment. We used a gold standard to reveal the optimal combination of parameters that maximise the F1 score.

The gold standard was collected broadly following the procedure in Hwang et al. (2015), annotated by one graduate student and two payed undergraduate students. Document

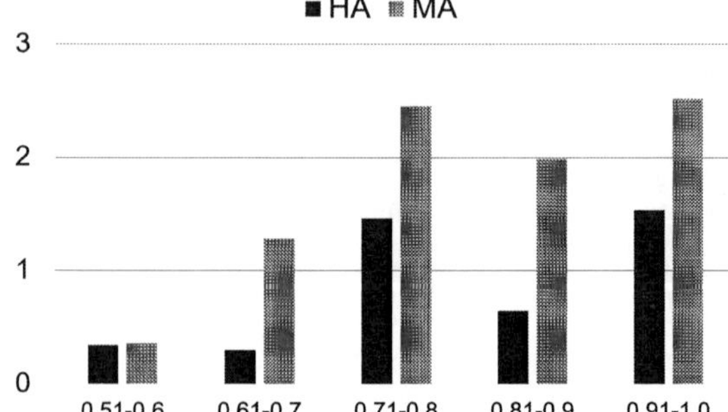

Figure 1: Average grade per interval, according to the web survey (where a value of 0 means that the sentences are not considered similar, and a value of 3 means that the sentences are considered very similar).

pairs (based on a title match) were presented to the annotators, and they were instructed to rate each sentence pair according to the descriptions of each point of the scale. If there were any doubts, they were instructed to focus on the semantic meaning rather than specific words. A training example was given prior to the annotation.

Only sentences with exactly three annotations were considered, which resulted in 4548 sentence pairs. Of these pairs, 4457 were rated as *Bad*, 37 were rated as *Bad Partial*, 24 were rated as *Good Partial*, and 30 were rated as *Good*.

The inter-annotator agreement was calculated using the Intra-class Correlation Coefficient (ICC), and revealed excellent agreement, $ICC(2,3) = 0.964$.

Since the gold standard was divided into four categories, we performed two experiments. In the first experiment (**GGPO**), the sentences rated as *Good* and *Good Partial* were considered correct alignments, and in the second experiment (**GO**) we restricted the correct alignments to only the sentences ranked as *Good*.

2.2.2. Results

As in the previous evaluation, the AA algorithm resulted in a very low number of aligned sentences for all given conditions when tested on the gold sentences.

	Max F1	No. sentences
AA	0.034	3
MA	0.758	39
HA	0.762	49

Table 2: The best-performing algorithm conditions in the GGPO setting.

In the **GGPO setting**, presented in Table 2, the results were as follows:

- The AA algorithm maximised its performance at $F1 = 0.034$, aligning 3 sentences (no difference was observed when changing parameters or vector conditions).

- The MA algorithm maximised its performance at $F1 = 0.758$, aligning 39 sentences (Mimick vectors, word similarity threshold of 0.39, sentence similarity threshold of 0.7).

- The HA algorithm maximised its performance at $F1 = 0.762$, aligning 49 sentences (Mimick vectors, word similarity threshold of 0.79, sentence similarity threshold of 0.7).

	Max F1	No. sentences
AA	0.060	2
MA	0.892	33
HA	0.800	38

Table 3: The best-performing algorithm conditions in the GO setting.

In the **GO setting**, presented in Table 3, we saw similar tendencies:

- The AA algorithm maximised its performance at $F1 = 0.060$, aligning 2 sentences (Mimick vectors, word similarity threshold of ≥ 0.29 and sentence similarity threshold of ≥ 0.4).

- The MA algorithm maximised its performance at $F1 = 0.892$, aligning 33 sentences (Mimick vectors, word similarity threshold of ≥ 0.39 and sentence similarity threshold of 0.8).

- The HA algorithm maximised its performance at $F1 = 0.800$, aligning 38 sentences (Mimick vectors, word similarity threshold of ≥ 0.59 and sentence similarity threshold of 0.9).

Generally, the conditions using Mimick for generating vectors for out-of-vocabulary words performed better in terms of precision, recall and number of aligned sentences. The best-performing algorithm was the MA in the GO setting, and HA in the GGPO setting.

2.2.3. The Corpus

After discovering the best-performing similarity thresholds for word and sentence alignment, the winning algorithm was re-run on the raw corpus of Swedish public authorities and municipalities web texts. The performance of MA and HA did not differ much in the GGPO setting, but MA was substantially better in the GO setting. Another benefit of MA is that it less computationally demanding, which could be important to consider when running on large corpora.

We chose to run the alignment with the MA algorithm, using a word similarity threshold of 0.39 and a sentence similarity threshold of 0.7.

This resulted in a resource of 45,671 sentence pairs. After removing duplicates, 15,433 sentence pairs remained.

2.3. Evaluation III: Text Characteristics

The aligned corpus was further analysed based on text characteristics. In this evaluation, we were interested in whether the sentence pairs in the aligned resource in fact differed in complexity.

2.3.1. Procedure

Since the aligned corpus contained duplicate sentences, we only considered the 15,433 unique sentence pairs for this analysis.

First, we performed a corpus-level surface analysis, using frequency and ratio measures to get a general overview of the corpus. The corpus-level measures have been previously used for analysing comparable corpora of texts in simple and standard Swedish (Heimann Mühlenbock, 2013). However, since this corpus does not include documents, but rather sentences, some of the measures used by Heimann Mühlenbock (2013) are not applicable. The measures we excluded from the analysis were LIX (Björnsson, 1968), type-token ratio and OVIX (Hultman and Westman, 1977).

The measures used for the corpus-level analysis were:

- **Total number of words**, calculated as the number of all the alphanumeric word tokens in the sub-corpus.

- **Number of unique words**, calculated as the number of all unique alphanumeric word tokens in the sub-corpus.

- **Ratio of long words**, defined as the ratio of words longer than 6 characters to the total number of words in the sub-corpus.

- **Ratio of extra long words**, defined as the ratio of words longer than 13 characters to the total number of words in the sub-corpus.

We then performed a sentence-level surface analysis of the collected corpora. The complexity measures were calculated for all sentences in the simple Swedish sub-corpus, and all sentences in the standard sub-corpus, and significance testing was performed using two-tailed t-test.

The measures considered for the sentence-level surface analysis were:

- **Word length (chars)**, calculated as the mean word length in number of characters. This value was calculated for each sentence, and then averaged over the entire sub-corpus.

- **Word length (syll)**, calculated as the mean word length in number of syllables. For simplicity, we let the number of vowels correspond to the number of syllables. This value was calculated for each sentence, and then averaged over the entire sub-corpus.

- **Sentence length (words)**, calculated as the number of tokens of a sentence. This value was calculated for each sentence, and then averaged over the entire sub-corpus.

- **Number of long words**, defined as the number of words longer than 6 characters. This value was calculated for each sentence, and then averaged over the entire sub-corpus.

- **Number of extra long words**, defined as the number of words longer than 13 characters. This value was calculated for each sentence, and then averaged over the entire sub-corpus.

Finally, we calculated the measures of a subset of a feature set used for text complexity classification (Falkenjack et al., 2013). The subset (hereafter: *SCREAM-sent*) consisted of the measures that were suitable for sentence-level analysis. The selection was done according to Falkenjack (2018).

A new version of SAPIS (Fahlborg and Rennes, 2016), an API service for text analysis and simplification, was used to calculate the linguistic measures used for the *SCREAM-sent* analysis. The new version has the same functionality as the original version of SAPIS, but now uses efselab[3] (Östling, 2018) for part-of-speech tagging. SAPIS uses MaltParser (Nivre et al., 2007) version 1.9.0 for dependency parsing.

Since the *SCREAM-sent* measures were calculated at the sentence level, all measures indicating an average should be regarded as absolute for a given sentence. The significance testing was performed using two-tailed *t*-tests, assuming non-equal variances.

The selected features were:

- **avg_dep_distance_dependent**, calculated as the average dependency distance in the document.

- **avg_n_syllables**, calculated as the average number of syllables per word in the document.

- **avg_prep_comp**, calculated as the average number of prepositional complements in the document.

- **avg_sentence_depth**, calculated as the average sentence depth.

- **avg_word_length**, calculated as the average word length in a document.

- **n_content_words**, calculated as the number of content words (nouns, verbs, adjectives and adverbs).

- **n_dependencies**, calculcated as the number of dependencies.

- **n_lix_long_words**, calculated as the number of long words as defined by the LIX formula; words with more than 6 characters.

- **n_nominal_postmodifiers**, calculated as the number of nominal pre-modifiers.

- **n_nominal_premodifiers**, calculated as the number of nominal post-modifiers.

- **n_right_dependencies**, calculated as the number of right dependencies.

- **n_sub_clauses**, calculated as the number of sub-clauses.

- **Lemma frequencies**, derived from the basic Swedish vocabulary SweVoc (Heimann Mühlenbock and Johansson Kokkinakis, 2012):

  - **n_swevoc_c**, calculated as the number of words that belong to the SweVoc C word list. SweVoc C contains lemmas that are fundamental for communication.

  - **n_swevoc_d**, calculated as the number of words that belong to the SweVoc D word list. SweVoc D contains lemmas for everyday use.

  - **n_swevoc_h**, calculated as the number of words that belong to the SweVoc H word list. SweVoc H contains other highly frequent lemmas.

  - **n_swevoc_s**, calculated as the number of words that belong to the SweVoc S word list. SweVoc S contains supplementary words from Swedish Base Vocabulary Pool.

  - **n_swevoc_total**, calculated as the number of words that belong to the total SweVoc word list. SweVoc Total contains SweVoc words of all categories.

- **n_syllables**, calculated as the number of syllables in the document.

- **n_tokens**, calculated as the number of tokens in the document.

- **n_unique_tokens**, calculated as the number of unique tokens in the document.

- **n_verbal_roots**, calculated as the number of sentences where the root is a verb.

- **n_verbs**, calculated as the number of verbs.

- **right_dependency_ratio**, calculated as the ratio of the number of right dependencies to the number of total dependencies.

- **sub_clause_ratio**, calculated as the ratio of sub-clauses to the total amount of sub-clauses.

- **total_token_length**, calculated as the length of all tokens of a document.

2.3.2. Results

We performed three sets of analyses: one corpus-level surface analysis, and two sentence-level analyses. The corpus-level analysis and the first sentence-level analysis account for the measures previously used by Heimann Mühlenbock (2013). The second sentence-level analysis accounts for the *SCREAM-sent* measures.

The results of the corpus-level surface analysis are presented in Table 4. The corpus of simple sentences is slightly smaller in size regarding the total number of words. The corpus of standard sentences exhibits a larger variety regarding word variation (number of unique word tokens), and has a slightly higher ratio of long and extra long word tokens.

The results of the sentence-level surface analysis is presented in Table 5. This analysis also shows a tendency of the corpus of simple sentences to have shorter word length (in both number of characters and number of syllables),

---

[3]https://github.com/robertostling/efselab

Measure	*simple*	*standard*
Total number of words	177,011	181,111
Number of unique words	10,373	11,593
Ratio of long words	22.55%	22.97%
Ratio of extra long words	3.28%	3.44%

Table 4: Overview of the characteristics of the sentences in the simple part of the corpus (*simple*) and the standard part of the corpus (*standard*).

Measure	$\overline{X}_{simple}$	$\overline{X}_{standard}$	t	p
Word length (chars)	5.36	5.40	-3.03	*
Word length (syll)	1.93	1.95	-3.67	*
Sentence length (words)	11.47	11.74	-3.96	**
Number of long words	2.96	3.10	-5.66	**
Number of extra long words	0.38	0.40	-3.47	**

** p<0.05, ** p<0.001*

Table 5: Sentence-level surface analysis.

shorter sentence length and a lower number of long and extra long words. The differences are statistically significant. The results of the sentence-level analysis using the *SCREAM-sent* measures are presented in Table 6. Statistically significant p-values are marked in bold.

Most measures show statistically significant differences. Measures related to the length of the sentence, such as the number of syllables and the number of tokens, are generally higher in the *standard* sentences. There is also a significant difference in sentence depth and number of right dependencies, which could indicate higher complexity in the *standard* sentences. The *simple* sentences generally exhibit shorter token length, and fewer long words (>6 characters). No difference could be observed regarding the SweVoc measures from category C (core vocabulary), D (words referring to everyday objects and actions, and H (highly frequent words). However, statistically significant differences were observed for the SweVoc category S (supplementary words from the Swedish Base Vocabulary Pool), and Swe-Voc Total.

3. Discussion

We have presented results from three evaluations. The first and second evaluation were done on the previously aligned corpus in order to find the optimal combination of settings for the corpus alignment. Then, the corpus was aligned with the best-performing parameter settings, and the third evaluation was conducted on the new resource of aligned sentences.

- Evaluation I, the human evaluation, indicated that sentence pairs produced by the MA algorithm were regarded more similar than sentence pairs produced by the HA algorithm. A sentence similarity threshold of 0.71 seemed to produce sentence pairs that were perceived as similar, but the results lack statistical power.

- Evaluation II, the evaluation on the gold standard, indicated that the best-performing combination of settings for the alignment in the GGPO condition was the HA algorithm, using Mimick vector generation, a word similarity threshold of 0.79, and a sentence similarity threshold of 0.7. In the GO condition, the best-performing combination of settings was the MA algorithm, using Mimick vector generation, a word similarity threshold of $\geq$ 0.39 and a sentence similarity threshold of 0.8.

- Evaluation III, the evaluation of text characteristics, revealed that there are many statistically significant differences between the sentences in the simple sub-corpus and the sentences in the standard sub-corpus. The standard part of the corpus generally scores higher on features used to predict text complexity, when compared sentence-wise to the sentences collected from the material in simple Swedish.

This work has resulted in a sentence-aligned Swedish corpus of sentence pairs that differ in complexity.

Many of the differences observed in the final text complexity evaluation are to be expected if we accept the hypothesis that the sentences belonging to the standard part of the corpus are more complex than the sentences in the simple Swedish sub-corpus. Such measures include the number of long words (in characters and syllables), sentence length (in tokens and syllables), and sentence depth. However, some of the measures are not straightforward to interpret. For example, Falkenjack et al. (2013) discuss the ratio of content words to be ambiguous, since a high ratio could be indicative of higher information density, while a low ratio could mean higher syntactic complexity.

We did not observe any statistically significant differences in the majority of the SweVoc measures, and this could possibly be explained by the nature of the used alignment algorithm. Since the algorithm aims to find semantically similar sentence pairs, it is likely that the aligned sentences will also be lexically similar.

The linguistic analysis of the different parts of the corpus in this study does not include pairwise comparison, which could reveal whether the complexity differs between the sentences in the sentence pairs.

The human evaluation performed shows tendencies of when the sentences are perceived as similar. However, due to the low sample size, these tendencies can not be confirmed without an additional study with a larger sample. It would also be interesting to see whether human readers experience differences in complexity when presented with the sentences in the sentence pairs.

The collected corpus contains texts written by expert writers, following general guidelines on how to write simple text. However, even though there are some general traits of what makes a text easy to read, one must remember that the needs of the different target groups may vary. Second language learners face other problems than persons with dyslexia or aphasia, and there can be large variations within each target group. The corpus collected in this study is restricted in this sense, and future work would benefit from a more target-centred approach.

For the purpose of ATS, sentence aligned resources can be sub-optimal, since simplification operations are not limited to the sentence level. The division of long or complex sentences into multiple shorter sentences is not an uncommon

Measure	$\overline{X}_{simple}$	$\overline{X}_{standard}$	t	p
avg_dep_distance_dependent	2.44	2.46	-3.81	**
avg_n_syllables	1.80	1.81	-3.24	**
avg_prep_comp	1.46	1.51	-3.77	**
avg_sentence_depth	5.95	6.01	-2.63	*
avg_word_length	5.07	5.11	-2.91	*
n_content_words	6.64	6.77	-3.51	**
n_dependencies	13.26	13.58	-4.46	**
n_lix_long_words	2.41	2.56	-6.64	**
n_nominal_postmodifiers	0.85	0.90	-4.06	**
n_nominal_premodifiers	0.28	0.30	-3.48	**
n_right_dependencies	9.18	9.39	-4.19	**
n_sub_clauses	0.26	0.26	-0.78	
n_swevoc_c	5.38	5.46	-1.89	
n_swevoc_d	0.26	0.26	-0.02	
n_swevoc_h	0.79	0.80	-0.73	
n_swevoc_s	0.61	0.63	-2.28	*
n_swevoc_total	6.32	6.44	-2.40	*
n_syllables	21.02	21.73	-5.96	**
n_tokens	13.26	13.58	-4.46	**
n_unique_tokens	12.45	12.73	-4.64	**
n_verbal_roots	0.81	0.80	3.32	**
n_verbs	2.45	2.46	-0.45	
right_dependency_ratio	0.70	0.70	0.63	
sub_clause_ratio	0.25	0.26	-0.89	
total_token_length	62.80	65.00	-6.18	**

*p<0.05, ** p<0.001*

Table 6: Results from the t-test comparing the sentences in the simple sub-corpus (*simple*) with the sentences in the standard sub-corpus (*standard*). The *n_lix_long_words* differs from the *Number of long words* in Table 5, since the former uses the lemma form in its calculation.

operation when simplifying text, as well as the addition of explanatory sentences to clarify one complex sentence. However, it has been pointed out that certain simplification approaches are best modelled with 1-to-1 alignments (see for example Alva-Manchego et al. (2017)), and that more complex operations might need other methods and data organised in a different manner.

A resource aligned at the sentence level can be used to investigate specific sentence-level simplification operations, but it is important to be aware of the limitations, and that additional resources, such as aligned text fragments or even full documents, are needed for a complete ATS analysis.

4. Conclusion

In this article, we have presented the work on creating and evaluating an aligned resource of Swedish sentence pairs that differ in complexity. The first two evaluations aimed to find the algorithm and the best combination of parameters to maximise alignment performance. The last evaluation investigated whether the sentences in the aligned sentence pairs in fact differed in complexity.

The resulting corpus consisted of 45,671 sentence pairs, of which 15,433 were unique. The statistical analysis indicates that the sentences belonging to the simple Swedish sub-corpus are generally less complex than the sentence be-

longing to the standard part of the corpus, according to both surface-level measures and analysis at a deeper linguistic level.

Future research includes further analysis of the sentence pairs to see what simplification operations that are present in the data, as well as making use of this resource in data-driven text simplification research for Swedish.

5. Bibliographical References

Alva-Manchego, F., Bingel, J., Paetzold, G., Scarton, C., and Specia, L. (2017). Learning how to simplify from explicit labeling of complex-simplified text pairs. In *Proceedings of the Eighth International Joint Conference on Natural Language Processing (Volume 1: Long Papers)*, pages 295—-305, Taipei, Taiwan. Asian Federation of Natural Language Processing.

Alva-Manchego, F., Scarton, C., and Specia, L. (2020). Data-driven sentence simplification: Survey and benchmark. *Computational Linguistics*, pages 1–87, 01.

Björnsson, C. H. (1968). *Läsbarhet*. Liber, Stockholm.

Coster, W. and Kauchak, D. (2011a). Learning to simplify sentences using wikipedia. In *Proceedings of the workshop on monolingual text-to-text generation*, pages 1–9. Association for Computational Linguistics.

Coster, W. and Kauchak, D. (2011b). Simple english

wikipedia: a new text simplification task. In *Proceedings of the 49th Annual Meeting of the Association for Computational Linguistics: Human Language Technologies: short papers-Volume 2*, pages 665–669. Association for Computational Linguistics.

Fahlborg, D. and Rennes, E. (2016). Introducing SAPIS - an API service for text analysis and simplification. In *The second national Swe-Clarin workshop: Research collaborations for the digital age, Umeå, Sweden*.

Falkenjack, J., Heimann Mühlenbock, K., and Jönsson, A. (2013). Features indicating readability in Swedish text. In *Proceedings of the 19th Nordic Conference of Computational Linguistics (NoDaLiDa-2013), Oslo, Norway*, number 085 in NEALT Proceedings Series 16, pages 27–40. Linköping University Electronic Press.

Falkenjack, J. (2018). Personal communication.

Fallgren, P., Segeblad, J., and Kuhlmann, M. (2016). Towards a standard dataset of swedish word vectors. In *Proceedings of the Sixth Swedish Language Technology Conference (SLTC), Umeå, Sweden*.

Heimann Mühlenbock, K. and Johansson Kokkinakis, S. (2012). SweVoc - a Swedish vocabulary resource for CALL. In *Proceedings of the SLTC 2012 workshop on NLP for CALL*, pages 28–34, Lund. Linköping University Electronic Press.

Heimann Mühlenbock, K. (2013). *I see what you mean. Assessing readability for specific target groups.* Dissertation, Språkbanken, Dept of Swedish, University of Gothenburg.

Hultman, T. G. and Westman, M. (1977). *Gymnasistsvenska*. LiberLäromedel, Lund.

Hwang, W., Hajishirzi, H., Ostendorf, M., and Wu, W. (2015). Aligning sentences from standard wikipedia to simple wikipedia. In *HLT-NAACL*, pages 211–217.

Kajiwara, T. and Komachi, M. (2016). Building a monolingual parallel corpus for text simplification using sentence similarity based on alignment between word embeddings. In *Proceedings of COLING, Osaka, Japan*, pages 1147–1158.

Nisioi, S., Štajner, S., Ponzetto, S. P., and Dinu, L. P. (2017). Exploring neural text simplification models. In *Proceedings of the 55th Annual Meeting of the Association for Computational Linguistics (Volume 2: Short Papers)*, pages 85–91.

Nivre, J., Hall, J., Nilsson, J., Chanev, A., Eryigit, G., Kübler, S., Marinov, S., and Marsi, E. (2007). MaltParser: A language-independent system for data-driven dependency parsing. *Natural Language Engineering*, 13(2):95–135.

Pinter, Y., Guthrie, R., and Eisenstein, J. (2017). Mimicking word embeddings using subword rnns. In *Proceedings of the 2017 Conference on Empirical Methods in Natural Language Processing*, pages 102–112.

Rennes, E. and Jönsson, A. (2016). Towards a corpus of easy to read authority web texts. In *Proceedings of the Sixth Swedish Language Technology Conference (SLTC2016), Umeå, Sweden*.

Saggion, H. (2017). *Automatic Text Simplification*. Number Vol. 32 in Synthesis Lectures on Human Language Technologies. Morgan & Claypool Publishers.

Scarton, C., Paetzold, G., and Specia, L. (2018). Text simplification from professionally produced corpora. In *Proceedings of the Eleventh International Conference on Language Resources and Evaluation (LREC 2018)*, Miyazaki, Japan. European Language Resources Association (ELRA).

Song, Y. and Roth, D. (2015). Unsupervised sparse vector densification for short text similarity. In *Proceedings of the 2015 Conference of the North American Chapter of the Association for Computational Linguistics: Human Language Technologies*, pages 1275–1280.

Specia, L. (2010). Translating from Complex to Simplified Sentences. In *Proceedings of the 9th international conference on Computational Processing of the Portuguese Language (PROPOR)*, pages 30–39.

Wubben, S., van den Bosch, A., and Krahmer, E. (2012). Sentence simplification by monolingual machine translation. In *Proceedings of the 50th Annual Meeting of the Association for Computational Linguistics (Volume 1: Long Papers)*, pages 1015–1024, Jeju Island, Korea.

Xu, W., Callison-Burch, C., and Napoles, C. (2015). Problems in current text simplification research: New data can help. *Transactions of the Association for Computational Linguistics*, 3:283–297.

Xu, W., Napoles, C., Pavlick, E., Chen, Q., and Callison-Burch, C. (2016). Optimizing statistical machine translation for text simplification. *Transactions of the Association for Computational Linguistics*, 4:401–415.

Zhang, X. and Lapata, M. (2017). Sentence simplification with deep reinforcement learning. In *Proceedings of the 2017 Conference on Empirical Methods in Natural Language Processing*, pages 584–594, Copenhagen, Denmark. Association for Computational Linguistics.

Zhang, Y., Ye, Z., Feng, Y., Zhao, D., and Yan, R. (2017). A constrained sequence-to-sequence neural model for sentence simplification. abs/1704.02312.

Zhu, Z., Bernhard, D., and Gurevych, I. (2010). A monolingual tree-based translation model for sentence simplification. In *Proceedings of the 23rd international conference on computational linguistics*, pages 1353–1361. Association for Computational Linguistics.

Östling, R. (2018). Part of speech tagging: Shallow or deep learning? *North European Journal of Language Technology*, 5:1–15.

1st Workshop on Tools and Resources to Empower People with REAding DIfficulties (READI2020), pages 14–19
Language Resources and Evaluation Conference (LREC 2020), Marseille, 11–16 May 2020
© European Language Resources Association (ELRA), licensed under CC-BY-NC

Incorporating Multiword Expressions in Phrase Complexity Estimation

Sian Gooding,[2] Shiva Taslimipoor,[1,2] Ekaterina Kochmar[1,2]
[1] ALTA Institute
[2] Department of Computer Science and Technology, University of Cambridge
{shg36, st797, ek358}@cam.ac.uk

Abstract

Multiword expressions (MWEs) were shown to be useful in a number of NLP tasks. However, research on the use of MWEs in lexical complexity assessment and simplification is still an under-explored area. In this paper, we propose a text complexity assessment system for English, which incorporates MWE identification. We show that detecting MWEs using state-of-the-art systems improves predicting complexity on an established lexical complexity dataset.

Keywords: Text simplification, MWE, Lexical simplification

1. Introduction

Complex Word Identification (CWI) is a well-established task in natural language processing, which deals with automated identification of words that a reader might find difficult to understand (Shardlow, 2013). As such, it is often considered the first step in a lexical simplification pipeline. For instance, after a CWI system identifies *sweeping* in:

(1) Prime Minister's government took the *sweeping* action

as complex, a simplification system might suggest replacing it with a simpler alternative, for example with *wide* or *broad*. However, CWI systems so far have been focusing on complexity identification at the level of individual words (Shardlow, 2013; Gooding and Kochmar, 2018; Yimam et al., 2018). At the same time, there is extensive evidence that complexity often pertains to expressions consisting of more than one word. Consider *ballot stuffing* in the following example from the dataset of Yimam et al. (2017):

(2) There have been numerous falsifications and *ballot stuffing*

A CWI system aimed at individual complex word identification would be of a limited use in this case, as trying to simplify *ballot stuffing* on an individual word basis is likely to produce nonsensical or semantically different expressions like *ballot *filling* or *vote stuffing*. *Ballot stuffing* is an example of a *multiword expression* (MWE), which has idiosyncratic interpretation that crosses word boundaries or spaces (Sag et al., 2002). Despite the fact that special consideration of MWEs has been shown to improve results in parsing (Constant et al., 2017), machine translation (Constant et al., 2017; Carpuat and Diab, 2010), keyphrase/index term extraction (Newman and Baldwin, 2012), and sentiment analysis (Williams et al., 2015) and is likely to improve the quality of lexical simplification approaches (Hmida et al., 2018), not much research addressed complexity identification in MWEs (Ozasa et al., 2007; François and Watrin, 2011).

In this paper, we show that identification of MWEs is a crucial step in a lexical simplification pipeline, and in particular

it is important at the stage of lexical complexity assessment. In addition, MWEs span a wide range of various expressions, including verbal constructions (*wind down*, *set aside*), nominal compounds (*sledge hammers*, *peace treaty*), named entities (*Barack Obama*, *Los Angeles*), and fixed phrases (*brothers in arms*, *show of force*), among others. Such expressions can be challenging, with various degrees of complexity, for both native and non-native readers. We show that identifying the type of an MWE is helpful at the complexity assessment stage. We also argue that knowing types of MWEs can further assist in selecting an appropriate simplification strategy: for instance, in case of many named entity MWEs and some nominal compounds like *prime minister* the best simplification strategy might consist in providing a reader with a link to a Wikipedia entry. We present a comprehensive system that:

- discovers MWEs in text;
- identifies MWE type using linguistic patterns; and
- incorporates MWE type into a lexical complexity assessment system.

Our system is trained on a novel lexical complexity dataset for English annotated with the types of MWEs (Kochmar et al., 2020), [1] consisting of 4732 expressions extracted from the complexity-annotated dataset of Yimam et al. (2017). We discuss this dataset in Section 2. Section 3. details our approach to MWE identification. We then present our lexical complexity assessment system in Section 4., and discuss the results of both MWE detection and complexity assessment systems in Section 5.

2. Complex Phrase Identification Dataset

The dataset of Yimam et al. (2017) is the most comprehensive dataset annotated for lexical complexity in context. It consists of 34879 lexemes annotated as simple or complex by 20 annotators, 10 of which are native and other 10 are non-native speakers of English, sourced via Amazon Mechanical Turk. Annotators were presented with text passages of 5−10 sentences from texts of one of three genres (professionally written NEWS, WIKINEWS written by amateurs,

---

[1] https://github.com/ekochmar/MWE-CWI

MWE Type	Examples	%
MW compounds:	*life threatening, property sector*	26.88
MW named entities:	*Alawite sect, Formica Fusca*	10.50
Verb-particle and other phrasal verbs:	*close down, get rid of*	2.51
Fixed phrase:	*conflict of interest, et al.*	1.52
Semi-fixed VP:	*flexed <their> muscles, close <the> deal*	0.82
Verb-preposition:	*morph into, shield against*	0.72
PP modifier:	*upon arrival, within our reach*	0.70
Conjunction / Connective:	*thus far, according to*	0.34
Verb-noun(-preposition):	*provides access to, bid farewell*	0.32
Coordinated phrase:	*shock and horror, import and export*	0.23
Support verb:	*make clear, has taken steps*	0.15
Not MWE:	*vehicle rolled over, IP address is blocked*	46.09
Not MWE but contains MWE(s):	*collapsed property sector, interior ministry troops*	9.21

Table 1: Classes of MWEs annotated in the dataset of Kochmar et al. (2020)

and WIKIPEDIA articles), and were asked to highlight words and sequences of words up to 50 characters in length that they considered difficult to understand. As a result, Yimam et al. (2017) collected a dataset of 30147 individual words and 4732 "phrases" annotated as simple or complex in context. The annotation follows one of the two settings: under *binary* setting a lexeme receives a label of 1 even if a single annotator selected it as complex (0 if none of the annotators considered it complex), and under *probabilistic* setting a lexeme receives a label on the scale of $[0.0, 0.05, ..., 1.0]$ representing the proportion of annotators among 20 that selected an item as complex.

During annotation, annotators were allowed to select any sequence of words, which resulted in selection of expressions that do not form MWEs proper (for instance, *his drive*), as well as sentence fragments and sequences of unrelated words (for instance, *authorities should annul the*). Since the annotators in Yimam et al. (2017) were not instructed to select proper MWEs in this data, Kochmar et al. (2020) first re-annotated the selection of 4732 sequences longer than one word from the original dataset with their MWE status and type.

In this annotation experiment, Kochmar et al. (2020) followed the annotation instructions and distinguished between the MWE types from Schneider et al. (2014), with a few modifications:

- Additional types for "phrases" that are not MWE proper were introduced. These types include `Not MWE` for cases like *authorities should annul the*, and `Not MWE but contains MWE(s)` for longer non-MWE expressions that contain MWEs as sub-units: for example, *collapsed property sector*.

- Two categories, `verb-particle` and `other phrasal verb`, were merged into one due to lack of distinguishing power between the two from the simplification point of view.

- Categories `phatic` and `proverb` were not used because examples of these types do not occur in this data.

Table 1 presents the full account of MWE types with examples and their distribution in the dataset of Kochmar et al. (2020). The dataset was annotated by 3 annotators, all trained in linguistics, over a series of rounds. The annotators achieved observed agreement of at least 0.70 and Fleiss κ (Fleiss, 1981) of at least 0.7145 across the annotation rounds, which suggests substantial agreement. We refer the readers to the original publication (Kochmar et al., 2020) for more details on the annotation procedure.

3. Multiword Expression Identification

We first need to train an MWE identification system to detect the expressions of interest for our study. MWE identification is the task of discriminating, in context, and linking those tokens that together develop a special meaning. This can be modestly modelled using sequence tagging systems. We experiment with two systems: one is BERT-based transformer (Devlin et al., 2018) for token classification, and the other is the publicly available graph convolutional neural network (GCN) based system, which is reported to achieve state-of-the-art results on MWE identification (Rohanian et al., 2019).

The BERT-based token classification system is designed by adding a linear classification layer on top of the hidden-states output of the BERT architecture. We use the pre-trained model of `bert-base` provided by 'Hugging Face' developers [2] and fine-tune the weights of the whole architecture for a few iterations (i.e. 5 epochs). We use the same configurations that they use for named entity recognition. Among various systems designed to tag corpora for MWEs (Ramisch et al., 2018) the best systems incorporate dependency parse information (Al Saied et al., 2017; Rohanian et al., 2019). The GCN-based system that we employ consists of GCN and LSTM layers with a linear classification layer on top. As in the original system, we use ELMo for input representation.

Since our complexity estimation dataset is not originally designed for MWE identification, we augment our training data with the STREUSLE dataset which is comprehensively annotated for MWEs (Schneider and Smith, 2015). In Section 5. we show how this addition helps better identification of MWEs.

---

[2] `https://github.com/huggingface/transformers`

Once MWEs are identified in text, their types are predicted based on linguistic patterns. For instance, an MWE detection system identifies *woke up* as an MWE in *He woke up in the morning as usual*. A linguistic patterns-based system then uses the information about the parts-of-speech in this expression to predict its type as `verb-particle and other phrasal verbs`. Next, the predicted MWE together with its type is passed on to the lexical complexity assessment system that assesses the complexity of the expression (see Section 4.).

In Section 5. we first compare the results of the two MWE identification systems. Then we use the best one in evaluating the performance of complexity assessment.

4. MWE Complexity Assessment Systems

We build a baseline MWE complexity system, whose goal is to assign a complexity score to identified MWEs. The complexity assessment system is trained on phrases that have been annotated as MWEs in our dataset, and tested using the MWEs extracted from the test portion of the shared task dataset (Yimam et al., 2018).

We run experiments using the probabilistic labels, which represent the complexity of phrases on a scale of $[0.0...0.70]$,[3] representing the proportion of 20 annotators that found a phrase complex. The MWE complexity assessment system is a supervised feature-based model.

4.1. Features

Our complexity assessment system relies on 6 features. First, we include two traditional features found to correlate highly with word complexity in previous research: *length* and *frequency*. These are adapted for phrases by considering (1) the number of words instead of the number of characters for *length*, and (2) using the average frequency of bigrams within the phrase, which is calculated using the Corpus of Contemporary American English (Davies, 2009) for *frequency*. Average bigram frequency is used rather than n-gram frequency to account for the differences in MWE lengths and to increase feature coverage.

The second category of features focuses on the complexity of words contained within the MWE. We use an open source system of Gooding and Kochmar (2019) to tag words with a complexity score. Since this system does not directly assign complexity scores to MWEs, we use the highest word complexity within the phrase as well as the average word complexity as features.

The source genre of the sentence where a phrase occurs (NEWS, WIKINEWS or WIKIPEDIA) is used as another feature, as we hypothesise that different domains (e.g., more general for the NEWS vs. more technical for the WIKIPEDIA articles) may challenge readers to a different extent. Finally, following Kochmar et al. (2020), who show that different types of MWEs show different complexity levels, we use the type of MWE predicted by the linguistic patterns-based system as a feature. An example of the feature set for the phrase *sledge hammers* is shown in Table 2.

	sledge hammers
MWE	MW Compounds
Length	2
Freq	39
Max CW	0.70
Mean CW	0.60
Genre	News

Table 2: Complexity prediction feature set for *sledge hammers*

4.2. System Implementation

A set of standard regression algorithms from the `scikit-learn`[4] library are applied to the dataset. Model predictions are rounded to the closest 0.05 interval. The best performing model, identified via stratified 5-fold cross validation, uses a Multi-layer Perceptron regressor with 6 hidden layers and the `lbfgs` optimiser, used due to the size of the dataset.

5. Experiments

5.1. MWE Identification Results

We report the results of our MWE identification systems compared to the gold standard annotation which is explained in Section 2. We evaluate the systems in terms of the MWE-based precision, recall and F1-score which are defined in Savary et al. (2017). MWE-based evaluation measures count the strict matching between the prediction and the gold labels where every component of an MWE should be correctly tagged in order for it to be considered true positive. In Table 3, we report the MWE-based measures for both positive (MWE) and negative (non-MWE) classes.[5]

As can be seen in Table 3, the graph convolutional neural network-based (GCN) system outperforms Bert-transformer token classification for identifying MWEs. We can also see that the addition of external MWE-annotated data from STREUSLE helps improving the overall results. As expected, the data augmentation is especially effective in increasing recall as well as the overall F-measure.

The best-performing system, GCN trained on both our MWE data and STREUSLE dataset, achieves the highest F1-scores of 0.72 on `not MWE` and 0.60 on `MW compounds` classes, which are also the most prevalent in our data. At the same time, it finds detection of less frequent classes like `verb-preposition`, `verb-noun(-preposition)` and `conjunction/connective` more challenging.

5.2. End-to-end Complexity System Results

We use a pipeline system consisting of three stages: (1) *MWE identification*, (2) *MWE type prediction*, and (3) *MWE complexity prediction*. In Table 4 we report the results on the MWE proportion of the 2018 shared task test sets (Yimam et

---

[3]The upper bound on this scale reflects the fact that at most 14 annotators agreed that a particular phrase is complex.

[4]`https://scikit-learn.org`

[5]The negative class (non-MWEs) includes expressions (sequences of words) that are present in the dataset of Yimam et al. (2018) but are not tagged as MWEs in Kochmar et al. (2020), e.g. *authorities should annul the*.

training data	model	MWE class			non-MWE class		
		P	R	F1	P	R	F1
Our data train	GCN	93.67	37.37	53.43	66.03	97.97	78.89
	BERT-transformer	90.62	29.29	44.27	63.16	97.56	76.68
Our data train +	GCN	90.80	39.90	**55.44**	66.67	96.75	**78.94**
STREUSLE	BERT-transformer	95.95	35.86	52.21	65.68	98.78	78.90

Table 3: Performance of MWE identification systems in the development phase

Test Set	MAE	
	System	CAMB
(3) Complexity Prediction		
News (133)	**0.0688**	0.0767
Wikipedia (84)	**0.0671**	0.0734
WikiNews (79)	0.0375	**0.0327**
(2,3) MWE Type Prediction +		
Complexity Prediction		
News (133)	**0.0745**	0.0767
Wikipedia (84)	**0.0720**	0.0734
Wikinews (79)	0.0474	**0.0327**
(1,2,3) MWE Identification +		
MWE Type Prediction +		
Complexity Prediction		
News (61)	**0.0889**	0.0984
Wikipedia (27)	**0.1221**	0.1283
WikiNews (23)	**0.0572**	0.0595

Table 4: Complexity assessment system results

al., 2018) for each stage of the pipeline. We compare our results to the strategy used by the winning shared task system CAMB (Gooding and Kochmar, 2018), where all phrases are simply assigned the complexity value of 0.05. This baseline is highly competitive, as 1074 of the 2551 examples have a probabilistic score of 0.05, with 61% of MWEs having a value of 0.00 or 0.05. We use Mean Absolute Error (MAE) as our evaluation metric, following the 2018 Shared Task official evaluation strategy (Yimam et al., 2018). This metric estimates average absolute difference between pairs of the predicted and the gold-standard complexity scores.

The initial results in Table 4 consider *complexity prediction* in isolation, by testing on valid MWEs and providing the gold labels for the MWE types. Our system achieves lower absolute error than the baseline on both NEWS and WIKIPEDIA test sets, but not on the WIKINEWS test set. However, the distribution of probabilistic scores in the WIKINEWS test set is highly skewed, with 79% having scores of 0.05 or 0.00 and the highest complexity score in the dataset being only 0.35; a graph in Figure 1 illustrates the distribution of labels across test sets.

In practice we do not have gold standard labels for the MWE types, therefore we use linguistic pattern analysis to predict the MWE labels. The results of combining type and complexity prediction (2,3) follow the same trend as complexity prediction alone, however they also show a decrease in performance across test sets. As Kochmar et al. (2020) show, the type of MWE is highly informative when considering phrase complexity, therefore misclassification at this stage negatively impacts subsequent complexity prediction. We note that our MWE-type detection system achieves the F1-scores around 0.70 on the `MW named entities`, `PP modifier`

and `verb-particle` or other phrasal verb classes, followed by F1-scores around 0.60 for the `MW compounds` and `verb-preposition` classes. The classes that our system most struggles in identifying include `conjunction/connective`, `coordinated phrase` and `verb-noun(-preposition)`.

Finally, we consider the entire pipeline including the initial step (1) of *MWE identification*. As complexity prediction can only be performed on MWEs identified by our system, the size of the test set is reduced, therefore results are not directly comparable to previous stages. However, we note that our system outperforms the baseline across all genres. The baseline performs worse on the MWEs identified by our system as the probabilistic average is higher (0.14 compared to 0.09). A point of interest is that of the MWEs identified by the system, only 0.08% have a complexity value of 0 compared to 18% of the initial test sets. This suggests that the MWE identification step is identifying 'strong' MWEs that are more likely to be considered complex by annotators. This further supports our hypothesis that an MWE identification system can be combined with complexity features into a unified system to provide better complexity identification at the level of phrases.

6. Conclusions

In this paper, we propose a complexity assessment system for predicting complexity of MWEs rather than single word units. We show that augmenting the system with the information about type of expressions improves the performance. Research on lexical complexity assessment would highly benefit from the proposed data and system.

Acknowledgements

The second and third authors' research is supported by Cambridge Assessment, University of Cambridge, via the ALTA

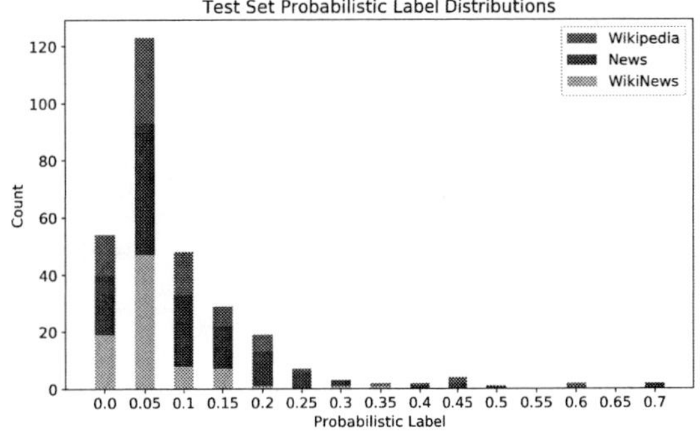

Figure 1: Probabilistic label counts across test sets

Institute. We are grateful to the anonymous reviewers for their valuable feedback.

7. Bibliographical References

Al Saied, H., Candito, M., and Constant, M. (2017). The ATILF-LLF System for Parseme Shared Task: a Transition-based Verbal Multiword Expression Tagger. In *13th Workshop on Multiword Expressions (MWE 2017)*, pages 127–132.

Carpuat, M. and Diab, M. (2010). Task-based evaluation of multiword expressions: a pilot study in statistical machine translation. In *Proceedings of NAACL-HLT*, pages 242–245.

Constant, M., Eryiğit, G., Monti, J., van der Plas, L., Ramisch, C., Rosner, M., and Todirascu, A. (2017). Multiword expression processing: A survey. *Computational Linguistics*, 43(4):837–892.

Davies, M. (2009). The 385+ million word corpus of contemporary american english (1990–2008+): Design, architecture, and linguistic insights. *International journal of corpus linguistics*, 14(2):159–190.

Devlin, J., Chang, M.-W., Lee, K., and Toutanova, K. (2018). Bert: Pre-training of deep bidirectional transformers for language understanding. *arXiv preprint arXiv:1810.04805*.

Fleiss, J. L. (1981). *Statistical methods for rates and proportions*. New York: John Wiley, 2nd edition.

François, T. and Watrin, P. (2011). On the contribution of MWE-based features to a readability formula for French as a foreign language. In *Proceedings of the International Conference Recent Advances in Natural Language Processing 2011*, pages 441–447, Hissar, Bulgaria, September. Association for Computational Linguistics.

Gooding, S. and Kochmar, E. (2018). CAMB at CWI shared task 2018: Complex word identification with ensemble-based voting. In *Proceedings of the Thirteenth Workshop on Innovative Use of NLP for Building Educational Applications*, pages 184–194, New Orleans, Louisiana, June. Association for Computational Linguistics.

Gooding, S. and Kochmar, E. (2019). Complex word identification as a sequence labelling task. In *Proceedings of the 57th Annual Meeting of the Association for Computational Linguistics*, pages 1148–1153, Florence, Italy, July. Association for Computational Linguistics.

Hmida, F., Billami, M., François, T., and Gala, N. (2018). Assisted lexical simplification for french native children with reading difficulties. In *Proceedings of the Workshop of Automatic Text Adaptation, 11th International Conference on Natural Language Generation*.

Kochmar, E., Gooding, S., and Shardlow, M. (2020). Detecting multiword expression type helps lexical complexity assessment. In *Proceedings of the Twelfth International Conference on Language Resources and Evaluation (LREC 2020)*.

Newman, David, K. N. L. J. H. and Baldwin, T. (2012). Bayesian text segmentation for index term identification and keyphrase extraction. In *Proceedings of COLING 2012*, pages 2077–2092.

Ozasa, T., Weir, G., and Fukui, M. (2007). Measuring readability for Japanese learners of English. In *Proceedings of the 12th Conference of Pan-Pacific Association of Applied Linguistics*, pages 122–125.

Ramisch, C., Cordeiro, S., Savary, A., Vincze, V., Mititelu, V., Bhatia, A., Buljan, M., Candito, M., Gantar, P., Giouli, V., et al. (2018). Edition 1.1 of the PARSEME Shared Task on Automatic Identification of Verbal Multiword Expressions.

Rohanian, O., Taslimipoor, S., Kouchaki, S., Ha, L. A., and Mitkov, R. (2019). Bridging the gap: Attending to discontinuity in identification of multiword expressions. In *Proceedings of the 2019 Conference of the North American Chapter of the Association for Computational Linguistics: Human Language Technologies, Volume 1 (Long and Short Papers)*, pages 2692–2698.

Sag, I. A., Baldwin, T., Bond, F., Copestake, A., and Flickinger, D. (2002). Multiword expressions: A pain in the neck for nlp. *Lecture Notes in Computer Science*, 2276:1–15.

Savary, A., Ramisch, C., Cordeiro, S., Sangati, F., Vincze, V., Qasemizadeh, B., Candito, M., Cap, F., Giouli, V., Stoyanova, I., et al. (2017). The PARSEME shared task on automatic identification of verbal multiword expressions. In *Proceedings of the 13th Workshop on Multiword Expressions (MWE 2017)*, pages 31–47.

Schneider, N. and Smith, N. A. (2015). A corpus and model integrating multiword expressions and supersenses. In *Proceedings of the 2015 Conference of the North American Chapter of the Association for Computational Linguistics: Human Language Technologies*, pages 1537–1547.

Schneider, N., Onuffer, S., Kazour, N., Danchik, E., Mordowanec, M. T., Conrad, H., and Smith, N. A. (2014). Comprehensive annotation of multiword expressions in a social web corpus. In *Proceedings of the Ninth International Conference on Language Resources and Evaluation (LREC'14)*, pages 455–461. European Language Resources Association (ELRA), May.

Shardlow, M. (2013). A comparison of techniques to automatically identify complex words. In *51st Annual Meeting of the Association for Computational Linguistics Proceedings of the Student Research Workshop*, pages 103–109, Sofia, Bulgaria, August. Association for Computational Linguistics.

Williams, L., Bannister, C., Arribas-Ayllon, M., Preece, A., and Spasić, I. (2015). The role of idioms in sentiment analysis. *Expert Systems with Applications*, 42(21):7375–7385.

Yimam, S. M., Štajner, S., Riedl, M., and Biemann, C. (2017). CWIG3G2 - complex word identification task across three text genres and two user groups. In *Proceedings of the Eighth International Joint Conference on Natural Language Processing (Volume 2: Short Papers)*, pages 401–407, Taipei, Taiwan, November. Asian Federation of Natural Language Processing.

Yimam, S. M., Biemann, C., Malmasi, S., Paetzold, G., Specia, L., Štajner, S., Tack, A., and Zampieri, M. (2018). A report on the complex word identification shared task 2018. In *Proceedings of the Thirteenth Workshop on Innovative Use of NLP for Building Educational Applications*,

pages 66–78, New Orleans, Louisiana, June. Association
for Computational Linguistics.

1st Workshop on Tools and Resources to Empower People with REAding DIfficulties (READI2020), pages 20–26
Language Resources and Evaluation Conference (LREC 2020), Marseille, 11–16 May 2020
© European Language Resources Association (ELRA), licensed under CC-BY-NC

Automatically Assess Children's Reading Skills

Ornella Mich, Nadia Mana, Roberto Gretter, Marco Matassoni, Daniele Falavigna
Fondazione Bruno Kessler (FBK), Trento, Italy
{mich, mana, gretter, matasso, falavi}@fbk.eu

Abstract

Assessing reading skills is an important task teachers have to perform at the beginning of a new scholastic year to evaluate the starting level of the class and properly plan next learning activities. Digital tools based on automatic speech recognition (ASR) may be really useful to support teachers in this task, currently very time consuming and prone to human errors. This paper presents a web application for automatically assessing fluency and accuracy of oral reading in children attending Italian primary and lower secondary schools. Our system, based on ASR technology, implements the Cornoldi's MT battery, which is a well-known Italian test to assess reading skills. The front-end of the system has been designed following the participatory design approach by involving end users from the beginning of the creation process. Teachers may use our system to both test student's reading skills and monitor their performance over time. In fact, the system offers an effective graphical visualization of the assessment results for both individual students and entire class. The paper also presents the results of a pilot study to evaluate the system usability with teachers.

Keywords: reading skills, reading assessment, language learning, automatic speech recognition, children's speech recognition

1. Introduction

Assessing reading skills is one of the important tasks that teachers usually perform at the beginning of the scholastic year to have all the information they need to build an overview of the students' reading level and consequently plan effective lessons. This assessment should also be repeated at regular intervals during the scholastic term in order to monitor students' progress and, when necessary, to reformulate the work plan, including specific exercises to strengthen the students' skills and overcome possible difficulties. One of the most well-known standardized tests used in Italy to assess reading skills is based on the MT battery (Cornoldi et al., 1998), which measures the reading fluency, accuracy and comprehension. If the comprehension test can be simultaneously administered to all students of a class, the fluency and accuracy tests must instead be individually administered, in a quiet room: the student is invited to read aloud the piece as best as he/she can, whereas the examiner times and marks the errors on a specific paper sheet. Although it would be desirable to have several evaluation moments during the scholastic term, since this activity is very time consuming, this aspect prevents to regularly repeat the assessment. Furthermore, this activity is also subject to human errors. For these reasons, a digital tool supporting teachers in the MT battery administration seems to be really helpful.

The paper presents a web application for automatically assessing the fluency and the accuracy of oral reading in children attending the primary and lower secondary school. A first prototype of this system was described in a previous paper (Artuso et al., 2017). Here, we will present an advanced version of it, especially focusing on the design of its front-end. We will also describe the new functionalities that support teachers in quickly evaluate reading skills of an entire group of students. Furthermore, the paper presents the results of a pilot study, carried out with teachers, to evaluate the system usability.

This paper is organized as follows: Section 2 reports on research studies related to the paper's topic, whereas Section 3 describes the whole architecture of the system, giving some details about (a) the server side and (b) the client side. Finally, Section 4 draws some conclusions by highlighting benefits and limitations of the system, and presenting directions for future work.

2. Related works

Many studies have demonstrated the effectiveness of technology supporting children's learning by strengthening and enhancing a variety of skills, including those related to reading accuracy, speed, fluency and comprehension (Dynarski et al., 2007; Kamil, 2012). In the last decades, useful applications have been developed to support the reading process through automatic assessment of oral reading by estimating reading errors (Mostow et al., 1993), (dis)fluency (Bolanos et al., 2013), or mispronunciations (Black et al., 2010). Most of these applications are based on automatic speech recognition (ASR) technology. Indeed, the recent advances in the ASR field by means of new hybrid Deep Neural Network–Hidden Markov Models (DNN-HMMs) (Serizel and Giuliani, 2016), trained on large children spoken language corpora or originally developed for adult speech and then adapted to children speech (Serizel and Giuliani, 2014; Giuliani and Babaali, 2015; Liao et al., 2015), have made possible significant improvements of ASR algorithms and fostered the spread of technology based on automatic recognition of children speech for computer-assisted language learning.

The adoption of this technology is fostered by a design process based on a participatory approach (Schuler and Namioka, 1993), where target users (children, parents or teachers) are actively involved in the development stage starting from the beginning. Following this approach, user requirements as well as user needs and expectations are investigated and collected by focus groups, brainstorming meetings, interviews or questionnaires. The gathered information is analyzed and a first draft of the graphical interface is usually elaborated in the form of mock-ups, discussed and commented with the end users in order to collect feed-

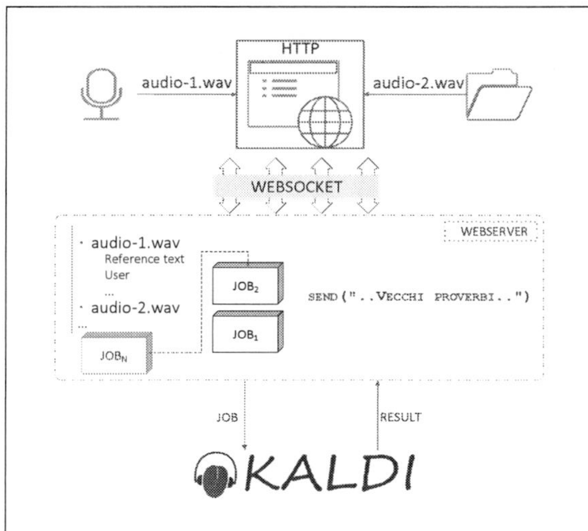

Figure 1: System overview.

back before the implementation stage. Finally, the system is usually tested and evaluated firstly by User Experience (UX) experts, and secondly by target users in order to assess its usability and accessibility (Nielsen, 2012).

3. System architecture

Our system is a web application based on an architecture formed by several modules distributed along both client and server sides. This architecture is illustrated in Figure 1.

On the client side, a web browser acquires audio files either directly from the microphone of the device (PC, laptop, mobile), or uploading them from the file system.

The collected audio files are then sent to the web server and here processed, i.e. compared to the reference reading. The resulting outputs are sent back to the client side, where they are visualized on a web page.

In the following, we briefly describe the server, which is the technological core of our system, and the client i.e. the front-end, which is the graphical interface between the technological core of our system and the user.

3.1. The server

The aim of the server is to process the audio file(s) sent from the client, and return the results to the client, which will visualize them. More specifically, first the server has to perform ASR on the incoming audio, then to compare the text automatically obtained by means of ASR algorithms with the expected text, and find out errors in reading, in particular those concerning speed and accuracy. The results of the comparison are also stored in a database, which allows teachers to create personalized visualizations of the data, for example data aggregated by class, novel, date, individual student, etc.

Our server is built up with the *Node.js*® framework[1]. The audio files acquired by means of the client, as explained in Section 3.2., are first transcribed by means of the ASR module which is based on the KALDI toolkit (Povey et al.,

---
[1]https://node.js.org

2011), an open source software toolkit largely used to develop state-of-the-art ASR systems for a variety of applications. Since the recorded audio files are related to a predefined set of texts, the automatic transcription related to a submitted job is then aligned with the reference transcription of the corresponding audio recording.

3.1.1. Acoustic models

The training corpus used by the ASR KALDI (Serizel and Giuliani, 2014; Giuliani and Babaali, 2015) consists of clean read speech from Italian children distributed by school grade, from grade 2 through grade 8, i.e. approximately aged from 7 to 13 years.

The training set was built by involving 115 children, each of whom was asked to read 58 or 65 sentences selected from digital texts of children's literature, appropriate for his/her school grade. Each speaker read a different set of sentences, including also 5-8 phonetically reach sentences. The number of utterances in the training set is 7,020 whereas their total duration is 7h:16m.

First, triphone hidden Markov models (HMMs) with gaussian mixture model (GMM) output densities are trained and used to align acoustic observations with tied HMMs states, obtained by means of a phonetic decision tree. Then, a deep neural network (DNN) with output nodes associated to tied HMMs states is trained using the resulting alignment. Acoustic observations are obtained from an eleven frames context window of features (5 frames at each side of the current frame).

Outputs of hidden layers are transformed by sigmoid functions, while softmax normalization is applied to the output layer. The DNN has 4 hidden layers each with 1536 neurons and 2410 output nodes (i.e. the same number of HMMs tied states). See (Artuso et al., 2017) for more details related to both acoustic modeling and decoding process.

3.1.2. Language models

To train the language models used in the ASR system we took advantage from the fact that the texts read by the pupils are those of predefined novels, and therefore known.

To both develop the ASR system and measure its performance, we have considered four different Italian novels, namely *I sette re di Roma* (The seven kings of Rome), *Vecchi proverbi* (Old proverbs), *La botte piena e la botte vuota* (The full barrel and the empty barrel), *I sovrani etruschi* (The Etruscan kings), taken from the Cornoldi's MT battery (Cornoldi et al., 1998), specifically designed and validated by experts to evaluate children's reading skills. A corpus of twenty readings was built by recording children (9 female and 11 male, aged 8-12 yeas) while reading aloud these novels. This corpus was used as testing set to assess the performance of the developed ASR system. Here below, we will give some details of the different language models (LM)s employed, while the reader is addressed to (Artuso et al., 2017) for examining the related achieved results more in details. The texts of all the four novels mentioned above were first normalized by: *a)* removing the punctuation, *b)* expanding numbers and acronyms and *c)* reducing all words to lowercase. Then the following three different 3-gram LMs were trained on the resulting text data, using the IRSTLM open source toolkit (Federico et al., 2008):

- Text To Read (TTR). The text training data are the reference texts of the novels, i.e. no attempts to train a reading error model is carried out.

- Automatic Error Model (AEM). The TTR data set is augmented with words formed by syllables obtained from the word beginnings (e.g., *bottiglia* – lit. bottle – generates *bot-* and *botti-*). With this approach we try to simulate false starts.

- Leave One Out (LOO). Both TTR and AEM text data are augmented with "exact" manual transcriptions of the sentences read by the pupil, so that a real reading error model can be trained. In this way the error model can account for non predictable reading errors leading to non-words, like for example mispronunciations of uncommon words or names (for instance *Tarquinio Prisco* often becomes *Tarquinio Parisco*, *proverbio* becomes *provervio*, etc.).

Table 1 shows some samples of the texts used to train the different LMs described above. The total number of words in the four stories is 606, the number of unigrams, bigrams and trigrams resulting after LM training on the TTR data set is: 332, 594 and 12, respectively.

3.2. The front-end

The structure of the front-end side of the second version of our system, i.e. the client, has been re-designed following the participatory design approach (Schuler and Namioka, 1993).

The system's designers involved end users - teachers - from the beginning of their work, organizing focus groups and brainstorming sessions with them to gather their needs and expectations. Pilot studies were performed to test the system between a process step and another.

The client is organized in three main parts: the acquisition page (Figure 3), the visualization of the assessment results of a single student (Figure 4), and the visualization of the assessment results of an entire class (Figures 5 and 6).

Table 1: Texts used to train the LMs. Pronunciation errors are highlighted in bold.

TTR
per la sorpresa e l' amarezza il vecchio proverbio . . .

AEM
pe- per la **so-** sorpresa e l' **ama-** amarezza il **ve-** vecchio **pro-** proverbio . . .
per la **sorpre-** sorpresa e l' **amare-** amarezza il vecchio **prove-** proverbio . . .

LOO
per la sorpresa **e l' amarezz-** e l' amarezza **del** vecchio proverbio . . .
per la sorpresa e l' amarezza il vecchio **provervio** . . .
per la **s-** sorpresa e l' amarezza il vecchio proverbio . . .
per la sorpresa e l' amarezza il vecchio proverbio . . .
per la sorpresa e l' **armarezza** il vecchio proverbio . . .
. . .

Figure 2: Material created and discussed during the focus group with teachers.

Before illustrating in detail each one of the client's parts, as an example of user involvement in the design process, we will describe one of the focus groups we performed with end users after the implementation of the first version of our system (Artuso et al., 2017) in order to collect information to design a better version.

3.2.1. Participatory design

Seven teachers coming from three different elementary schools in our area were involved in the focus group organized to discuss the first version of our system and find out its weaknesses and strengths, to be overcome and emphasized respectively.

The involved teachers were invited to discuss the following topics: (1) the MT battery, (2) the reading aloud practice, (3) possible new functionalities to be added to improve the system, and (4) what are the potentials of our system. For each of the above topics, the teachers first individually worked writing their thoughts on post-its (Figure 2) and then discussing them in group, chaired by two researchers.

Concerning the MT battery, the teachers affirmed that they usually perform the test individually, outside of the classroom, and use it to measure the reading fluency, whereas they globally evaluate the student considering not only the result of the test but also considering the individual progress during the previous scholastic years. The involved teachers also highlighted the fact that the novels proposed by the MT battery are easier than those proposed in the current school textbooks and also than those used in the official national screening - Prove INVALSI[2].

Concerning the reading aloud practice, the involved teachers said it is an important activity: they usually invite students to train this skill at home and then they evaluate the students with reading aloud sessions at school.

Concerning the first version of our system, after working individually with it, the teachers suggested some improvements: (1) adding the possibility of using it in the classroom, where each student has his/her computer and each one can perform the reading test in parallel with other students, because this would allow to save a lot of time; however, this function implies that the system is able to capture

---

[2]https://www.invalsi.it/

only the audio recorded more closely to the microphone and filter out any noise, which is technically difficult; (2) they suggested to implement a version of the system running on tablet-PCs because they affirm that it is easier for students reading on the display of tablet PCs than on that of desktop PCs; (3) they would like having the possibility of printing the results of the audio elaboration performed by our system to discuss them with other class teachers, as well as with pupils' parents; (4) teachers suggested to also find out the missing pauses and not only highlight those that are too long; (5) teachers would prefer not having a global score including both fluency and accuracy, but having two separated scores.

Concerning the potentials of our application, the teachers stated that it is really interesting because (a) it allows an objective evaluation, (b) it can be used more often than the paper version, (c) it is useful to have a view of the reading skill progress over time. They proposed to also add the possibility of evaluating the reading comprehension skills.

After analysing the results of this focus group, our software programmers implemented the request (5) - having two separated scores and the request (3) - printing the results. The other requests are considered as future work.

3.2.2. The acquisition page

At the beginning of an assessment session, the teacher inserts the name of the student involved in the test and the class he/she is attending; then, the teacher selects the title of the novel on which the student is evaluated. Now, the system is ready to receive the audio file to be elaborated. Concerning this point, our system may work in two different ways: (a) the teacher first records offline the oral reading of the student and then uploads the audio file using the arrow on the right part of the page (see Figure 3 on the top-right); (b) the student reads real time the chosen novel using the PC microphone; in this case, the teacher clicks on the microphone icon (see Figure 3 on the top-left) to start the audio recording. When the system has acquired the entire file (case (a)) or the student has finished to read the text (case (b)), the teacher listens to the recorded audio by clicking on the play button. If he/she is satisfied with it, he/she lets start the audio processing by clicking on the button "TRASCRIVI" ("Transcribe") to launch the ASR algorithms and perform the automatic assessment. Otherwise, the reading can be recorded again.

Figure 3: How to insert new registrations.

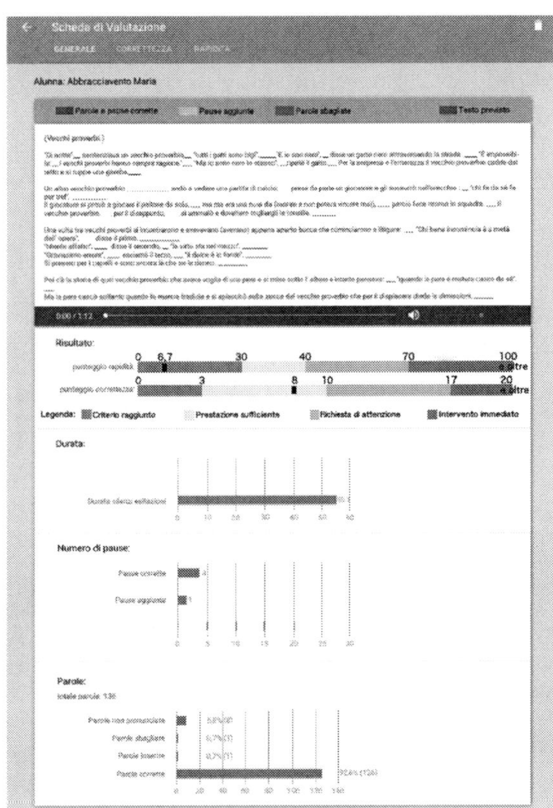

Figure 4: Assessment results of a single student.

3.2.3. Visualization of a student's assessment

At the end of the audio processing made by the ASR on the server-side, our system opens a web page as that shown in Figure 4, which represents the output of our system for a student attending the fifth class of the primary school and reading the novel "I vecchi proverbi". The web page is divided in three main areas: on the top side of the page, the transcription of the read text is visualized; then, there is a box where the scores are visualized, and on the third area, three charts are visualized, reporting results statistics.

The text area Here, words and pauses, represented by means of underscores, are visualized in different colors, chosen by following the rules of the color psychology (Elliot and Maier, 2014), as explained in the following: the green color is used to indicate both the words correctly read and the pauses correctly done; the yellow color is used to indicate the pauses added where not necessary; the red color is used to indicate those words that are not correctly read; the blue color is used to indicate the skipped words, i.e. the words present in the text but not read by the student. This kind of visualization makes the whole area a sort of *picture* of the reading: the teacher has an immediate feeling of the student's performance, without listening the recording.

Individual Scores Our system assesses the reading skills computing the two scores proposed by Cornoldi et al. (1998): (1) speed of reading and (2) accuracy. The speed

Table 2: Schema for placing scores in reading the text *Old Proverbs* (see Figure 4), used to assess students attending the fifth class of the primary school.

	fullness criterion reached	sufficient performance against the criterion	attention required	immediate intervention request
Speed (in cs)	< 31	$31 - 40$	$41 - 70$	> 70
Accuracy (in #errors)	$0 - 3$	$4 - 10$	$11 - 17$	> 18

of reading is computed as the total amount of hundredth of seconds spent by the reader to complete the entire reading divided by the number of read syllables. The accuracy is associated to the total number of errors. An error is the missing of a (group of) syllable(s) or a word, the adding of a (group of) syllable(s) or a word, a pause longer than five seconds, the wrong reading of a syllable.

Cornoldi et al. (1998) measure the reading skills according to four levels: (1) fullness criterion reached, (2) sufficient performance against the criterion, (3) attention required and (4) immediate intervention request. In the case of the text reported in Figure 4, the values associated to each level are reported in Table 2. These values, depending on the number of words and syllables presented in a text, change from text to text.

Individual Statistics In this area, three charts summarize some information about the text's pauses (duration, number of correct ones, number of missed ones) and words (the number of those correctly read, those wrong read, the missed ones). Having a graphical representation of these information helps teachers quickly have highlighted the aspects on which the student is struggling: if the timing, i.e. the pauses, or the spelling.

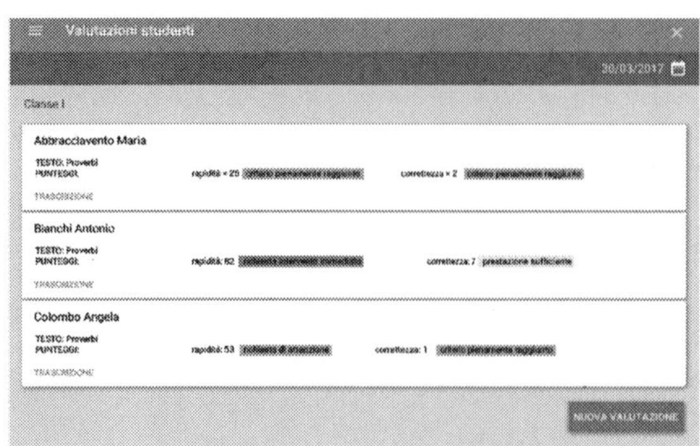

Figure 5: Assessment results of a class.

3.2.4. Visualization of a class's assessment

The two pages summarizing the results of the entire class (Figures 5 and 6) complete the visualization of the outputs of our system. The first summary page reports the single scores of each student in the class, scores related to the reading done in the specific day, which is selected on the calendar that the teacher can open clicking on the icon at the top right of the page (Figure 5). Clicking on the button "Trascrizione", the teacher can directly go to the result page of a specific student (Figure 4).

The second summary page (Figure 6) reports three types of charts: the first one visualizes the mean of the speed and accuracy of the entire class over time (Figure 6 on the top); the second one details the scores of all the students in the class, for a specific day (Figure 6 on the middle and on the bottom); the third one reports the scores of a single student over time.

3.2.5. Usability evaluation with end users

In order to evaluate the usability, meant as ease of access and use (Nielsen, 2012), of our system, we conducted a pilot study by involving three Primary school teachers who teach Italian. One, 28 year old, daily accesses Internet and has a medium level of digital skills, whereas the other two, aged 53 and 56 respectively, are less tech savvy and have a low level of digital skills. After receiving a short description of the application and of the aim of the study, the participants were asked to individually perform the following four tasks: 1. upload a new audio file from the local file system; 2. record a new audio file on the spot by using the PC microphone; 3. launch the automatic transcription and assessment process; 4. search for one of the past transcrip-

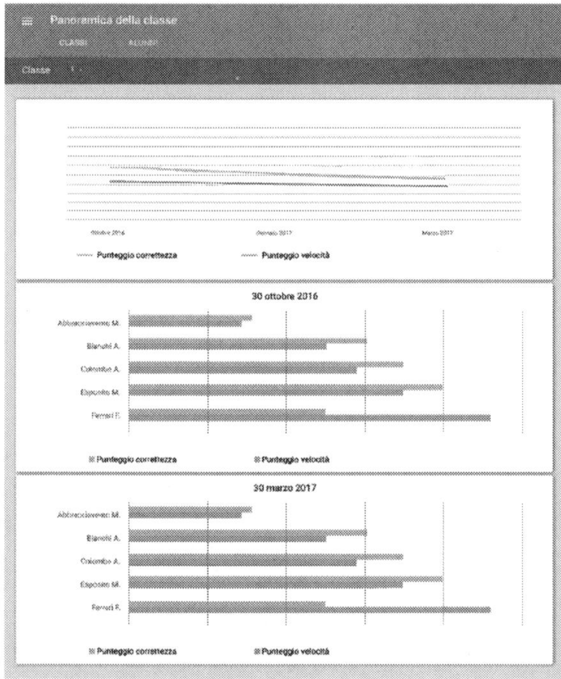

Figure 6: Monitoring of a class over time.

tions and check it.

The participants were observed during the tasks in order to: (a) check if and how they could complete the tasks, (b) see which difficulties they met, and (c) collect any comment during the task performing.

The first participant (the youngest and most tech savvy one) quickly completed all the proposed tasks, without any particular difficulty. The other two participants performed without problems tasks 1 and 4, but they both had an hesitation on the task 2 and the third one needed the help of the observer to complete the task 3.

At the end of the experimental session, the participants were interviewed to collect appreciations, criticisms and any suggestion useful to improve the system. In particular, it was explicitly asked (1) do you think that this application would be useful for your job? and (2) what would you improve?

All three participants really appreciated the application and positively replied to the first question. Only one participant added that it would be more useful if the application could work without the Internet connection. Regarding the second question: two participants stated that they would like to have the possibility of loading and processing more than one audio file at a time, and one participant asked for a search bar, supporting a quick search among all the stored transcriptions by student's name.

Given the findings of this pilot study, both the suggestion about the multiple file loading and that about the quick search by name were implemented in the current version of our system, whereas we are investigating the possibility of also making a stand-alone version.

4. Conclusion

In this paper we have presented a web application for automatically assessing the oral reading skills of children. Given audio recordings of oral readings, the system applies ASR algorithms and automatically estimates reading errors, disfluency, hesitations. The system aims to support teachers in assessing reading skills in their students. Starting from a first version presented in (Artuso et al., 2017) the front-end side of the system has been completely redesigned by following a participatory approach that involved a group of teachers both in focus groups and in pilot studies.

At the moment, the system has two main limitations: (a) it only estimates reading accuracy and speed but not comprehension and (b) it does not work on any text but on a set of pre-defined and pre-processed texts.

However, the system offers several advantages by: (a) speeding up the assessment based on the tests of MT battery (Cornoldi et al., 1998), (b) preventing humans errors in timing the task and marking errors, (c) memorizing in the server's database more assessment sessions along the year, so to allow teachers to better monitor and compare students' performance over time, (d) giving details on the errors, helpful for the teacher to suggest specific exercises to overcome students' difficulties, (e) both individual and class monitoring over time, (f) giving a quick visual overview of the errors by means of an effective graphical visualization. The next steps will be to: 1) add the automatic reading comprehension assessment, and 2) carry out a massive evalua-

tion of the system with teachers of several schools by assessing (a) the accuracy of ASR algorithms and therefore the system precision compared to the humans, (b) the efficiency in terms of time-saving, and (c) the usability of the graphical interface. Future work will also include the design and implementation of (a) a version for students for doing exercises with self-assessment in order to consolidate the reading skills, and (b) an enhanced version of ASR models able to process audio files of any text, instead of a pre-defined set of texts. Finally, in order to make the automatic task even more efficient, we are also going to explore the feasibility of performing parallel assessments in a noise environment such as a classroom where all students are in front of his/her computer, each one performing the reading test in parallel with other students. That means to try to face the limitations due to noisy recordings and to overcome the technical difficulties negatively impacting on the speech recognition accuracy by trying to use appropriate filtering.

5. Acknowledgements

The authors would like to thank all the children who contributed to the corpus of oral readings, as well as all the teachers who participated to the design and experimental sessions. Special thanks also go to Kaleidoscopio Social Cooperative and the school directors for their valuable collaboration in finding participants for our data collections and testing.

6. Bibliographical References

Artuso, S., Cristoforetti, L., Falavigna, D., Gretter, R., Mana, N., and Schiavo, G. (2017). A system for asessing children readings as school. In *SLaTE*, pages 115–120.

Black, M. P., Tepperman, J., and Narayanan, S. S. (2010). Automatic prediction of children's reading ability for high-level literacy assessment. *IEEE Transactions on Audio, Speech, and Language Processing*, 19(4):1015–1028.

Bolanos, D., Cole, R. A., Ward, W. H., Tindal, G. A., Schwanenflugel, P. J., and Kuhn, M. R. (2013). Automatic assessment of expressive oral reading. *Speech Communication*, 55(2):221–236.

Cornoldi, C., Colpo, G., and Gruppo, M. (1998). Nuove prove di lettura mt. *Giunti OS*.

Dynarski, M., Agodini, R., Heaviside, S., Novak, T., Carey, N., Campuzano, L., Means, B., Murphy, R., Penuel, W., Javitz, H., et al. (2007). Effectiveness of reading and mathematics software products: Findings from the first student cohort. IES Report - hal-00190019.

Elliot, A. J. and Maier, M. A. (2014). Color psychology: Effects of perceiving color on psychological functioning in humans. *Annual review of psychology*, 65:95–120.

Federico, M., Bertoldi, N., and Cettolo, M. (2008). IRSTLM: an Open Source Toolkit for Handling Large Scale Language Models. In *Proc. of Interspeech*, pages 1618–1621, Brisbane, Australia, September.

Giuliani, D. and Babaali, B. (2015). Large Vocabulary Children's Speech Recognition with DNN-HMM and

SGMM Acoustic Modeling. In *Proc. of Interspeech*, pages 1635–1639, Dresden (Germany), September.

Kamil, M. L., (2012). *Current and historical perspectives on reading research and instruction*, pages 161–188. American Psychological Association.

Liao, H., Pundak, G., Siohan, O., Carroll, M., Coccaro, N., Jiang, Q.-M., Sainath, T. N., Senior, A., Beaufays, F., and Bacchiani, M. (2015). Large vocabulary automatic speech recognition for children. In *Interspeech*.

Mostow, J., Hauptmann, A. G., Chase, L. L., and Roth, S. (1993). Towards a reading coach that listens: Automated detection of oral reading errors. In *AAAI*, pages 392–397.

Nielsen, J. (2012). Usability 101: Introduction to usability (2012). *URL: http://www. nngroup. com/articles/usability-101-introduction-to-usability/[Accessed November 2016]*, 9:35.

Povey, D., Ghoshal, A., Boulianne, G., Burget, L., Glembek, O., Goel, N., Hannemann, M., Motlicek, P., Qian, Y., Schwarz, P., et al. (2011). The kaldi speech recognition toolkit. In *IEEE 2011 Workshop on Automatic Speech Recognition and Understanding*. IEEE Signal Processing Society.

Schuler, D. and Namioka, A. (1993). *Participatory design: Principles and practices*. CRC Press.

Serizel, R. and Giuliani, D. (2014). Vocal tract length normalisation approaches to DNN-based children's and adults' speech recognition. In *Proc. of IEEE SLT Workshop*, South Lake Tahoe, (California and Nevada), December, 7-10.

Serizel, R. and Giuliani, D. (2016). Deep-neural network approaches for speech recognition with heterogeneous groups of speakers including children. *Natural Language Engineering*, FirstView:1–26, 7.

1st Workshop on Tools and Resources to Empower People with REAding DIfficulties (READI2020), pages 27–32
Language Resources and Evaluation Conference (LREC 2020), Marseille, 11–16 May 2020
© European Language Resources Association (ELRA), licensed under CC-BY-NC

Text Simplification to Help Individuals With Low Vision Read More Fluently

Lauren Sauvan[1*], Natacha Stolowy[1*], Carlos Aguilar[2], Thomas François[3], Núria Gala[4], Frédéric Matonti[5], Eric Castet[6], Aurélie Calabrèse[7]

[1] North Hospital, Marseille France; [2] Mantu Lab, Amaris Research Unit, Sophia Antipolis, France; [3] UCLouvain, IL&C, CENTAL, Belgique; [4] Aix-Marseille Univ. Laboratoire Parole et Langage, CNRS UMR 7309, Aix-en-Provence, France; [5] Centre Paradis Monticelli, Marseille, France; [6] Aix-Marseille Univ., Laboratoire de Psychologie Cognitive, CNRS UMR 7290, Marseille, France; [7] Université Côte d'Azur, Inria, Sophia Antipolis, France.
* These authors contributed equally
aurelie.calabrese@inria.fr

Abstract

The objective of this work is to introduce text simplification as a potential reading aid to help improve the poor reading performance experienced by visually impaired individuals. As a first step, we explore what makes a text especially complex when read with low vision, by assessing the individual effect of three word properties (frequency, orthographic similarity and length) on reading speed in the presence of Central visual Field Loss (CFL). Individuals with bilateral CFL induced by macular diseases read pairs of French sentences displayed with the self-paced reading method. For each sentence pair, sentence n contained a target word matched with a synonym word of the same length included in sentence n+1. Reading time was recorded for each target word. Given the corpus we used, our results show that (1) word frequency has a significant effect on reading time (the more frequent the faster the reading speed) with larger amplitude (in the range of seconds) compared to normal vision; (2) word neighborhood size has a significant effect on reading time (the more neighbors the slower the reading speed), this effect being rather small in amplitude, but interestingly reversed compared to normal vision; (3) word length has no significant effect on reading time. Supporting the development of new and more effective assistive technology to help low vision is an important and timely issue, with massive potential implications for social and rehabilitation practices. The end goal of this project will be to use our findings to custom text simplification to this specific population and use it as an optimal and efficient reading aid.

Keywords: low vision, lexical simplification, word frequency, word neighborhood size, word length

1. Introduction

Age-related macular degeneration (AMD) accounts for 8.7% of all blindness worldwide and is the most common cause of blindness in developed countries. Older adults suffering from AMD often lose the ability to use central vision after developing a central scotoma. Despite advances in the treatment of AMD (Miller, 2013), central vision cannot be restored and difficulty with reading is often the primary complaint of patients with central field loss (CFL) (Brown et al., 2014), who have to use their eccentric vision for reading. The number of Europeans with AMD being expected to reach 60 million by 2030 (Wong et al., 2014), there is a real societal need to understand the reading deficit of these patients in order to help restore their functional reading.

Over the past twenty years, different approaches have been taken to explore this still unresolved matter. First, great effort has been invested in determining whether manipulations of text display (magnification, line spacing, etc.) could improve reading performance (Calabrèse et al., 2010). However, no modification of text presentation has proven to significantly increase reading speed for people with central vision loss. Another approach, extensively explored recently, is to optimize the capabilities of the remaining peripheral vision for reading through perceptual learning. Unfortunately, studies investigating training benefits in people with AMD show a very wide and uneven range of reading speed improvement (Calabrèse et al., 2017). A third approach lies in the development of cutting-edge reading aids targeted towards central vision loss to increase reading accessibility. The current works falls directly within this scope with the innovative idea to use text simplification as a new reading aid for individuals with CFL.

Text simplification is a growing domain in the field of Natural Language Processing (NLP), combining computer science, psycholinguistics and computational linguistics. Given a text, its main objective is to identify difficult linguistic forms for a given population and then remove or substitute them with simpler equivalents, customized to the needs of this specific population. The aim is to produce an equivalent version while keeping the meaning unchanged (Saggion, 2017). Text simplification has been used to make texts more accessible to various populations: people with low-literacy (Watanabe et al., 2009), second language learners (Crossley et al., 2014), deaf people (Inui et al., 2003), autistic readers (Barbu et al., 2013) or individuals with reading disorders, such as dyslexia (Rello et al., 2013; Ziegler et al., 2015). Text simplification can be achieved through: (1) the addition of information (definitions, explanations, etc.), (2) the deletion of unnecessary information or (3) the reduction of linguistic complexity using simpler equivalents (Shardlow, 2014). These three types of linguistic simplification can be carried at different linguistic levels: lexical (through synonym substitution), morpho-syntactic (through word-form variation, sentence splitting, clause deletion, among others), or discursive (expliciting pronouns by their referent, expliciting discourse relations through discourse markers, etc.). Although very promising in its current application fields, text simplification has never been applied to low vision before.

The general objective of the present work is to investigate whether text simplification can promote higher reading performance with AMD by reducing the linguistic complexity of text for individuals with low vision. By investigating which lexical transformation(s) can most benefit reading with central field loss, our long-term goal is to provide a first set of useful guidelines to design reading aids using text simplification that will promote reading performance improvement for this population.

Word frequency, word length and word neighborhood size are some of the most important linguistic factors known to affect text complexity and reading performance in normal vision (Adelman & Brown, 2007; Leroy & Kauchak, 2014). The neighborhood of a given word (*e.g.,* FIST) being defined as all the words of the same length varying from it by only one letter (*e.g.,* GIST, FAST, etc. (Coltheart et al., 1977)). In the case of CFL, visual input is deteriorated and access to text is only partial (Taylor et al., 2018). When reading the word "halte" with a scotoma (Figure 1), eccentric or incomplete letters may not be properly identified, leading to many possible misidentifications ("halle", "balte", "balle", "batte", etc.). Because bottom-up visual input is less reliable, CFL individuals must rely much more on top-down linguistic inference than readers with normal vision (Bullimore, 1995; Fine & Peli, 1996). Thus, we hypothesize that the effect of linguistic factors on reading performance should be much different in CFL patients than reported before with normally sighted readers. In a recent work, we started investigating this hypothesis by inspecting the effect of word frequency on the reading performance of 28 readers with CFL (Stolowy et al., 2019). As expected, results showed that low-frequency words significantly decrease reading speed. However, the amplitude of this effect was much larger for the visually impaired (differences in the range of seconds) than reported before for normal readers (range of milliseconds) (Khelifi et al., 2019; Schuster et al., 2016).

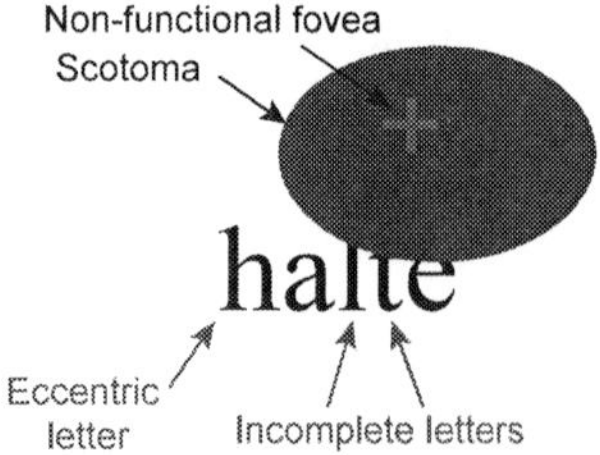

Figure 1: Partial access to text in the presence of a scotoma leads to a greater need for linguistic inference

In the current paper, we increment on our previous work by inspecting the respective effects of frequency, length and the number of neighbor words on reading speed in CFL individuals. In the following sections we will describe the methodology of our experiment (Section 2), presents its outcome results (Section 3) and discuss these results while proposing some future work directions (Section 4).

2. Methods

2.1 Participants

31 participants (18 women) were recruited from the Low-Vision Clinic of La Timone Hospital (Marseille, France). We selected our patients on three criteria: (1) presence of a bilateral central scotoma with monocular acuity of 4/10 (0.4 logMAR) or worse in their better eye; (2) absence of eye pathology other than maculopathy; (3) be fluent French readers. A total of six pathologies inducing CFL were present in our sample: atrophic AMD (n = 15), exudative AMD (n = 4), Stargardt's disease (n = 4), diabetic retinopathy (n = 1), cone dystrophy (n = 1) and myopic retinopathy (n = 6). Recruited participants ranged in age from 32 to 89 years.

2.2 Apparatus & stimuli

Sentences were displayed on an LCD monitor and presented on a window that subtended 56° x 42° at 40 cm. Sentences were aligned to the left and displayed in Courier (non-proportional font) in black on a white background. Print size was chosen optimally for each participant as the value of his/her critical print size, measured before testing with a French computerized version of MNREAD (Calabrèse et al., 2014; Calabrèse et al., 2019). Reading was monocular (eye with better visual acuity) with an appropriate correction for near vision.

2.3 Reading material

Reading material was created in French using ReSyf, a French lexicon with graded synonyms (Billami et al., 2018) and Lexique3, a lexical database providing word frequencies (in occurrences / million) and word neighborhood size (Coltheart's N) of standard written and oral French (New et al., 2001). The whole material was created in three steps, in order to generate pairs of synonyms with constrained linguistic properties (i.e. target words) embedded within pairs of interchangeable sentences. An example (in English) is given in Table 1.

Synonym pair	coast *characters = 5 / frequency = 48 / neighbors = 3* shore *characters = 5 / frequency = 24 / neighbors = 13*
Sentence pair	**You should go for a walk along the […] to relax** *44 characters / target word = n-2* **My parents have worked by the […] for many years** *45 characters / target word = n-3*
Cond. 1	**You should go for a walk along the** coast **to relax** **My parents have worked by the** shore **for many years**
Cond. 2	**You should go for a walk along the** shore **to relax** **My parents have worked by the** coast **for many years**

Table 1: Reading material example

First, we created a pool of target words, by selecting 32 pairs of synonyms matching the following criteria: (1) equal number of characters within a pair, with a length comprised between 3 and 8 characters; (2) frequency ratio between a high-frequency word and its low-frequency synonym comprised between 2 and 10; (3) difference in number of orthographic neighbors between the two synonyms comprised between 5 and 10.

Second, 32 pairs of short matching sentences were created so that each word from a pair could fit within either sentence of the corresponding sentence pair. Three criteria were used: (1) within a pair, sentences could have a maximum difference of 5 characters. Overall, sentences ranged in length from 42 to 65 characters (mean ± SD = 54 ± 6); (2) within each sentence, comprised of 'n' words, the target word could be located in any of these four locations: 'n', 'n-1', 'n-2', or 'n-3'; (3) pairs of sentences were specifically designed to fit the single and most frequent common sense for both words of a synonym pair.

Third, we generated our final reading material by combining sentence pairs with their matching pairs of synonym. In Condition 1, the first word of a pair was assigned to the first sentence of the corresponding pair, while the second word was assigned to the second sentence, thus creating 64 full sentences. In Condition 2, the "sentence – word" pairing was reversed to create a different set of 64 full sentences. These two experimental conditions allowed us to counterbalance any potential effect of the sentence itself (structure, complexity, predictability) by randomly assigning participants to Condition 1 or 2 (Steen-Baker et al., 2017).

2.4   Reading procedure & experimental design

Sentences were presented within 4 blocks of 16 trials (8 pairs of sentences) each. Participants were randomly assigned to Condition 1 or 2 and read between two to four blocks, depending on their reading speed and level of fatigue. Sentences were displayed randomly within each block with non-cumulative self-paced reading, where sentences appear as a whole but with all words masked by strings of "x" (Aaronson & Scarborough, 1976; Just et al., 1982). Participants were instructed to read each sentence aloud as quickly and accurately as possible while revealing each word one at a time using keyboard presses. Reading accuracy (correct *vs.* incorrect) and total reading time (in seconds) were recorded for each target word.

2.5   Statistical analysis

Statistical analyses were carried out in R (R Core Team, 2018). Reading accuracy (*i.e.,* binary variable) was analyzed by fitting a generalized linear mixed-effects model (GLME). Reading time (*i.e.,* continuous variable) was analyzed with a linear mixed-effects model (LME). In each model, two kinds of independent variables were included: (1) characteristics of the target word, *i.e.* their frequency, their length and their number of orthographic neighbors; (2) individual characteristics of the participants, *i.e.* their age and daily reading habits. The random structure of both models included a random intercept for participants, assuming a different "baseline" performance level for each individual. Reading time and word frequency were transformed in natural logarithm (ln) units to satisfy the assumptions of parametric statistical tests (Howell, 2009; Tabachnick et al., 2007). All continuous variables were centered around their mean. Optimal model structures were assessed using the Akaike Information Criterion (AIC) and likelihood-ratio tests (Zuur et al., 2010). In the Results section, fixed-effects estimates are reported along with their p-values and 95% confidence intervals (Bates et al., 2015).

3.   Results

3.1   Effect of frequency, length and neighborhood size on reading accuracy

On average, target words were read accurately 94% of the time, with individual variations ranging from 62 to 100% depending on participants. When all implemented in a single GLME model, word frequency (in occurrences/million), word length (in number of characters) and number of orthographic neighbors showed no significant effect on accuracy.

3.2   Effect of frequency, length and neighborhood size on reading time

Word frequency, word length and number of orthographic neighbors were all included in a single LME model in order to assess the individual influence of each factor (when partialling out the effect of the other two) on word reading time. Fixed effects results from this model are presented in Table 2.

	Estimate	SE	t-value	p-value	95% CI
Intercept *(ln(seconds))*	1.308	0.156	8.39	<0.001	[0.99; 1.62]
Frequency *(ln(occurrences/million))*	**-0.088**	**0.010**	**-9.03**	**<0.001**	**[-0.11; -0.07]**
Number of neighbors	**0.011**	**0.005**	**2.09**	**0.03**	**[0.001; 0.020]**
Length *(characters)*	0.006	0.021	0.26	0.79	[-0.04; 0.05]
Age *(years)*	0.003	0.006	0.45	0.66	[-0.01; 0.01]
Still reading *No*	-0.228	0.181	-1.26	0.22	[-0.60; 0.15]

Table 2: Results from the LME model; SE stands for Standard Error; CI stands for Confidence Interval. Factors showing a significant effect are highlighted in bold font.

As given by the model, average reading time when all factors are at their mean value is 3.7 seconds (exp(1.31)). Word frequency has a significant effect with a regression coefficient estimate of -0.088 (t = -9.03, p = <0.001, 95% CI = [-0.11; -0.07]; Figure 2). This means that multiplying frequency (in original units) by 10 multiplies reading time (in original units) by 0.82 (10 ^ -0.088), *i.e.,* a 18 % decrease. Similarly, multiplying frequency (in original units) by 1000 (*i.e.,* from 0.5 to 500, where most of our values lie) multiplies reading time (in original units) by 0.54 (1000 ^ -0.088), *i.e.,* a 56 % decrease.

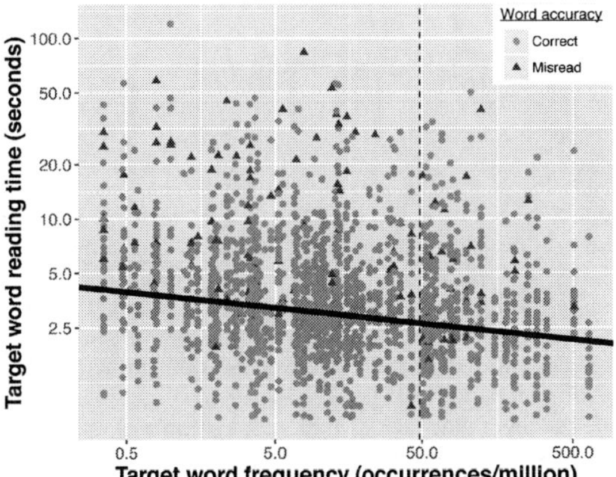

Figure 2: Scatterplot of target word reading time as a function of word frequency

The number of neighbors also has a significant effect on reading time but of smaller amplitude: when increasing neighborhood size by one neighbor, reading time is multiplied by 1.01 (exp(0.011)), representing a 1.01% increase (estimate = 0.011, t = 2.09, p = 0.03, 95% CI = [0.001; 0.020]; Figure 3). In other words, increasing the number of neighbors by 10 (*i.e.,* where most of our values lie from, 0 to 10) increases reading time by 10%.

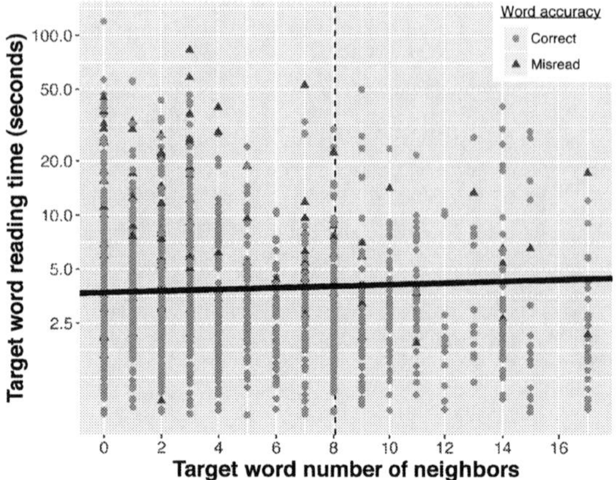

Figure 3: Scatterplot of target word reading time as a function of word number of neighbors

Word length has no significant effect on reading time (estimate = 0.006, t = 0.26, p = 0.79, 95% CI = [-0.04; 0.05]). It is notable that low-frequency words are on average longer than high-frequency words (Kliegl et al., 1982; Rayner & Duffy, 1986). Plus, within the specific range of word length represented in our experiment (3 to 8 characters), word neighborhood size and word length co-vary, with longer words having less neighbors (r = -0.44, t = -15, 95% CI = [-0.48, -0.39]). Therefore, the effects of frequency and neighborhood size reported above could have been induced by the confound between word length and each of these factors. However, including all three variables in our model enabled to rule out this possibility by partialling out the effect of word length. The age of the participant and the fact that they still maintain a daily reading activity shows no significant effect on reading time either.

4. Conclusions

In this work, we investigated for the first time the respective effects of multiple lexical factors on the reading performance of low-vision individuals with CFL.

Our first result is the facilitator effect of word frequency on reading time: the more frequent in the language, the faster a word is read. This result confirms what has been reported recently with CFL readers (Calabrèse et al., 2016b; Stolowy et al., 2019) and is also in line with the effect reported in the literature for subjects with normal vision (Kliegl et al., 2006). However, the effect of word frequency found in our CFL population is much greater than what has been reported before for normally sighted subjects, suggesting that low-vision individuals do rely more on lexical inference to support eccentric reading (Legge et al., 2001).

Our second result is the small but significant effect of word neighborhood size on reading time with CFL: the more neighbors, the slower a word is read. For normal readers however, word neighborhood size has long been known to have a facilitator effect on word recognition (the more neighbors, the easier to identify) (Vergara-Martínez & Swaab, 2012). We hypothesize that the reversed effect we report in CFL individuals is due to the visual constraint imposed by the presence of a central scotoma, hiding portions of the text (*i.e.,* letters) and forcing to use eccentric vision. The lack of high resolution coupled with missing visual information, would lead CFL readers to confuse one word with its orthographic neighbors, creating even more uncertainty for large word neighborhood size. Here are a couple of examples using the word "salle" that has 14 neighbors in French: *"Je vois la salle de ma fenêtre"* could be confused with *"Je vois le sable de ma fenêtre"*; *"J'ai loué une salle pour demain"* could be confused with *"J'ai loué une selle pour demain"* Although one could argue that the context normally helps the reader choose the correct statement, it is important to keep in mind that if a lot of relevant words are misidentified, there is no meaningful context to rely on, therefore leading to confusion.

Our third result is the absence of significant effect of word length on word reading time. For normal vision however, this effect is commonly reported in eye movement research as word reading time increasing with word length, mainly as a result of the increasing number of "refixations" (Kliegl et al., 2004; Vitu et al., 2001).

Trying to reduce reading deficits in AMD is a hot topic in the low-vision community. To our knowledge, the present project is the first one to propose the investigation of the linguistics aspects of this reading deficit by combining psycholinguistics, psychophysics of reading and ophthalmology. The long-term challenge of this work is to investigate what aspects of a text make it specifically complex for individuals with CFL (e.g., visual, lexical, syntactic, etc.) in order to provide simplification guidelines to promote reading performance improvement for this population. For instance, the present results suggest that when simplifying a text by substituting a "complex" word with a simpler synonym, one should preferably choose a synonym with higher frequency rather than one with few neighbors, no matter what length they are. Furthermore, despite its small amplitude, the reverse effect of word neighborhood size that we report is of great fundamental interest, as it confirms that the characteristics of text complexity differs when reading with CFL and should be investigated, rather than extrapolated from results with normal vision.

In the future, other aspects of text complexity, namely syntactic and discursive, should be investigated with CFL readers to build upon this work. The long-term objective will be to provide full comprehensive guidelines to design reading aids using text simplification tailored to low vision users. Furthermore, recent advances in the domain of natural language processing should allow a large-scale implementation of such reading aids, using automated text simplification algorithms. Assistive technology could be developed (in the form of web plug-ins or dedicated software) and used by individuals with visual impairment to enhance daily reading performance on computers, tablets, e-readers, etc. Optometrists in charge of visual readaptation in eye clinics could also benefit from this approach. In this context, text simplification would be used to train reading under the optometrist's supervision and advice. Our hope is that reducing the complexity of lexical units in text, without changing their meaning, should improve overall reading performance of low-vision readers.

5. Acknowledgements

This work was supported by the Fondation de France and by the Belgian FNRS. The authors thank Dr. Frédéric Chouraqui and Dr. Alban Comet for their help in recruiting the participants.

6. Bibliographical References

Aaronson D, Scarborough HS (1976) Performance theories for sentence coding: Some quantitative evidence. Journal of Experimental Psychology: Human Perception and Performance 2: 56-70.

Adelman JS, Brown GDA (2007) Phonographic neighbors, not orthographic neighbors, determine word naming latencies. Psychonomic Bulletin & Review 14: 455--459.

Barbu E, Martín-Valdivia MT, Ureña-López LA (2013) Open Book: a tool for helping ASD users' semantic comprehension. Proceedings of the Workshop on Natural Language Processing for Improving Textual Accessibility: 11--19.

Bates D, Mächler M, Bolker B, Walker S (2015) Fitting Linear Mixed-Effects Models Using lme4. Journal of Statistical Software 67: 1--48.

Brown JC, Goldstein JE, Chan TL, Massof R, Ramulu P, Low Vision Research Network Study Group (2014) Characterizing functional complaints in patients seeking outpatient low-vision services in the United States. Ophthalmology 121: 1655-62.e1.

Bullimore BI M. (1995) Reading and eye movements in age related maculopathy. Optometry and Vision Science.

Calabrèse A, Bernard J, Faure G, Hoffart L, Castet E (2014) Eye movements and reading speed in macular disease: the shrinking perceptual span hypothesis requires and is supported by a mediation analysis. Invest Ophthalmol Vis Sci 55: 3638-45.

Calabrèse A, Bernard J, Faure G, Hoffart L, Castet E (2016) Clustering of Eye Fixations: A New Oculomotor Determinant of Reading Speed in Maculopathy. Invest Ophthalmol Vis Sci 57: 3192-202.

Calabrèse A, Bernard J, Hoffart L, Faure G, Barouch F, Conrath J, et al. (2010) Small effect of interline spacing on maximal reading speed in low-vision patients with central field loss irrespective of scotoma size. Invest Ophthalmol Vis Sci 51: 1247-54.

Calabrèse A, Liu T, Legge GE (2017) Does Vertical Reading Help People with Macular Degeneration: An Exploratory Study. PLoS One 12: e0170743.

Calabrèse A, Mansfield JS, Legge GE (2019) mnreadR, an R package to analyze MNREAD data. version 2.1.3 https://CRAN.R-project.org/package=mnreadR.

Coltheart M, Davelaar E, Jonasson JE, Besner D (1977) Access to the internal lexicon. In: Dornio S, editor. Attention and performance VI. Hillsdale, NJ: Erlbaum: pp. 535--555.

Crossley SA, Yang HS, McNamara DS (2014) What's so simple about simplified texts? A computational and psycholinguistic investigation of text comprehension and text processing. Reading in a Foreign Language 26: 92-113.

Fine EM, Peli E (1996) The role of context in reading with central field loss. Optom Vis Sci 73: 533-9.

Howell DC (2009) Statistical methods for psychology. Cengage Learning.

Inui K, Fujita A, Takahashi T, Iida R, Iwakura T (2003) Text Simplification for Reading Assistance: A Project Note. Proceedings of the Second International Workshop on Paraphrasing 16: 9–16.

Just MA, Carpenter PA, Woolley JD (1982) Paradigms and processes in reading comprehension. J Exp Psychol Gen 111: 228-38.

Khelifi R, Sparrow L, Casalis S (2019) Is a Frequency Effect Observed in Eye Movements During Text Reading? A Comparison Between Developing and Expert Readers. Scientific Studies of Reading 0: 1-14.

Kliegl R, Grabner E, Rolfs M, Engbert R (2004) Length, frequency, and predictability effects of words on eye movements in reading. European Journal of Cognitive Psychology 16: 262-284.

Kliegl R, Nuthmann A, Engbert R (2006) Tracking the mind during reading: the influence of past, present, and future words on fixation durations. J Exp Psychol Gen 135: 12-35.

Kliegl R, Olson RK, Davidson BJ (1982) Regression analyses as a tool for studying reading processes: comment on Just and Carpenter's eye fixation theory. Mem Cognit 10: 287-96.

Legge GE, Mansfield JS, Chung ST (2001) Psychophysics of reading XX - Linking letter recognition to reading speed in central and peripheral vision. Vision Res 41: 725-43.

Leroy G, Kauchak D (2014) The effect of word familiarity on actual and perceived text difficulty. J Am Med Inform Assoc 21: e169-72.

Miller JW (2013) Age-related macular degeneration revisited--piecing the puzzle: the LXIX Edward Jackson memorial lecture. Am J Ophthalmol 155: 1-35.e13.

Rayner K, Duffy SA (1986) Lexical complexity and fixation times in reading: effects of word frequency, verb complexity, and lexical ambiguity. Mem Cognit 14: 191-201.

R Core Team (2018) R: A Language and Environment for Statistical Computing. Vienna, Austria: R Foundation for Statistical Computing. , https://www.R-project.org/.

Saggion, H. (2017) Automatic Text Simplification. Synthesis Lectures in Human Language Technologies. California, Morgan & Claypool Publishers.

Schuster S, Hawelka S, Hutzler F, Kronbichler M, Richlan F (2016) Words in Context: The Effects of Length, Frequency, and Predictability on Brain Responses During Natural Reading. Cereb Cortex 26: 3889-3904.

Shardlow M (2014) A survey of automated text simplification. Int. J. Adv. Comput. Sci. Appl. Special Issue on Natural Language Processing 2014: doi:10.14569.

Steen-Baker AA, Ng S, Payne BR, Anderson CJ, Federmeier KD, Stine-Morrow EAL (2017) The effects of context on processing words during sentence reading among adults varying in age and literacy skill. Psychol Aging 32: 460-472.

Stolowy N, Calabrèse A, Sauvan L, Aguilar C, François T, Gala N, et al. (2019) The influence of word frequency on word reading speed when individuals with macular diseases read text. Vision Research 155: 1 - 10.

Tabachnick BG, Fidell LS, Ullman JB (2007) Using multivariate statistics. Pearson Boston, MA.

Taylor DJ, Edwards LA, Binns AM, Crabb DP (2018) Seeing it differently: self-reported description of vision loss in dry age-related macular degeneration. Ophthalmic Physiol Opt 38: 98-105.

Vergara-Martínez M, Swaab TY (2012) Orthographic neighborhood effects as a function of word frequency: an event-related potential study. Psychophysiology 49: 1277-89.

Vitu F, McConkie GW, Kerr P, O'Regan JK (2001) Fixation location effects on fixation durations during reading: an inverted optimal viewing position effect. Vision Res 41: 3513-33.

Wong WL, Su X, Li X, Cheung CMG, Klein R, Cheng C, et al. (2014) Global prevalence of age-related macular degeneration and disease burden projection for 2020 and 2040: a systematic review and meta-analysis. Lancet Glob Health 2: e106-16.

Ziegler JC, Gala N, Brunel A, Combes M (2015) Text Simplification to increase Readability and facilitate Comprehension: a proof-of-concept pilot study. Workshop Brain and Language Cargèse.

Zuur AF, Ieno EN, Elphick CS (2010) A protocol for data exploration to avoid common statistical problems. Methods in Ecology and Evolution 1: 3-14.

7.   Language Resource References

Billami M, François T, Gala N (2018) ReSyf: a French lexicon with ranked synonyms. In Proceedings of the 27th Conference on Computational Linguistics (COLING 2018), Santa Fe, USA.: 2570-2581 https://cental.uclouvain.be/resyf/

New B, Brysbaert M, Veronis J, Pallier C (2007) The use of film subtitles to estimate word frequencies. Applied Psycholinguistics 28: 661-677.

1st Workshop on Tools and Resources to Empower People with REAding DIfficulties (READI2020), pages 33–40
Language Resources and Evaluation Conference (LREC 2020), Marseille, 11–16 May 2020

Identifying Abstract and Concrete Words in French to Better Address Reading Difficulties

Daria Goriachun, Núria Gala

Aix Marseille Univ., Laboratoire Parole et Langage (LPL UMR 7309)
5 Avenue Pasteur, 13100 Aix en Provence, France
dariagoryachun@gmail.com, nuria.gala@univ-amu.fr

Abstract

Literature in psycholinguistics and neurosciences has showed that abstract and concrete concepts are perceived differently by our brain, and that the abstractness of a word can cause difficulties in reading. In order to integrate this parameter into an automatic text simplification (ATS) system for French readers, an annotated list with 7,898 abstract and concrete nouns has been semi-automatically developed. Our aim was to obtain abstract and concrete nouns from an initial manually annotated short list by using two distributional approaches: nearest neighbors and syntactic co-occurrences. The results of this experience have enabled to shed light on the different behaviors of concrete and abstract nouns in context. Besides, the final list, a resource *per se* in French available on demand, provides a valuable contribution since annotated resources based on cognitive variables such as concreteness or abstractness are scarce and very difficult to obtain. In future work, the list will be enlarged and integrated into an existing lexicon with ranked synonyms for the identification of complex words in text simplification applications.

Keywords: text simplification, abstract and concrete nouns, semantic annotation, lexicon.

1. Introduction

The existence of differences in the brain for processing abstract and concrete words has been proven by researchers in the field of cognitive sciences. The basis for these studies is a dual-coding theory, described by Pavio (1965; 1991) consisting of two separate cognitive subsystems – two ways, verbal and non-verbal, of decoding the information. Their activation would depend on the degree of abstractness of the word. If concrete words use these two systems equally because they have an image as a support in the memory of the speaker, abstract words can only be decoded by a verbal system. Later this theory has also been proved by event-related potential (ERP) and functional magnetic resonance imaging (fMRI) tests (Just et al., 2004), which showed the detailed distinction between different brain zones activation during the processing of abstract and concrete words.

Relying on this theory, one could presuppose that concrete words have an advantage over abstract words in the task of word recall, since they beneficiate of two ways of decoding. The hypothesis has been confirmed by Kroll & Merves (1986) and James (1975) who refer to the ease with which a word evokes a mental image, as to the semantic factor which facilitates the recognition of words in the lexical decision task. And also by Shallice (1988) and Schwanenflugel (1991), who state that highly imaginable words have a richer or more easy accessible semantic representation.

Recently, Crutch and Warrington (2005) proposes that representations of concrete words are organized in a hierarchical structure (categorical organization), while abstract words are mainly represented by semantic associations. This theory maintains that concrete words share more representations with other similar words (for example, cow - sheep) than with other associated words (for example, cow - barn), while abstract words share more representations with other associated words (for example, theft - punishment) than with other similar words (for example, theft - crime). This can be reviewed from the point of view of another explanation for the concreteness effect in the framework of context availability theory (Schwanenflugel et al., 1988; Schwanenflugel & Shoben, 1983; Schwanenflugel & Stowe, 1989), which argues that concrete words are strongly associated with some contexts, while abstract words are weakly associated with many contexts, and the representations of abstract words have less conceptual overlap because these words appear in more disparate contexts, although they are semantically related (Schwanenflugel & Shoben, 1983).

In the 60s – 80s of the twentieth century, the question of the influence of the word's imageability on its perception and its impact in the complexity of texts was raised, particularly in people with deep dyslexia, and later on in normal readers. Paivio (1968) and Jones (1985) conducted a series of experiments separately to determine the level of word iconicity and the factors influencing the perception of the word as an abstract word in English (Canadian English in the first case and British English in the second). Jones (1985) conducted a study in non-dyslexic subjects with the task to annotate a list of words with high and low level of imageability, and to determine on a scale from 1 to 7 the ease of putting these words into simple factual statements. The results coincided with the researcher's hypotheses (except for a few words): concepts such as 'dog' are easy to put into simple factual statements (ex., the dog has four legs, the dog is a pet, the dog barks) than more abstract words such as 'idea'.

In this paper, we aim at identifying abstract and concrete words in French to develop a lexical database for French by bootstrapping from an initial manually annotated short list. In the following sections, we first address the issue of characterizing abstract and concrete words (section 2). In section 3, we describe the methodology to annotate French nouns bootstrapped from an initial short list by using two distributional approaches, nearest neighbors and syntactic co-occurrences. In section 4 we present the experimental setup, the initial word list and the results of the first two stages for extending the database. We finally conclude with an analysis of the results obtained after a comparison with human judgements and a discussion on the possible usages of the resource, namely its integration into an automatic text simplification (ATS) system to measure the impact of the abstract/concrete notion in the identification of complex words during reading.

2. Identifying Abstract and Concrete words

2.1 On the notions of Abstractness and Concreteness

Concreteness is the quality or state of being concrete, i.e. relating to an actual, specific thing or instance. The 'concreteness effect' refers "to the observation that concrete nouns are processed faster and more accurately than abstract nouns in a variety of cognitive tasks" (Jessen et al., 2000). Various theories explaining this effect in normal readers and people with reading disabilities are proposed in the literature. Plaut and Shallice (1993), in their connectionist model, consider an advantage for reading concrete words, due to the facility of their characterization. This is confirmed by a recent study that has showed an impact of word imageability and word regularity in word reading accuracy and word learning efficiency (Steacy & Compton, 2019). There is an evidence that imageability, the feature that describes the degree of ease with which a word provokes the appearance of a mental image in the reader's mind (Paivio et al., 1968), significantly impacts word reading accuracy and rate of word learning.

Categorizing words into concrete and abstract remains a difficult task. According to Tellier and colleagues (2018), concrete words are associated to great iconicity, particularly in terms of mental representation, while abstract words are rather verbally encoded (Paivio, 1986). Concrete words are more associated with contextual information and sensorimotor experiences than abstract words, insofar as, as pointed out, among others, concrete words are linked to high imageability and abstract words to low imageability (Paivio, 1986 and Palmer et al., 2013).

Following Gorman (1961), the notion of 'concrete noun' refers to objects, materials, sources of *relatively direct* sensation, while the notion of 'abstract noun' refers to objects, materials, and sources of *relatively indirect* sensation, with social or introspective information (Danguecan & Buchanan, 2016), see Table 1. However, Gorman (1961) claims that both abstract and concrete words can be general (name a group or a category) or specific (name a specific idea or an object).

A clear division of words into an abstract or a concrete category, however, remains quite subjective due to the fact that, firstly, each person has a different language experience and background, and secondly, in the vocabulary of any language, there are many polysemic words that often have meanings related to different categories on the concreteness scale.

Abstract words		Concrete words	
Processes, states and periods	lockdown, hope, month	Spatially perceptible	table, tree
Measures and qualities	degree, kindness	Physically perceptible by one of the five senses	music, rainbow, bitterness
Phenomena and events	advice, party	All living beings	women, cat
Human features	liar, genius	Mythological creatures	troll, dragon

Table 1. Abstract/Concrete typology (Danguecan & Buchanan, 2016; Dove, 2016)

Even though the binary nature of such a division may seem an obstacle to the accuracy of the classification, in our work we adhere to such a categorization. We believe that if previous studies were able to prove the difference in the perception of abstract and concrete words by the human brain, the line between abstractness and concreteness exists in the lexicon and can be reflected in specific inherent features in the vocabulary.

With the advent of automatic tools for natural language processing (NLP), an increasing interest has been shown in the possibility of automatic disambiguation of semantic features. Automatic annotation of abstract/concrete words remains nevertheless an area that is not sufficiently covered in research papers. Abstractness and concreteness being semantic properties, with no link with formal features (length, frequency, etc.), this increases the difficulty to obtain accurate annotations from raw corpora. The existing databases reported in the literature are usually based on the results of human annotations (Brysbaert et al., 2014). Databases for French are rare and contain a small amount of information (Bonin et al., 2003; Ferrand, 2001; Ferrand & Alario, 1998). They have mainly been developed for psycholinguistic experiments.

2.2 State-of-the-Art Methods to Annotate abstract and concrete words

Different attempts to build annotated lists of abstract and concrete words are reported on the literature. Rabinovich and colleagues (2018) use a weakly supervised approach to infer the abstraction property of words and expressions in the complete absence of labeled data. They exploit morphological cues as suffixes and prefixes and the contextual surroundings of a word as it appears in text. Their results show that the proposed heuristics are powerful enough to obtain a high correlation with human labels. The results also demonstrate that a minimum morphological information and a text corpus are enough to provide predictions (the authors used a set of "abstractness indicators" in English, i.e. suffixes like *-ness, -ence, -ety,-ship* etc.).

Other research (Marslen-Wilson et al., 2013) shows different degrees of concreteness for derived word-forms on the mental representation in English. Words with an opaque structure, i.e. words with a meaning that is not clearly linked to their stem in synchronic linguistics (for instance, "department") can be more difficult to categorize than words that can be easily decomposed into a stem with a transparent meaning and a suffix ("friendship").

With the rising of word embedding techniques the direction of the research has slightly changed, since this method allows to automatically extend distributional networks using the semantic proximity information presented as vectors. Studies involving the use of the word embedding algorithms for predicting the concreteness of words in one language and between languages have been proposed by Ljubešić and colleagues (2018). The question of the stability in word embeddings, depending on the assignment to the category of concrete or abstract, has also been studied by Pierrejean & Tanguy (2019). The results of this study have shown better stability of concrete words compared to abstract. Finally, Abnar and colleagues (2018) have carried experiments using multiple algorithms to compare their performance to the results of brain activity with the goal to find a better solution for the future word-sense disambiguation in abstract and concrete nouns. With word embeddings, as abstract concepts are mostly associated with abstract concepts, they appear in similar contexts and overall behave alike in a semantic space. Concrete concepts are also strongly associated with concrete concepts and appear in similar contexts.

There is no doubt that word embeddings are very powerful methods in NLP. However, as well as many other machine learning mechanisms, they often represent a 'black box' for the researcher: what is happening inside the algorithm operation remains vague and limits the interpretability of the results (Chen et al., 2018).

3.   Experimental setup

3.1   Objectives

In our study we are interested not only in what is happening after the application of a NLP algorithm, but also in what is happening inside the 'black box', i.e. how close is one or another algorithm of word embedding to a human judgement, and for which category, Abstract or Concrete, we can obtain better results. Our aim is to identify whether it is possible to bootstrap from a manually annotated list of words in order to enrich an existing database where words have been ranked according to their reading difficulty (Billami et al., 2018). We also aim at finding out whether this bootstrapping works better for abstract or for concrete nouns. Our hypothesis is that abstract nouns are semantically linked to other abstract nouns and concrete nouns are semantically linked to concrete nouns. We avoid using the term "synonyms" because this term has a restricted connotation. The distributional methods we use in our study, in addition to synonyms, may include other lexical relations such as analogies, antonyms and word associations.

3.2   Methodology

In order to enrich our initial short list of abstract and concrete nouns, we used two different types of relations: nearest neighbors (*voisins distributionnels*) and syntactic co-occurrences (*co-occurrents syntaxiques*) extracted from the French lexical database Le Voisins De Le Monde[3]. Nearest neighbors are words that share the same contexts, while syntactic co-occurrences are words that frequently appear next to a target word (van der Plas, 2009). For instance, 'plante' (plant) and 'fleur' (flower) are nearest neighbors of the concrete word 'arbre' (tree), while 'branche' (branch) and 'ombre' (shadow) are syntactic co-occurrents. 'Inquiétude' (worry) and 'peur' (fear) are nearest neighbors of the abstract word 'crainte' (dread), while 'dissipation' (dissipation) and 'reflet' (reflect) are found as syntactic co-occurrents.

We decided to base our research on these two methods because they show two distinct relations of semantical bonds in context. We made the hypothesis that this would be crucial for automatically identifying and distinguishing abstract and concrete words in context. In our study we investigated which of these two approaches was closer to human judgements: how many units from the output subset of nearest neighbors and syntactic co-occurrences obtained would better correspond to the human evaluation results.

We were also interested in differences in accuracy of prediction between abstract and concrete words and in the differences in the size of semantic networks of abstract and concrete words, if there were any. According to the theory of Schwanenflugel & Shoben (1983), abstract words appear in more varied contexts while concrete words appear in less contexts. Crutch & Warrington (2005) suggest that concrete words are organized following a semantic similarity principle, whereas abstract words are organized by their association with other words. In this work, we wanted to study if a quantitative prevalence and/or a greater homogeneity could be found in the results for abstract or concrete words during the extension of the primary list and/or as a result of the human evaluation.

3.3   Data

To automatically annotate words by using nearest neighbors and syntactic co-occurrences, we first created an initial short list of words from two studies for French (Ferrand, 2001; Ferrand & Alario, 1998) which contain 260 and 366 nouns respectively, with annotations according to abstractness and concreteness scales (see Appendix A).

To create our initial list, we chose 19 abstract nouns (Ferrand, 2001) and 42 concrete nouns (Ferrand and Alario, 1998) with a high frequency score (>=40) according to the lexical database for French Lexique 3[1]. Abstract nouns are monosemic according the lexical resource with graded synonyms ReSyf[2] (Billami et al., 2018). Nouns from the study of Ferrand and Alario (1998) annotated with a high concrete value and with a high frequency indicator[1] were often polysemic[2]. We decided to avoid them and to keep only monosemic concrete words (without abstract meanings, e.g. bread, hand, house, journal, etc.). Unlike concrete words, abstract words were mostly monosemic (they did not have other concrete meanings, e.g. joy, friendship, hatred, happiness, etc.).

The next step was to manually extract syntactic co-occurrences and nearest neighbors from the distributional database Les Voisins De le Monde[3] available online: 50 lexical units for each noun for the further bootstrapping process. The initial experimental dataset was reduced to only 50 nearest neighbors as we identified that after 50 first neighbors the distance from the target word according to the values given by the database became more important. In short, the relations became too distanced (according to the distance scores provided by Les Voisins De Le Monde). After these first two steps, we had a first list of 2,503 words from which we removed repetitions, non-nouns and words with a different part-of-speech of the target word. Finally, we obtained a full experimental list consisting of 369 units (180 concrete ad 189 abstract nouns) (see Table 2).

Category	Abstract	Concrete	Total
Initial short lists	19	42	61
Before manual filtering	909	1,594	2,503
After manual filtering: removing non-nouns, repetitions, errors, etc.	**189**	**180**	**369**

Table 2. Manual extension of the initial short list.

The next step was to automatically extract, for each of these 369 words, the 50 nearest neighbors and 50 syntactic co-occurrences obtained from the resource Les Voisins De le Monde[3] and to compare the output of each approach (a sample of the list can be found in the Appendix B).

4. Results and Discussion

4.1 Results

From the list of 369 words we gathered a quantitatively different output among the categories: 62,174 abstract words and 31,333 concrete words, which means that the number of concrete words gathered with nearest neighbors and syntactic co-occurrences is half the number of the gathered abstract words. After eliminating all the repetitions, we obtained 4,222 unique concrete words and 3,676 unique abstract words, as shown in Table 3:

Category	Abstract	Concrete	Total
Raw list	62,174	31,333	93,507
Filtered data	3,675	4,223	**7,898**

Table 3. Number of abstract and concrete annotated words automatically obtained from the initial lists.

These figures show that it seems easier to obtain abstract nouns than concrete nouns straight away. This is not because there is a larger number of abstract words in French but rather because of the closeness of abstract concepts in context. In other words, if we choose a pair of random abstract nouns X and Y and a random pair of concrete words Z and W, a random abstract word X is more likely to have another random abstract word Y as a nearest neighbor or as a syntactic co-occurrence, than a random

pair of concrete words Z and W to appear in the same semantic network as nearest neighbors or semantic co-occurrences.

Differences between the two distributional approaches, nearest neighbors and syntactic co-occurrences, were also found. For concrete nouns, the output obtained through the nearest neighbors and syntactic co-occurrences is almost equal (cf. Table 4), but for abstract nouns these numbers are uneven (45,340 *vs* 16,834). Nearest neighbors is the method that worked better for abstract words quantitatively, and syntactic co-occurrences is the method which, as we observed in the processed dataset, worked slightly better for concrete words. This result confirms the hypothesis that there are differences in the semantic representations between concrete and abstract words.

Category	Abstract	Concrete	Total
Raw data nearest neighbors	45,340	16,223	61,563
Raw data co-occurrences	16,834	15,110	31,944
Filtered data nearest neighbors	**2,129**	1,631	3,760
Filtered data co-occurrences	1,546	**2,592**	4,138

Table 4. Number of abstract and concrete words obtained after bootstrapping from the experimental list using two different distributional methods.

After filtering the lists (removing repetitions and part-of-speech errors), the differences among the categories were narrow: we finally obtained 3,675 abstract and 4,223 concrete nouns.

4.2 Evaluation

We used an online platform to annotate through crowdsourcing a sample of 120 nouns randomly selected from the filtered data obtained after the extension of the list of 369 nouns: 60 concrete nouns (30 nearest neighbors and 30 syntactic co-occurrences from the initial list of 180 concrete nouns) and 60 abstracts (30 nearest neighbors and 30 syntactic co-occurrences from the initial list of 189 abstract nouns). The sample was randomly selected from the data to avoid sampling bias.

By means of an online questionnaire addressed to Aix-Marseille Univ. staff and students, the participants had to annotate each word using a slider scale between -100 (very abstract) on the left of the interface and 100 (very concrete) on the right (see Figure 1). Participants were advised not to use the 'both concrete and abstract' option in the middle of the scale (position 0) very often (those who did it were automatically excluded from the experiment by the system).

4 word-fillers were also added to the 120 stimuli: 2 abstract words with a low score of iconicity ('haine' and 'espoir', hatred and hope, respectively) and 2 concrete words with a high score of concreteness and iconicity ('ananas' and 'guitare', pineapple and guitar). This is a common precaution to know if the participant has understood the instructions and if he has accomplished the task honestly

(the annotations of these words are not considered in the evaluation). In the instructions for the participants at the beginning of the test, we advised to make an intuitive choice without overthinking. 1,083 individuals participated in the test in only 4 hours (after this period the link to the platform was disabled).

Figure 1: Screenshot of the test online (for the word 'bourdonnement', buzz).

The results of the annotations were subjected to statistical analysis with R. All the choices lower than 0 were considered as choices towards 'abstractness' and all the choices higher than 0 were considered as choices towards 'concreteness'. This scale allows us (i) to observe the degree of these notions according to human judgment and (ii) to identify polysemic words (we hypothesize that polysemic words are close to 0 values). Human annotations were compared with the results of the automatic annotation on a binary basis. To convert the data gathered from the annotation, the means for each stimulus were calculated based on the 1,083 responses.

Starting from the fact that the semantic decision task is complex and ambiguous even for a human, we obtained better agreements with the method of nearest neighbors. For both methods, the correspondences were better for concrete than for abstract words, as it is showed in Table 5.

Category	Abstract	Concrete	Total
Nearest Neighbors Precision score	21 out of 30 **70%**	25 out of 30 **83,3%**	**77 %**
Syntact. Co-occurrences Precision score	15 out of 30 50%	19 out of 30 63,3%	57 %

Table 5. Number of correspondences human judgement/automatic annotation and Precision.

The standard deviation of human annotations was large which further confirms the difficulty of the task and the importance of our results. The stimuli with the smaller standard deviations (< 40) were all concrete names, among the stimuli with the larger standard deviations (> 65) there were abstract nouns and polysemic concrete names. We observed a strong correlation ($r = -0.6210$) between the means of stimuli (degree of concreteness) and the standard deviation (hesitation level): the greater the degree of concreteness, the lower the value of standard deviation. In general, the more a word is considered as concrete, the less hesitations appear during the annotation.

Using Fleiss' kappa formula, we obtained an inter-annotator agreement equal to 0.256, which is a weak agreement, but in line with other experiments on lexical semantic decision, particularly with a large scale from -100 to 100.

Our data analysis revealed that in the case of polysemy, a person chooses a concrete meaning rather than an abstract one, which is consistent with another research (Kwong, 2013). For example, the words 'cadre', 'échelle', 'cote', 'espèce', 'réserve', 'secours' (frame, scale, rating, specie, reserve, rescue) were classified as concrete.

We investigated the influence of the frequency of individual words on our results, but we did not find any relationship between frequency and means ($r = -0.0039$), and frequency and standard deviation ($r = -0.0901$). Finally, the results from two groups of participants (not native French speakers and participants with speech or language problems) were analyzed apart, however no significant differences were found in the results from these two groups and the others.

4.3 Discussion and future work

Since the nearest neighbors method showed its performativity in the task of automatically expanding the initial list of words and confirmed its conformity to a human's judgment at a fairly high level (77 % compared to the overall 57 % of syntactic co-occurrences), we plan to continue to use this distributional method in order to enlarge the list of 7,898 words already obtained. It will be also interesting to compare the results with results obtained with word embeddings.

The present list and its enlarged versions will also be integrated into the lexical resource ReSyf to be used in a text simplification system. It will also be utilized to future studies on the impact of word concreteness/abstractness in the reading process in normal and poor readers, and people with reading disabilities. These studies can be relevant for French, as previous researches have been mostly conducted for English (Sandberg & Kiran, 2014; Crutch & Warrington, 2005; Kiran et al., 2009; Palmer et al., 2013; Schwanenflugel & Stowe, 1989; Schwanenflugel et al., 1988).

5. Conclusion

Guided by the idea that abstract and concrete words have different semantic organizations, in this paper we confirmed our first hypothesis: abstract nouns are semantically linked to other abstract nouns and concrete nouns are semantically linked to concrete nouns in context. We also verified that nearest neighbors and syntactic co-occurrences methods work differently depending on the concreteness of the word. We found differences in the two approaches explored: nearest neighbors permitted to obtain more abstract nouns, while for concrete nouns both nearest neighbors and syntactic co-occurrences showed similar results from a quantitatively point of view. However, after removing repetitions, we obtained two lists of almost equal size, even if we finally gathered more concrete words.

These results would suggest that abstract words have a richer semantic network (i.e. more words in common) than concrete words. The difference between nearest neighbors and syntactic co-occurrences methods shows that the nearest neighbors method seems more suited for gathering abstract words, while the syntactic co-occurrences method seems more suitable to enrich a list of concrete words (see Table 4).

Having compared the sample from our automatically annotated data with the results of human evaluation, we conclude that the nearest neighbors method shows better precision rates for both abstract and concrete words. Annotating concreteness is prevalent using both methods according to human judgement, which can be related to the fact that in case of polysemy a participant is more likely to choose a concrete meaning than an abstract one.

In future work, we plan to continue the extension of the existent list with the nearest neighbors method and compare the results with other methods such as word embeddings. Besides, we foresee to study abstract and concrete words in authentic texts to evaluate their impact on reading (e.g. in primary schools with different reader profiles). In doing this, we aim to verify to what extent the 'concreteness effect' impacts word reading and comprehension in beginning readers of French.

6. Acknowledgements

This work has been funded by the French Agence Nationale pour la Recherche, through the ALECTOR project (ANR-16-CE28-0005). We deeply thank our colleague Frank Sajous for providing access to the complete data from Les Voisins De Le Monde database, as well as Johannes Ziegler and two anonymous reviewers for their valuable insights.

7. Bibliographical References

Billami, M. B., François, T. & Gala, N. (2018). ReSyf: a French lexicon with ranked synonyms. 27th International Conference on Computational Linguistics (COLING 2018), Santa Fe, New Mexico, United States, 2570-2581.

Bonin, P., Méot, A., Aubert, L.-F., Malardier, N., Niedenthal, P., & Capelle-Toczek, M.-C. (2003). Normes de concrétude, de valeur d'imagerie, de fréquence subjective et de valence émotionnelle pour 866 mots. L'Année psychologique, 103(4), 655–694. https://doi.org/10.3406/psy.2003.29658

Brysbaert, M., Warriner, A. B., & Kuperman, V. (2014). Concreteness ratings for 40 thousand generally known English word lemmas. Behavior Research Methods, 46(3), 904–911. https://doi.org/10.3758/s13428-013-0403-5

Chen, Z., He, Z., Liu, X., & Bian, J. (2018). Evaluating semantic relations in neural word embeddings with biomedical and general domain knowledge bases. BMC Medical Informatics and Decision Making, 18(S2), 65. https://doi.org/10.1186/s12911-018-0630-x

Crutch, S. J., & Warrington, E. K. (2005). Abstract and concrete concepts have structurally different representational frameworks. Brain, 128(3), 615–627. https://doi.org/10.1093/brain/awh349

Danguecan, A. N., & Buchanan, L. (2016). Semantic Neighborhood Effects for Abstract versus Concrete Words. Frontiers in Psychology, 7. https://doi.org/10.3389/fpsyg.2016.01034

Dove, G. (2016). Three symbol ungrounding problems: Abstract concepts and the future of embodied cognition. Psychonomic Bulletin & Review, 23(4), 1109–1121. https://doi.org/10.3758/s13423-015-0825-4

Ferrand, L. (2001). Normes d'associations verbales pour 260 mots « abstraits ». L'année Psychologique, 101(4), 683–721. https://doi.org/10.3406/psy.2001.29575

Ferrand, L., & Alario, F.-X. (1998). Normes d'associations verbales pour 366 noms d'objets concrets. L'année psychologique, 98(4), 659–709. https://doi.org/10.3406/psy.1998.28564

James, C. T. (1975). The role of semantic information in lexical decisions. Journal of Experimental Psychology: Human Perception and Performance, 1(2), 130–136. https://doi.org/10.1037/0096-1523.1.2.130

Jessen, F., Heun, R., Erb, M., Granath, D.-O., Klose, U., Papassotiropoulos, A., & Grodd, W. (2000). The Concreteness Effect: Evidence for Dual Coding and Context Availability. Brain and Language, 74(1), 103–112. https://doi.org/10.1006/brln.2000.2340

Jones, G. V. (1985). Deep dyslexia, imageability, and ease of predication. Brain and Language, 24(1), 1–19. https://doi.org/10.1016/0093-934X(85)90094-X

Just, M. A., Newman, S. D., Keller, T. A., McEleney, A., & Carpenter, P. A. (2004). Imagery in sentence comprehension: An fMRI study. NeuroImage, 21(1), 112–124. https://doi.org/10.1016/j.neuroimage.2003.08.042

Kiran, S., Sandberg, C., & Abbott, K. (2009). Treatment for lexical retrieval using abstract and concrete words in persons with aphasia: Effect of complexity. Aphasiology, 23(7–8), 835–853. https://doi.org/10.1080/02687030802588866

Kroll, J. F., & Merves, J. S. (1986). Lexical access for concrete and abstract words. Journal of Experimental Psychology: Learning, Memory, and Cognition, 12(1), 92–107. https://doi.org/10.1037/0278-7393.12.1.92

Kwong, O. Y. (2013). New Perspectives on Computational and Cognitive Strategies for Word Sense Disambiguation. Springer New York. https://doi.org/10.1007/978-1-4614-1320-2

Marslen-Wilson, W. D., Tyler, L. K., Waksler, R., & Older, L. (2013). Abstractness and transparency in the mental lexicon.

Paivio, A. (1986). Mental representations: A dual coding approach. Oxford University Press ; Clarendon Press.

Paivio, A. (1991). Dual coding theory: Retrospect and current status. Canadian Journal of Psychology/Revue Canadienne de Psychologie, 45(3), 255–287. https://doi.org/10.1037/h0084295

Paivio, A., Yuille, J. C., & Madigan, S. A. (1968). Concreteness, imagery, and meaningfulness values for 925 nouns. Journal of Experimental Psychology, 76(1, Pt.2), 1–25. https://doi.org/10.1037/h0025327

Palmer, S. D., MacGregor, L. J., & Havelka, J. (2013). Concreteness effects in single-meaning, multi-meaning and newly acquired words. Brain Research, 1538, 135–150. https://doi.org/10.1016/j.brainres.2013.09.015

Plaut, D. C., & Shallice, T. (1993). Deep dyslexia: A case study of connectionist neuropsychology. Cognitive Neuropsychology, 10(5), 377–500. https://doi.org/10.1080/02643299308253469

Rabinovich, E., Sznajder, B., Spector, A., Shnayderman, I., Aharonov, R., Konopnicki, D., & Slonim, N. (2018). Learning Concept Abstractness Using Weak Supervision. Proceedings of the 2018 Conference on

Empirical Methods in Natural Language Processing, 4854-4859. https://doi.org/10.18653/v1/D18-1522

Sandberg, C., & Kiran, S. (2014). Analysis of abstract and concrete word processing in persons with aphasia and age-matched neurologically healthy adults using fMRI. Neurocase, 20(4), 361–388. https://doi.org/10.1080/13554794.2013.770881

Schwanenflugel, P. J. (1991). Why are abstract concepts hard to understand? In The psychology of word meanings (pp. 223–250). Lawrence Erlbaum Associates, Inc.

Schwanenflugel, P. J., Harnishfeger, K. K., & Stowe, R. W. (1988). Context availability and lexical decisions for abstract and concrete words. Journal of Memory and Language, 27(5), 499–520. https://doi.org/10.1016/0749-596X(88)90022-8

Schwanenflugel, P. J., & Shoben, E. J. (1983). Differential Context Effects in the Comprehension of Abstract and Concrete Verbal Materials. 21.

Schwanenflugel, P. J., & Stowe, R. W. (1989). Context availability and the processing of abstract and concrete words in sentences. Reading Research Quarterly, 24(1), 114–126. https://doi.org/10.2307/748013

Shallice, T. (1988). From neuropsychology to mental structure. Cambridge University Press. https://doi.org/10.1017/CBO9780511526817

Steacy, L. M., & Compton, D. L. (2019). Examining the role of imageability and regularity in word reading accuracy and learning efficiency among first and second graders at risk for reading disabilities. Journal of Experimental Child Psychology, 178, 226–250. https://doi.org/10.1016/j.jecp.2018.09.007

van der Plas, L. (2009). Combining syntactic co-occurrences and nearest neighbours in distributional methods to remedy data sparseness. Proceedings of the Workshop on Unsupervised and Minimally Supervised Learning of Lexical Semantics - UMSLLS '09, 45–53. https://doi.org/10.3115/1641968.1641974

8.   Language Resource References

[1] Lexique org. Retrieved February 4, 2020, from http://www.lexique.org/

[2] ReSyf: a French lexicon with ranked synonyms. Retrieved February 4, 2020, from https://cental.uclouvain.be/resyf/index.html

[3] Les Voisins De Le Monde. Retrieved February 4, 2020, from http://redac.univ-tlse2.fr/voisinsdelemonde/

Appendix A. Initial short lists.

19 Abstract words of the initial list (Ferrand, 2001)		42 Concrete words of the initial list (Ferrand and Alario, 1998)			
amitié	joie	arbre	chat	livre	poignée
colère	peur	avion	chemise	main	poisson
courage	santé	bateau	cheval	maison	porte
crainte	sécurité	boîte	chien	manteau	pomme
effort	siècle	bouteille	cigarette	marteau	robe
espoir	succès	bras	église	montagne	sucre
gloire	tristesse	bureau	ferme	montre	table
haine	usage	café	feuille	mur	téléphone
idée	vérité	camion	fleur	oiseau	train
imagination		carte	journal	pain	voiture
		chaîne	lettre		

Appendix B. Examples from filtered data.

The 'relation' is the method by which a word has been obtained: nearest neighbor (NN) or syntactic cooccurrence (SC). The category corresponds to concrete (C) and Abstract (A) nouns, we note with * the errors from the automatic annotation.

Id Stimulus	Stimulus	Id Output	Output	Relation	Category
1	aéroport	1	port	NN	C
1	aéroport	2	gare	NN	C
1	aéroport	3	parc	NN	C
1	aéroport	4	station	NN	C
1	aéroport	5	tarmac	SC	C
1	aéroport	6	atterrissage*	SC	C
1	aéroport	7	ravitaillement*	SC	C

1	aéroport	8	airbus	SC	C
2	ballon	9	balle	NN	C
2	ballon	10	objet	NN	C
2	ballon	11	vélo	NN	C
2	ballon	12	cassette	NN	C
2	ballon	13	nacelle	SC	C
2	ballon	14	manieur	SC	C
2	ballon	15	tour	SC	C
2	ballon	16	tentative*	SC	C
3	câble	17	téléphone	NN	C
3	câble	18	bouquet	NN	C
3	câble	19	télécommunication*	NN	C
3	câble	20	satellite	NN	C
3	câble	21	abonné*	SC	C
3	câble	22	gaine	SC	C
3	câble	23	abonnement	SC	C
3	câble	24	raccordement	SC	C
4	dessin	25	photo	NN	C
4	dessin	26	photographie	NN	C
4	dessin	27	peinture	NN	C
4	dessin	28	portrait	NN	C
4	dessin	29	ensemble	SC	C
4	dessin	30	dossier	SC	C
4	dessin	31	carton	SC	C
4	dessin	32	accompagné*	SC	C
5	abus	33	recel	NN	A
5	abus	34	détournement	NN	A
5	abus	35	escroquerie	NN	A
5	abus	36	fraude	NN	A
5	abus	37	information	SC	A
5	abus	38	complicité	SC	A
5	abus	39	rencontre	SC	A
5	abus	40	juge*	SC	A
6	chance	41	possibilité	NN	A
6	chance	42	capacité	NN	A
6	chance	43	avantage	NN	A
6	chance	44	potentiel	NN	A
6	chance	45	scepticisme	SC	A
6	chance	46	égalité	SC	A
6	chance	47	égalisation	SC	A
6	chance	48	illusion	SC	A
7	décision	49	choix	NN	A
7	décision	50	mesure	NN	A
7	décision	51	accord	NN	A
7	décision	52	déclaration	NN	A
7	décision	53	félicité	SC	A
7	décision	54	cassation	SC	A
7	décision	56	pourvoi	SC	A
7	décision	57	réaction	SC	A
8	émotion	58	inquiétude	NN	A
8	émotion	59	angoisse	NN	A
8	émotion	60	sentiment	NN	A
8	émotion	61	plaisir	NN	A
8	émotion	62	capteur*	SC	A
8	émotion	63	chantage	SC	A
8	émotion	64	larme*	SC	A
8	émotion	65	moment	SC	A

1st Workshop on Tools and Resources to Empower People with REAding DIfficulties (READI2020), pages 41–48
Language Resources and Evaluation Conference (LREC 2020), Marseille, 11–16 May 2020
© European Language Resources Association (ELRA), licensed under CC-BY-NC

Benchmarking Data-driven Automatic Text Simplification for German

Andreas Säuberli, Sarah Ebling, Martin Volk
Department of Computational Linguistics, University of Zurich
Andreasstrasse 15, 8050 Zurich, Switzerland
andreas.saeuberli@uzh.ch, {ebling,volk}@cl.uzh.ch

Abstract

Automatic text simplification is an active research area, and there are first systems for English, Spanish, Portuguese, and Italian. For German, no data-driven approach exists to this date, due to a lack of training data. In this paper, we present a parallel corpus of news items in German with corresponding simplifications on two complexity levels. The simplifications have been produced according to a well-documented set of guidelines. We then report on experiments in automatically simplifying the German news items using state-of-the-art neural machine translation techniques. We demonstrate that despite our small parallel corpus, our neural models were able to learn essential features of simplified language, such as lexical substitutions, deletion of less relevant words and phrases, and sentence shortening.

Keywords: Simplified German, automatic text simplification, neural machine translation

1 Introduction

Simplified language is a variety of standard language characterized by reduced lexical and syntactic complexity, the addition of explanations for difficult concepts, and clearly structured layout.[1] Among the target groups of simplified language are persons with cognitive impairment and learning disabilities, prelingually deaf persons, functionally illiterate persons, and foreign language learners (Bredel and Maaß, 2016).

Automatic text simplification, the process of automatically producing a simplified version of a standard-language text, was initiated in the late 1990s (Carroll et al., 1998; Chandrasekar et al., 1996) and since then has been approached by means of rule-based and statistical methods. As part of a rule-based approach, the operations carried out typically include replacing complex lexical and syntactic units by simpler ones. A statistical approach generally conceptualizes the simplification task as one of converting a standard-language into a simplified-language text using machine translation techniques.

Research on automatic text simplification has been documented for English (Zhu et al., 2010), Spanish (Saggion et al., 2015), Portuguese (Aluisio and Gasperin, 2010), French (Brouwers et al., 2014), and Italian (Barlacchi and Tonelli, 2013). To the authors' knowledge, the work of Suter (2015) and Suter et al. (2016), who presented a prototype of a rule-based text simplification system, is the only proposal for German.

The paper at hand presents the first experiments in data-driven simplification for German, relying on neural machine translation. The data consists of news items manually simplified according to a well-known set of guidelines. Hence, the contribution of the paper is twofold:

1. Introducing a parallel corpus as data for automatic text simplification for German

2. Establishing a benchmark for automatic text simplification for German

---

[1]The term *plain language* is avoided, as it refers to a specific level of simplification. *Simplified language* subsumes all efforts of reducing the complexity of a text.

Section 2 presents the research background with respect to parallel corpora (Section 2.1) and monolingual sentence alignment tools (Section 2.2) for automatic text simplification. Section 3 introduces previous approaches to data-driven text simplification. Section 4 presents our work on automatic text simplification for German, introducing the data (Section 4.1), the models (Section 4.2), the results (Section 4.3), and a discussion (Section 4.4).

2 Parallel Corpora and Alignment Tools for Automatic Text Simplification

2.1 Parallel Corpora

Automatic text simplification via machine translation requires pairs of standard-language/simplified-language texts aligned at the sentence level, i.e., parallel corpora. A number of parallel corpora have been created to this end. Gasperin et al. (2010) compiled the PorSimples Corpus consisting of Brazilian Portuguese texts (2,116 sentences), each with two different levels of simplifications ("natural" and "strong"), resulting in around 4,500 aligned sentences. Bott and Saggion (2012) produced the Simplext Corpus consisting of 200 Spanish/simplified Spanish document pairs, amounting to a total of 1,149 (Spanish) and 1,808 (simplified Spanish) sentences (approximately 1,000 aligned sentences).

A large parallel corpus for automatic text simplification is the Parallel Wikipedia Simplification Corpus (PWKP) compiled from parallel articles of the English Wikipedia and the Simple English Wikipedia (Zhu et al., 2010), consisting of around 108,000 sentence pairs. Application of the corpus has been criticized for various reasons (Štajner et al., 2018); the most important among these is the fact that Simple English Wikipedia articles are often not translations of articles from the English Wikipedia. Hwang et al. (2015) provided an updated version of the corpus that includes a total of 280,000 full and partial matches between the two Wikipedia versions.

Another frequently used data collection, available for English and Spanish, is the Newsela Corpus (Xu et al., 2015) consisting of 1,130 news articles, each simplified into four school grade levels by professional editors.

Klaper et al. (2013) created the first parallel corpus for German/simplified German, consisting of 256 texts each (approximately 70,000 tokens) downloaded from the Web. More recently, Battisti et al. (2020) extended the corpus to 6,200 documents (nearly 211,000 sentences).

The above-mentioned PorSimples and Newsela corpora present standard-language texts simplified into multiple levels, thus accounting for a recent consensus in the area of simplified-language research, according to which a single level of simplified language is not sufficient; instead, multiple levels are required to account for the heterogeneous target usership. For simplified German, *capito*,[2] the largest provider of simplification services (translations and translators' training) in Austria, Germany, and Switzerland, distinguishes between three levels along the Common European Framework of Reference for Languages (CEFR) (Council of Europe, 2009): A1, A2, and B1.[3] Each level is linguistically operationalized, i.e., specified with respect to linguistic constructions permitted or not permitted at the respective level.

2.2 Sentence Alignment Tools for Simplified Texts

A freely available tool exists for generating sentence alignments of standard-language/simplified-language document pairs: *Customized Alignment for Text Simplification (CATS)* (Štajner et al., 2018). *CATS* requires a number of parameters to be specified:

- **Similarity strategy:** *CATS* offers a lexical (character-n-gram-based, CNG) and two semantic similarity strategies. The two semantic similarity strategies, WAVG (Word Average) and CWASA (Continuous Word Alignment-based Similarity Analysis), both require pretrained word embeddings. WAVG averages the word vectors of a paragraph or sentence to obtain the final vector for the respective text unit. CWASA is based on the alignment of continuous words using directed edges.

- **Alignment strategy:** *CATS* allows for adhering to a monotonicity restriction, i.e., requiring the order of information to be identical on the standard-language and simplified-language side, or abandoning it.

3 Data-Driven Automatic Text Simplification

Specia (2010) introduced statistical machine translation to the automatic text simplification task, using data from a small parallel corpus (roughly 4,500 parallel sentences) for Portuguese. Coster and Kauchak (2011) used the original PWKP Corpus (cf. Section 2.1) to train a machine translation system. Xu et al. (2016) performed syntax-based statistical machine translation on the English/simplified English part of the Newsela Corpus.

Nisioi et al. (2017) introduced neural sequence-to-sequence models to automatic text simplification, performing experiments on both the Wikipedia dataset of (Hwang et al., 2015) and the Newsela Corpus for English, with automatic alignments derived from *CATS* (cf. Section 2.2). The authors used a Long Short-term Memory (LSTM) architecture (Hochreiter and Schmidhuber, 1997) as instance of Recurrent Neural Networks (RNNs).

Surya et al. (2019) proposed an unsupervised or partially supervised approach to text simplification. Their model is based on a neural encoder-decoder but differs from previous approaches by adding reconstruction, adversarial, and diversification loss, which allows for exploiting non-parallel data as well. However, the authors' results prove that some parallel data is still essential.

Finally, Palmero Aprosio et al. (2019) experimented with data augmentation methods for low-resource text simplification for Italian. Their unaugmented dataset is larger than the one presented in this paper but includes more low-quality simplifications due to automatic extraction of simplified sentences from the Web. Our work differs in that we benchmark and compare a wider variety of low-resource methods.

The most commonly applied automatic evaluation metrics for text simplification are BLEU (Papineni et al., 2002) and SARI (Xu et al., 2016). BLEU, the *de-facto* standard metric for machine translation, computes token n-gram overlap between a hypothesis and one or multiple references. A shortcoming of BLEU with respect to automatic text simplification is that it rewards hypotheses that do not differ from the input. By contrast, SARI was designed to punish such output. It does so by explicitly considering the input and rewarding tokens in the hypothesis that do not occur in the input but in one of the references (addition) and tokens in the input that are retained (copying) or removed (deletion) in both the hypothesis and one of the references.

SARI is generally used with multiple reference sentences, which are hard to obtain. Due to this limitation, human evaluation is often needed. This mostly consists of three types of ratings: how well the content or meaning of the standard-language text is preserved, how fluent or natural the simplified output is, and how much simpler the output is compared to the standard-language original. Each simplified unit (in most cases, a sentence) is typically rated on a 5-point scale with respect to each of the three dimensions.

4 Automatic Text Simplification for German

4.1 Training Data

All data used in our experiments was taken from the Austria Press Agency (*Austria Presse Agentur*, APA) corpus built by our group. At this press agency, four to six news items covering the topics of politics, economy, culture, and sports are manually simplified into two language levels, B1 and A2, each day following the *capito* guidelines introduced in Section 2.1. The subset of data used for the experiments reported in this paper contains standard-language news items along with their simplifications on level B1 between August 2018 and December 2019. The dataset will be described in more detail in a separate publication.

---

[2]https://www.capito.eu/ (last accessed: February 3, 2020)

[3]Note that while the CEFR was designed to measure foreign language skills, with simplified language, it is partly applied in the context first-language acquisition (Bredel and Maaß, 2016).

	Original	*Jedes Kalb erhält spätestens sieben Tage nach der Geburt eine eindeutig identifizierbare Lebensnummer, die in Form von Ohrmarken beidseitig eingezogen wird.*
		('At the latest seven days after birth, each calf is given a unique identification number, which is recorded on ear tags on both sides.')
B1		*In Österreich bekommt jedes Kalb spätestens 7 Tage nach seiner Geburt eine Nummer, mit der man es erkennen kann.*
		('In Austria, at the latest 7 days after birth, each calf receives a number, with which it can be identified.')
	Original	*US-Präsident Donald Trump hat in seiner mit Spannung erwarteten Rede zur Lage der Nation seine politischen Prioritäten betont, ohne große wirtschaftliche Initiativen vorzustellen.*
		('In his eagerly awaited State of the Union address, U.S. President Donald Trump stressed his political priorities without presenting any major economic initiatives.')
B1		*US-Präsident Donald Trump hat am Dienstag seine Rede zur Lage der Nation gehalten.*
		('U.S. President Donald Trump gave his State of the Union address on Tuesday.')
	Original	*Sie stehe noch immer jeden Morgen um 6.00 Uhr auf und gehe erst gegen 21.00 Uhr ins Bett, berichtete das Guinness-Buch der Rekorde.*
		('She still gets up at 6:00 a.m. every morning and does not go to bed until around 9:00 p.m., the Guinness Book of Records reported.')
B1		*Sie steht auch heute noch jeden Tag um 6 Uhr in der Früh auf und geht um 21 Uhr schlafen.*
		('Even today, she still gets up at 6 every morning and goes to bed at 9.')

Table 1: Examples from the Austria Press Agency (APA) corpus

We aligned the sentences from the original German news articles with the simplified articles using *CATS* (cf. Section 2.2). We chose the WAVG similarity strategy in conjunction with fastText embeddings (Bojanowski et al., 2017). fastText offers pretrained word vectors in 157 languages, derived from Wikipedia and Common Crawl (Grave et al., 2018).[4] As our alignment strategy, we dismissed the monotonicity restriction due to our observation that the order of information in a simplified-language text is not always preserved compared to that of the corresponding standard-language text.

CATS is built on the heuristic that every simplified-language sentence is aligned with one or several standard-language sentences. For 1-to-n and n-to-1 alignments, each of the n sentences forms a separate sentence pair with its counterpart, i.e., the single counterpart is duplicated. This leads to oversampling of some sentences and—as we will discuss in Section 4.4—poses a significant challenge for learning algorithms, but it is inevitable because we cannot assume that the order of information is preserved after simplification.[5] Sentence pairs with a similarity score of less than 90% were discarded (this threshold was established based on empirical evaluation of the tool on a different dataset), which resulted in a total of 3,616 sentence pairs. Table 1 shows examples, which are also representative of the wide range of simplifications present in the texts. Table 2 shows the number of German and simplified German sentences that we used for training and evaluation. The sets are all disjoint, i.e., there are no cross-alignments between any of them. Since the dataset is already very small

German	Simplified German	Alignment	Usage
3316	3316	1:1, 1:n, n:1	training
300	300	1:1	validation
	3316	–	data augmentation
50		–	evaluation

Table 2: Number of sentences from the Austria Press Agency (APA) corpus in our experiments

and the automatic alignments are not perfect, we decided not to use a parallel test set but to select models based on their best performance on the validation set and evaluate manually without a target reference. We chose the number of sentences for data augmentation to match the number of parallel sentences during training, in accordance with Sennrich et al. (2016a).

We applied the following preprocessing steps:

- In the simplified German text, we replaced all hyphenated compounds (e.g., *Premier-Ministerin* 'female prime minister') with their unhyphenated equivalents (*Premierministerin*), but only if they never occur in hyphenated form in the original German corpus.

- We converted all tokens to lowercase. This reduces the subword vocabulary and ideally makes morpheme/subword correspondences more explicit across different parts of speech, since nouns are generally capitalized in German orthography.

- We applied byte-pair encoding (BPE) (Sennrich et al., 2016b), trained jointly on the source and target text. BPE splits tokens into subwords based on the frequencies of their character sequences. This decreases the total vocabulary size and increases overlap between source and target.

---

[4]`https://fasttext.cc/docs/en/crawl-vectors.html` (last accessed: November 25, 2019)

[5]Another possibility to deal with 1-to-n and n-to-1 alignments would be to merge them into single alignments by concatenation. However, in our case, this would have resulted in many segments becoming too long to be processed by the sequence-to-sequence model.

4.2 Neural Models in Our Experiments

All models in our experiments are based on the Transformer encoder-decoder architecture (Vaswani et al., 2017). We used *Sockeye* version 1.18.106 (Hieber et al., 2017) for training and translation into simplified German. Unless otherwise stated, the hyperparameters are defaults defined by *Sockeye*. The following is an overview of the models:

BASE baseline model; embedding size of 256

BPE5K same as BASE but with less BPE merge operations ($10{,}000 \rightarrow 5{,}000$) (Sennrich and Zhang, 2019)

BATCH1K same as BASE but with a smaller token-based batch size ($4096 \rightarrow 1024$) (Sennrich and Zhang, 2019)

LINGFEAT same as BASE but extending embedding vectors with additional linguistic features (lemmas, part-of-speech tags, morphological attributes, dependency tags, and BIEO tags marking where subwords begin or end) (Sennrich and Haddow, 2016)

NULL2TRG same as BASE but with additional *<null>*-to-target sentence pairs generated from non-parallel simplified sentences, doubling the size of the training set (Sennrich et al., 2016a)

TRG2TRG same as BASE but with additional target-to-target sentence pairs (same simplified sentence in source as in target), doubling the size of the training set (Palmero Aprosio et al., 2019) (cf. Section 3)

BT2TRG same as BASE but with additional backtranslated-to-target sentence pairs (source sentence is machine-translated from target sentence), doubling the size of the training set (Sennrich et al., 2016a)

For LINGFEAT, all linguistic features were obtained with *ParZu* (Sennrich et al., 2013), using *clevertagger* (Sennrich et al., 2013) for part-of-speech tags and *Zmorge* (Sennrich and Kunz, 2014) for morphological analysis. The embedding sizes for these features are: 221 for lemmas, 10 each for part-of-speech, morphology, and dependency tags, and 5 for subword BIEO tags, thus extending the total embedding size to 512.

For the backtranslation system, we used the same architecture, the same method, and the same set of sentence pairs as in LINGFEAT, and the added non-parallel sentences were the same for all models trained with augmented data (NULL2TRG, TRG2TRG, BT2TRG).

Moreover, each model type was trained three times, with three different random seeds for shuffling and splitting the training and validation set, in order to reach statistical significance.

After running preliminary trainings, it became clear that all of these models overfit quickly. Validation perplexity regularly reached its minimum before sentences of any kind of fluency were produced, and BLEU scores only started to increase *after* this point. Therefore, we decided to optimize for the BLEU score instead, i.e., stop training when BLEU scores on the validation set reached the maximum. We will discuss more specific implications of this decision in Section 4.4.

4.3 Results of Our Simplication Experiments

We report case-insensitive BLEU and SARI on the validation set, calculated using *SacreBLEU* (Post, 2018). Since we optimized the models for the BLEU score, these values may be taken as a kind of "upper bound" rather than true indicators of their performance.

Figure 1 shows results for the models listed in Section 4.2. TRG2TRG is the only model whose improvements compared to the baseline reached high statistical significance ($p = 0.00014$ for BLEU, $p = 0.00050$ for SARI), although improvements by LINGFEAT look promising ($p = 0.10$ for BLEU, $p = 0.020$ for SARI). The low performance of BT2TRG is surprising, considering the significant BLEU score improvements we observed in a previous experiment with a different German dataset (Battisti et al., 2020). BPE5K and BATCH1K, both proposed as low-resource optimizations in machine translation, do not have much of an effect in this context, either.

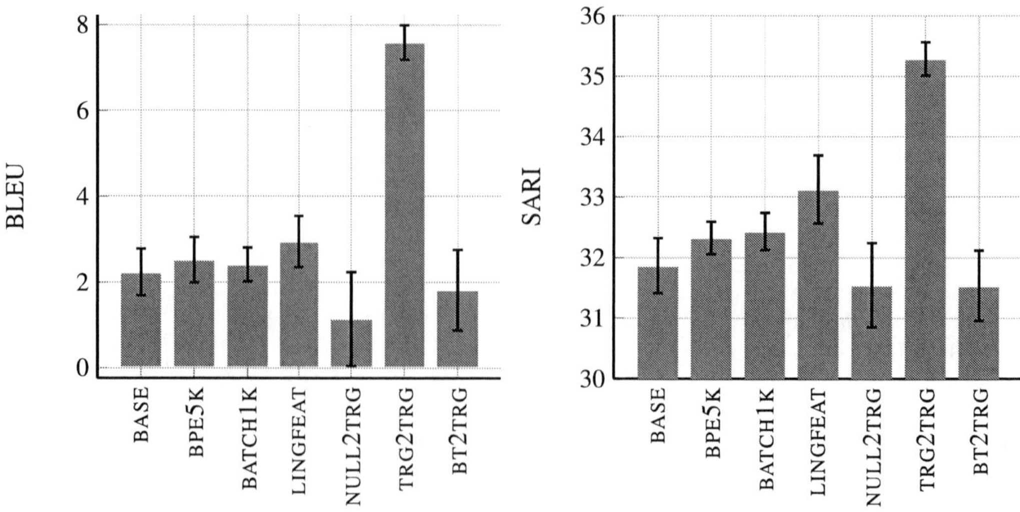

Figure 1: BLEU and SARI scores on the validation set (means and standard errors from three runs)

| | BASE | | +TRG2TRG | | +BT2TRG | |
	BLEU	SARI	BLEU	SARI	BLEU	SARI
BASE	2.23 ± 0.55	31.87 ± 0.46	$\mathbf{7.59 \pm 0.40}$	$\mathbf{35.29 \pm 0.28}$	1.81 ± 0.94	31.54 ± 0.58
+LINGFEAT	2.94 ± 0.60	$\mathbf{33.13 \pm 0.56}$	$\mathbf{9.75 \pm 0.63}$	$\mathbf{36.88 \pm 0.67}$	3.11 ± 0.56	$\mathbf{32.96 \pm 0.59}$

Table 3: BLEU and SARI scores of final model configurations on the validation set (means and standard errors from three runs). Bold font indicates significant improvements ($p < 0.05$) with respect to BASE

We also trained additional models which combined the data augmentation methods (TRG2TRG and BT2TRG) with the linguistic features (LINGFEAT) to see if there was a combined effect. The validation scores of all six configurations are presented in Table 3. These results suggest that linguistic features are beneficial even with synthetic data, and that augmentation with target-to-target pairs is more effective than backtranslation.

In addition to automatic evaluation, we translated a test set of 50 sentences using the above models and manually evaluated the output. This was done by the first author, a native speaker of German, with reference to the original sentence along the three criteria shown in Table 4. These are based on Surya et al. (2019) but adapted to capture more specific weaknesses arising from the low-resource setting.

The results are in Figure 2. They provide a clearer picture of the strengths and weaknesses of the configurations. In general, the models have no difficulty producing fluent sentences. However, most of the time, these sentences have little in common with the original but are exact or partial copies of other sentences in the training set. In the worst cases, 60–80% of output sentences are exact copies from the training set. This is a direct consequence of overfitting. Only TRG2TRG (especially in combination with linguistic features) managed to preserve content in a significant portion of the cases. Very often, this was accompanied by decreased fluency in the produced sentences, as in the following examples from the test set, produced by TRG2TRG+LINGFEAT (non-words are marked with '*'):

(1) **Source:**
Die Österreichischen Lotterien rechnen mit rund acht Millionen Tipps auf etwa eineinhalb Millionen Wettscheinen.
('The Austrian lotteries are expecting around eight million games played on about one and a half million play slips.')

Output (TRG2TRG+LINGFEAT):
Die österreichischen loinnen und rechnen mit 8 Millionen Tipps auf nur auf einhalb Millionen Euro mitscheinen scheinen Millionen.
('The Austrian *loinnen and are expecting 8 million games played on only on a half million Euro *withslips slips millions.')

(2) **Source:**
Sobald die Temperaturen steigen und mit Schnee nicht mehr zu rechnen ist, sollten Sommerreifen aufgezogen werden.
('As soon as the temperatures rise and snow is no longer to be expected, summer tires should be mounted.')

Output (TRG2TRG+LINGFEAT):
Sobald die Temperaturen steigen und Schnee nicht mehr zu aufgehoben werden.
('As soon as the temperatures rise and snow no longer to be lifted.')

(3) **Source:**
Aber wir werden unser Öl weiter verkaufen, ... die Sanktionen brechen", sagte Präsident Hassan Rouhani am Montag.
('But we will continue selling our oil, ... break the sanctions," said president Hassan Rouhani on Monday')

Output (TRG2TRG+LINGFEAT):
Aber sie werden nicht Öl weiter verkaufen, sagte am Montag verhani.
('But they will not continue selling oil, said *verhani on Monday.')

In these cases, the system attempts sentence shortening and lexical simplification (note the numeral replacement in Example 1). Generally, the model copies less from training targets (about 10%) and tends more towards transferring tokens from the input.

The results for BT2TRG confirm that backtranslation was not effective in this setting. Given the low content preservation scores in our baseline model for backtranslating, this is not surprising.

4.4 Discussion

As reported in Section 4.2, we optimized our models for BLEU scores. This resulted in models which strongly favored fluency over content preservation by mainly reproducing training material exactly and thus acted more like translation memories. The fact that augmenting the data with simple-to-simple pairs was relatively successful shows that the main difficulty for the other models was finding relevant correspondences between source and target. In the augmented data, these correspondences are trivial to find, and apparently, the model partly succeeded in combining knowledge from this trivial copying job with knowledge about sentence shortening and lexical simplification, as demonstrated by Examples 1–3.

In higher-resource scenarios, a frequent problem is that neural machine translation systems used for text simplification tasks are "over-conservative" (Sulem et al., 2018; Wubben et al., 2012), i.e., they tend to copy the input without simplifying anything. One possible solution to this is to enforce a less probable output during decoding, which is more likely to contain some changes to the input (Štajner and Nisioi, 2018). However, in the present setting, it is

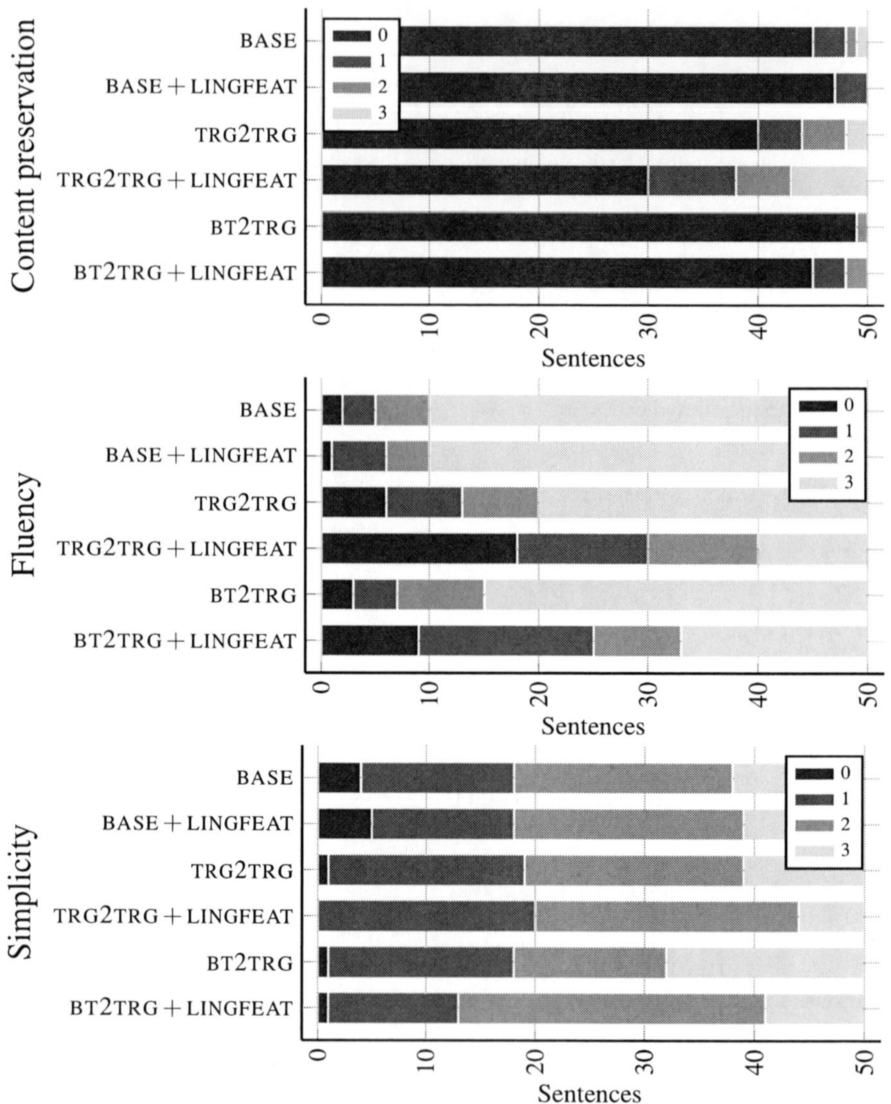

Figure 2: Human evaluation results

Criterion	Values	
content preservation	0	no content preserved
	1	general topic preserved, but wrong in specifics
	2	main statement recognizable, but wrong in details
	3	all relevant content preserved
fluency of output	0	gibberish, completely incomprehensible
	1	fluent in parts
	2	mostly fluent (modifying a word or two would make it acceptable)
	3	perfectly natural
relative simplicity	0	more complex than original
	1	equally complex
	2	somewhat simpler
	3	significantly simpler

Table 4: Criteria and values for human evaluation

quite the opposite: The models fail to reproduce most of the content, and adding simple-to-simple pairs can help in this case. However, as datasets grow larger, it may be challenging to balance the effects of real and synthetic data appropriately. To this end, approaches such as the semi-supervised one by Surya et al. (2019), where reconstruction of the input sequence is explicitly built into the model architecture, may be interesting to explore further.

When inspecting the model predictions in the test set, it also became clear that there was a considerable bias towards reproducing one of a handful of sentences in the training set. These are simplified sentences which occur more than once in training, because they are aligned with multiple original sentences. This suggests that including n-to-1 alignments in this way is a bad idea for sentence-to-sentence simplification.

Overall, even with a limited quantity of data, our models were able to learn essential features of simplified language, such as lexical substitutions, deletion of less relevant words and phrases, and sentence shortening. Although the performance of the models is not yet mature, these observations give a first idea about which types of texts are important in different settings. In particular, transformations of more complex syntactic structures require substantial amounts of data. When aiming for higher-quality output in low-resource settings, for example, it may be advisable to filter the texts to focus on lexical simplification and deletion, in order not to confuse the model with phenomena it will not learn anyway, and use the discarded sentences for data augmentation instead.

5 Conclusion

This paper introduces the first parallel corpus for data-driven automatic text simplification for German. The corpus consists of 3,616 sentence pairs. Since simplification of Austria Press Agency news items is ongoing, the size of our corpus will increase continuously.

A parallel corpus of the current size is generally not sufficient to train a neural machine translation system that produces both adequate and fluent text simplifications. However, we demonstrated that even with the limited amount of data available, our models were able to learn some essential features of simplified language.

6 Acknowledgments

The authors are indebted to *Austria Presse Agentur* (APA) and *capito* for providing the parallel corpus of standard-language and simplified-language news items.

7 Bibliographical References

Aluisio, S. M. and Gasperin, C. (2010). Fostering Digital Inclusion and Accessibility: The PorSimples project for Simplification of Portuguese Texts. In *Proceedings of the NAACL HLT 2010 Young Investigators Workshop on Computational Approaches to Languages of the Americas*, pages 46–53, Los Angeles, CA.

Barlacchi, G. and Tonelli, S. (2013). ERNESTA: A Sentence Simplification Tool for Children's Stories in Italian. In *Proceedings of the 14th Conference on Intelligent Text Processing and Computational Linguistics (CICLing)*, pages 476–487, Samos, Greece.

Battisti, A., Pfütze, D., Säuberli, A., Kostrzewa, M., and Ebling, S. (2020). A Corpus for Automatic Readability Assessment and Text Simplification of German. In *Proceedings of the 12th International Conference on Language Resources and Evaluation (LREC)*, Marseille, France.

Bojanowski, P., Grave, E., Joulin, A., and Mikolov, T. (2017). Enriching word vectors with subword information. *Transactions of the Association for Computational Linguistics*, 5:135–146.

Bott, S. and Saggion, H. (2012). Automatic simplification of Spanish text for e-Accessibility. In *Proceedings of the 13th International Conference on Computers Helping People with Special Needs (ICCHP)*, pages 527–534, Linz, Austria.

Bredel, U. and Maaß, C. (2016). *Leichte Sprache: Theoretische Grundlagen. Orientierung für die Praxis*. Duden, Berlin.

Brouwers, L., Bernhard, D., Ligozat, A., and Francois, T. (2014). Syntactic Sentence Simplification for French. In *Proceedings of the 3rd Workshop on Predicting and Improving Text Readability for Target Reader Populations (PITR)*, pages 47–56, Gothenburg, Sweden.

Carroll, J., Minnen, G., Canning, Y., Devlin, S., and Tait, J. (1998). Practical simplification of English newspaper text to assist aphasic readers. In *Proceedings of the AAAI'98 Workshop on Integrating aI and Assistive Technology*, pages 7–10.

Chandrasekar, R., Doran, C., and Srinivas, B. (1996). Motivations and methods for text simplification. In *Proceedings of the 16th Conference on Computational Linguistics*, pages 1041–1044, Copenhagen, Denmark.

Coster, W. and Kauchak, D. (2011). Learning to simplify sentences using Wikipedia. In *Proceedings of the Workshop on Monolingual Text-To-Text Generation (MTTG)*, pages 1–9, Portland, OR.

Council of Europe. (2009). *Common European Framework of Reference for Languages: Learning, teaching, assessment*. Cambridge University Press, Cambridge.

Gasperin, C., Maziero, E., and Aluisio, S. M. (2010). Challenging Choices for Text Simplification. In *Computational Processing of the Portuguese Language. Proceedings of the 9th International Conference, PROPOR 2010*, pages 40–50, Porto Alegre, Brazil.

Grave, E., Bojanowski, P., Gupta, P., Joulin, A., and Mikolov, T. (2018). Learning word vectors for 157 languages. In *Proceedings of the International Conference on Language Resources and Evaluation (LREC 2018)*.

Hieber, F., Domhan, T., Denkowski, M., Vilar, D., Sokolov, A., Clifton, A., and Post, M. (2017). Sockeye: A toolkit for neural machine translation. *arXiv preprint arXiv:1712.05690*, December.

Hochreiter, S. and Schmidhuber, J. (1997). Long short-term memory. *Neural computation*, 9(8):1735–1780.

Hwang, W., Hajishirzi, H., Ostendorf, M., and Wu, W. (2015). Aligning Sentences from Standard Wikipedia to Simple Wikipedia. In *Proceedings of NAACL-HLT*, pages 211–217.

Klaper, D., Ebling, S., and Volk, M. (2013). Building a German/Simple German Parallel Corpus for Automatic Text Simplification. In *ACL Workshop on Predicting and Improving Text Readability for Target Reader Populations*, pages 11–19, Sofia, Bulgaria.

Nisioi, S., Štajner, S., Ponzetto, S. P., and Dinu, L. P. (2017). Exploring Neural Text Simplification Models. In *Proceedings of the 55th Annual Meeting of the Association for Computational Linguistics*, pages 85–91, Vancouver, Canada, July.

Palmero Aprosio, A., Tonelli, S., Turchi, M., Negri, M., and Di Gangi, M. A. (2019). Neural text simplification in low-resource conditions using weak supervision. In *Proceedings of the Workshop on Methods for Optimizing and Evaluating Neural Language Generation*, pages 37–44, Minneapolis, Minnesota, June.

Papineni, K., Roukos, S., Ward, T., and Zhu, W.-J. (2002). BLEU: A method for automatic evaluation of machine translation. In *Proceedings of the 40th Annual Meeting of the Association for Computational Linguistics (ACL)*, pages 311–318, Philadelphia, PA.

Post, M. (2018). A call for clarity in reporting BLEU scores. In *Proceedings of the Third Conference on Machine Translation: Research Papers*, pages 186–191, Brussels, Belgium, October.

Saggion, H., Štajner, S., Bott, S., Mille, S., Rello, L., and Drndarević, B. (2015). Making it Simplext: Implementation and evaluation of a text simplification system for Spanish. *ACM Transactions on Accessible Computing (TACCESS)*, 6(4):14.

Sennrich, R. and Haddow, B. (2016). Linguistic input features improve neural machine translation. In *Proceedings of the First Conference on Machine Translation: Volume 1, Research Papers*, pages 83–91, Berlin, Germany, August.

Sennrich, R. and Kunz, B. (2014). Zmorge: A German morphological lexicon extracted from Wiktionary. In *LREC*, pages 1063–1067.

Sennrich, R. and Zhang, B. (2019). Revisiting low-resource neural machine translation: A case study. In *Proceedings of the 57th Annual Meeting of the Association for Computational Linguistics*, pages 211–221, Florence, Italy, July.

Sennrich, R., Volk, M., and Schneider, G. (2013). Exploiting synergies between open resources for german dependency parsing, pos-tagging, and morphological analysis. In *Proceedings of the International Conference Recent Advances in Natural Language Processing RANLP 2013*, pages 601–609.

Sennrich, R., Haddow, B., and Birch, A. (2016a). Improving neural machine translation models with monolingual data. In *Proceedings of the 54th Annual Meeting of the Association for Computational Linguistics (Volume 1: Long Papers)*.

Sennrich, R., Haddow, B., and Birch, A. (2016b). Neural machine translation of rare words with subword units. In *Proceedings of the 54th Annual Meeting of the Asso-*

ciation for Computational Linguistics (Volume 1: Long Papers), pages 1715–1725, Berlin, Germany, August.

Specia, L. (2010). Translating from Complex to Simplified Sentences. In *Computational Processing of the Portuguese Language. Proceedings of the 9th International Conference, PROPOR 2010*, pages 30–39, Porto Alegre, Brazil.

Štajner, S. and Nisioi, S. (2018). A detailed evaluation of neural sequence-to-sequence models for in-domain and cross-domain text simplification. In *Proceedings of the 11th Language Resources and Evaluation Conference*, Miyazaki, Japan.

Štajner, S., Franco-Salvador, M., Rosso, P., and Ponzetto, S. (2018). CATS: A Tool for Customized Alignment of Text Simplification Corpora. In *Proceedings of the Eleventh International Conference on Language Resources and Evaluation (LREC 2018)*, pages 3895–3903, Miyazaki, Japan.

Sulem, E., Abend, O., and Rappoport, A. (2018). Simple and effective text simplification using semantic and neural methods. In *Proceedings of the 56th Annual Meeting of the Association for Computational Linguistics (Volume 1: Long Papers)*, pages 162–173, Melbourne, Australia, July.

Surya, S., Mishra, A., Laha, A., Jain, P., and Sankaranarayanan, K. (2019). Unsupervised neural text simplification. In *Proceedings of the 57th Annual Meeting of the Association for Computational Linguistics*, pages 2058–2068, Florence, Italy, July.

Suter, J., Ebling, S., and Volk, M. (2016). Rule-based Automatic Text Simplification for German. In *Proceedings of the 13th Conference on Natural Language Processing (KONVENS 2016)*, pages 279–287, Bochum, Germany.

Suter, J. (2015). Rule-based text simplification for German. Bachelor's thesis, University of Zurich.

Vaswani, A., Shazeer, N., Parmar, N., Uszkoreit, J., Jones, L., Gomez, A. N., Kaiser, Ł., and Polosukhin, I. (2017). Attention is all you need. In *Advances in neural information processing systems*, pages 5998–6008.

Wubben, S., van den Bosch, A., and Krahmer, E. (2012). Sentence simplification by monolingual machine translation. In *Proceedings of the 50th Annual Meeting of the Association for Computational Linguistics (Volume 1: Long Papers)*, pages 1015–1024, Jeju Island, Korea, July. Association for Computational Linguistics.

Xu, W., Callison-Burch, C., and Napoles, C. (2015). Problems in Current Text Simplification Research: New Data Can Help. *Transactions of the Association for Computational Linguistics*, 3:283–297.

Xu, W., Napoles, C., Pavlick, E., Chen, Q., and Callison-Burch, C. (2016). Optimizing statistical machine translation for text simplification. *Transactions of the Association for Computational Linguistics*, 4:401–415.

Zhu, Z., Bernhard, D., and Gurevych, I. (2010). A monolingual tree-based translation model for sentence simplification. In *Proceedings of the International Conference on Computational Linguistics*, pages 1353–1361, Beijing, China.

1st Workshop on Tools and Resources to Empower People with REAding DIfficulties (READI2020), pages 49–56
Language Resources and Evaluation Conference (LREC 2020), Marseille, 11–16 May 2020
© European Language Resources Association (ELRA), licensed under CC-BY-NC

Visualizing Facets of Text Complexity across Registers

Marina Santini[*], **Arne Jönsson**[†], **Evelina Rennes**[†]

[*]RISE, Research Institutes of Sweden
Linköping, Sweden
marina.santini@ri.se
[†]Department of Computer and Information Science
Linköping University, Linköping, Sweden
{arne.jonsson, evelina.rennes}@liu.se

Abstract

In this paper, we propose visualizing results of a corpus-based study on text complexity using radar charts. We argue that the added value of this type of visualisation is the polygonal shape that provides an intuitive grasp of text complexity similarities across the registers of a corpus. The results that we visualize come from a study where we explored whether it is possible to automatically single out different facets of text complexity across the registers of a Swedish corpus. To this end, we used factor analysis as applied in Biber's Multi-Dimensional Analysis framework. The visualization of text complexity facets with radar charts indicates that there is correspondence between linguistic similarity and similarity of shape across registers.

Keywords: radar charts, text complexity, readability, Multi-Dimensional Analysis

1. Introduction

Data visualization refers to the graphical representation of information, data, results or findings. Graphical representations like charts, graphs, and maps, help the human brain understand and interpret trends and patterns in data. Effective data visualizations place meaning into complex information because they help disentangle complexities and unveil underlying patterns in a clear and concise way. The easiest and most common way to create a data visualization is to use bar graphs, pie charts or line graphs. These types of charts are effective and widely used. Recently, more sophisticated visualizations have been introduced, such as bullet graphs, heat maps, radial trees, radar charts or infographics. It goes without saying that the effectiveness of the visualization depends on the purpose and on the type of data. In this paper, we ponder about the best way to "shape" the results of a corpus-based study on text complexity in order to show how different registers differ according to a number of text complexity features. The insights provided by this study may be useful to understand how to visually represent a complex notion like text complexity.

Text complexity is an important dimension of textual variation. It is crucial to pin it down because texts can be customised to different types of audiences, according to cognitive requirements (e.g. texts for the dyslectic), social or cultural background (e.g. texts for language learners) or the text complexity that is expected in certain genres or registers (e.g. academic articles vs. popularised texts). Text complexity can be analysed in several ways. The approach we used is based on factor analysis as applied in Biber's Multi-Dimensional Analysis framework (Biber, 1988) (henceforth MDA). The corpus used in our analysis was the Swedish national corpus, called Stockholm-Umeå Corpus or SUC. Results are described in detail in Santini and Jönsson (2020), and indicate that it is indeed possible to elicit and interpret facets of text complexity using MDA, regardless some caveats due to the small size of the corpus. When we tabulated the results (see Table 1) and plotted them in a bar chart (see Figure 1), we observed that tabulation and a bar chart were useful for the identification of the text complexity similarities and dissimilarities across the registers, but their interpretation required some effort and time even for linguists. At this point we were intrigued by the following question: how can we visually shape the different facets of text complexity generated by the study in an efficient and intuitive way? In this paper, we focus on this research question and we argue that the type of visualization that seems to be the most appropriate for this type of results is the radar chart because it plots a polygonal "shape" that helps emphasise similarities and dissimilarities across categories.

2. Previous Work

To our knowledge, radar charts have never been used to visualize text complexity across registers. Since there is no previous work that explores this topic, we divide this section into two separate parts, the first one focusing on text complexity, and the second one listing linguistic studies that relied on radar charts visualization.

2.1. Text Complexity

Broadly speaking, text complexity refers to the level of cognitive engagement a text provides to human understanding (Vega et al., 2013). If a text is difficult, it requires more cognitive effort than an easy-to-read text and vice versa. Text complexity is a multifarious notion, since the complexity can affect the lexicon of a text, its syntax, how the narration of the text is organised, etc. For this reason, several definitions and several standards of text complexity exist. For instance, in theoretical linguistics Dahl (2004) puts forward an interpretation of "complexity" that is not synonymous with "difficulty". Rather, in his interpretation complexity is "an objective property of a system", i.e. "a measure of the amount of information needed to describe or reconstruct it". In his view, "[g]rammatical complexity is the result of historical processes often subsumed under the rubric of grammaticalization and involves what can be called mature linguistic phenomena, that is, features that take time to develop".

Another linguistic field where there is a persistent interest in the study of language complexity is second language (L2) research. For instance, Pallotti (2015) notes that the notion of linguistic complexity is still poorly defined and often used with different meanings. He proposes a simple, coherent view of the construct, which is defined in a purely structural way, i.e. the complexity directly arising from the number of linguistic elements and their interrelationships. More recently, Housen et al. (2019) present an overview of current theoretical and methodological practices in L2 complexity research and describe five empirical studies that investigate under-explored forms of complexity from a cross-linguistic perspective or that propose novel forms of L2 complexity measurements.

In education, one of the more comprehensive text complexity models that has been devised for teaching is the CCSS - Common Core State Standards (Hiebert, 2012). This model, mostly applied in the United States, is a three-parts model geared towards the evaluation of text complexity gradients from three points of view: qualitative, quantitative and by assessing the interaction between the reader and the task. Its benefits and drawbacks have been analysed by Fang (2016). Many other models of text complexity have been proposed for educational purposes, but none of them has gained universal status.

In recent years, the concept of text complexity has drawn the attention not only of linguists and educators, but also of consumer-oriented terminologists, of specialists dealing with writing and reading disorders and more recently also of researchers working in computational and language technology (LT). In LT, text complexity is tightly linked to corpus-based and data-driven analysis of textual difficulty, e.g. in second language acquisition (Lu, 2010) and to the development of LT applications, such as automatic readability assessment (Feng, 2010) or the automatic text simplification for those who have dyslexia (Rello et al., 2013a). Text complexity can also be seen as a sub-field of Text Simplification, which is currently a well-developed LT research area (Saggion, 2017).

Text complexity is a concept inherently tied to the notion of readability. According to Wray and Janan (2013), readability can be redefined in terms of text complexity. As pointed out by Falkenjack (2018), readability incorporates both the actual text and a specific group of readers, such as middle school students (Dale and Chall, 1949) or dyslectic people (Rello et al., 2013b), while text complexity seems to pertain to the text itself, or the text and a generalised group of readers. Readability indices are practical and robust but coarse since they cannot provide the nature of the complexity. Critics of readability indices have also pointed out some genre-based discrepancies and the bias caused by short sentences and high frequency vocabulary on the readability scores (Hiebert, 2012). It must be noted, however, that no perfect method exists to date to gauge text complexity and readability infallibly. Therefore, complexity and readability scores are useful, although they must be taken with a grain of salt.

2.2. Radar Charts

A radar chart is a type of 2D chart presenting multivariate data where each variable is given an axis and the data are plotted as a polygonal shape over all axes. Each axis starts from the centre. All axes are arranged radially, with equal distances between each other and with the same scale. Grid lines that connect from axis-to-axis are often used as a guide (Jelen, 2013). Radar charts have already been used to display linguistic data, but not text complexity across registers. For instance, Branco et al. (2014) used a radar chart for their tool that "supports human experts in their task of classifying text excerpts suitable to be used in quizzes for learning materials and as items of exams that are aimed at assessing and certifying the language level of students taking courses of Portuguese as a second language". In their tool, the arms of the radar chart are the reference scales obtained from 125 texts. When a new text is fed into the tool, its values are mapped into the radar chart to visualize its linguistic profile. Egbert and Biber (2018) plotted six radar charts to profile linguistic variation across registers. Each register has five pairs of textual dimensions. One member of the pair has been obtained with MDA, the other one with Canonical Discriminant Analysis (CDA). The purpose was to show the extent of the overlap between the two statistical methods when analysing linguistic data. Jönsson et al. (2018) used a radar chart to display text complexity analysed with Principal Component Analysis (PCA). Their radar chart displays the principal components (not registers) and how text complexity varies across them.

3. MDA and Text Complexity

In this section, we summarise the main findings of our study on text complexity variation in the SUC. Full details can be found in Santini and Jönsson (2020). Below, we briefly describe the SUC corpus and dataset, and present MDA, together with the 3-factor solution used in the study.

3.1. SUC Corpus and Dataset

The SUC (Gustafson-Capková and Hartmann, 2006) is a collection of Swedish texts and represents the Swedish language as used by native Swedish adult speakers in the 90s. The SUC includes a wide variety of texts written for several types of audiences, from academics, to newspapers' readers, to fictions' readers and contains subject-based text varieties (e.g. Hobby), press genres (e.g. Editorials), and mixed categories (e.g. Miscellaneous). We call them collectively "registers", as defined in Biber and Conrad (2009). Given the composition of the SUC, we assume the presence of different levels of text complexity across SUC registers. This assumption underlies the rationale of the study, which is to identify how linguistic features co-occur in texts that have different levels of text complexity. Arguably, text complexity in children's books is low, while specialised professionals, such as lawyers and physicians, must be able to understand very complex texts in order to practise their professions. In between easy texts for children and the domain-specific jargon used by specialised professionals, there exist texts that present different levels of textual difficulty.

From the SUC, a text complexity dataset has been extracted via SAPIS (Fahlborg and Rennes, 2016), an API Service for

SUC Registers	Number of texts per SUC register	Mean of normalised LIX scores	Mean of normalised Dim1+ scores	Mean of normalised Dim1- scores	Mean of normalised Dim2+ scores	Mean of normalised Dim3+ scores	Mean of normalised Dim3- scores
		Readabilty level	Pronominal-Adverbial (Spoken-Emotional) Facet	Nominal (In-formational) Facet	Adjectival (Information Elaboration) Facet	Verbal (Engaged) Facet	Appositional (Information Expansion) Facet
a_reportage_genre	269	53.82	27.62	69.47	28.25	26.61	85.25
b_editorial_genre	70	57.56	36.56	66.76	19.82	54.94	62.30
c_review_genre	127	52.91	32.11	68.71	31.07	32.24	79.29
e_hobby_domain	124	54.25	23.09	72.00	22.58	37.28	83.34
f_popular_lore_domain	62	38.72	46.54	76.06	27.81	45.38	61.24
g_bio_essay_genre	27	44.99	49.44	0	35.52	33.17	60.35
h_miscellaneous_mixed	145	47.58	19.14	57.56	24.07	30.44	66.00
j_scientific_writing_genre	86	53.16	23.12	57.72	27.60	37.25	80.25
k_imaginative_prose_genre	130	50.50	52.55	0	33.58	35.21	71.20
Total	**1040**						

Table 1: Summary table of all the facets and readability level across the SUC registers.

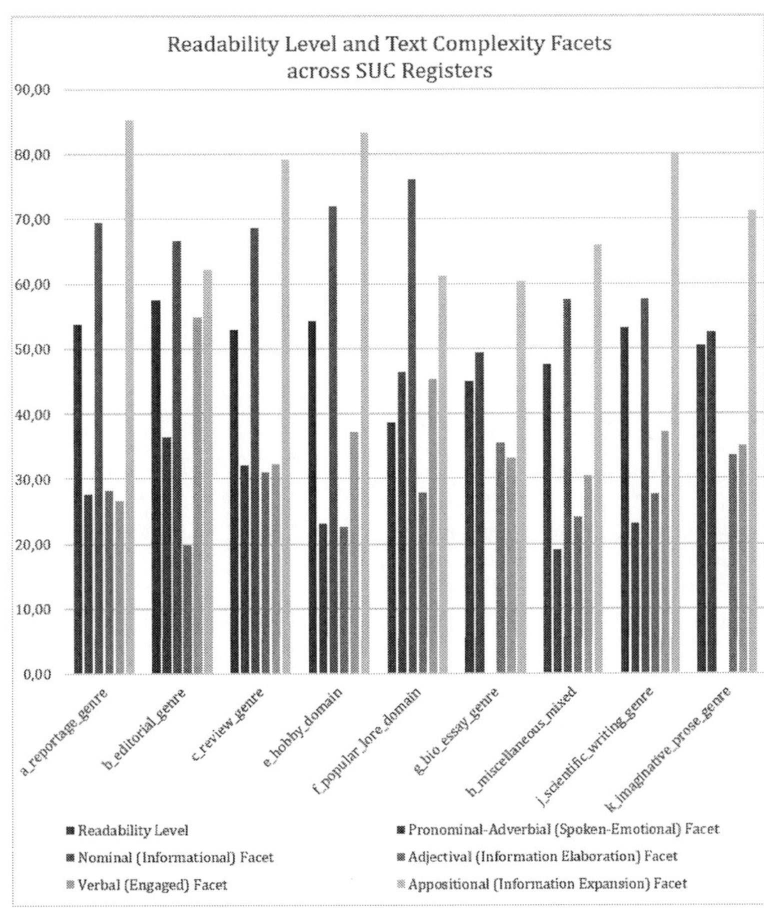

Figure 1: Summary chart of all the facets and readability levels across SUC registers.

Text Analysis and Simplification of Swedish text. The SUC dataset returned by SAPIS contains 120 linguistic features described in Falkenjack et al. (2013). This dataset is the source dataset used in the study.

3.2. MDA

Biber (1988) describes in detail the application of factor analysis to linguistic data. Biber's Multi-Dimensional Analysis refers to factor analysis (a bottom-up multivariate statistical method) to uncover patterns of linguistic variation across the registers collected in a corpus. The basic idea of MDA builds on the notion of "co-occurring linguistic features that have a functional underpinning" (Biber, 1988, p. 121). The co-occurrence of linguistic features across registers into factors is interpreted in terms of underlying textual dimensions.

There are three main steps in MDA, variable screening, running MDA proper, and the interpretation of the factors.

3.2.1. Variable Screening

We started off from the SUC dataset extracted from the SUC corpus via SAPIS. The dataset contains 1,040 records and 120 features. We noticed that some of the linguistic features in the dataset were somewhat redundant. For example, both *pos_det* and *dep_det* refer to the number of the determiners. This redundancy is detrimental for MDA because it causes multicollinearity, a statistical phenomenon that may lead to distorted results. We ditched out multicollinear features and ended up with 45 linguistic features that are listed in the Appendix.

3.2.2. Running MDA

After having screened the variables, we carried out MDA by building a correlation matrix, checking the determinant, assessing the sample adequacy and finally determining the number of factors. The key concept of factor analysis is that multiple observed variables have similar patterns of responses because they are all associated with a latent (i.e. not directly measured) "factor". Deciding the number of factors is not easy. Traditionally, the decision is made by looking at the scree plot. More recently, it has been shown that parallel analysis (Hayton et al., 2004) can help identify the most suitable number of factors. We then ran parallel analysis that suggested three significant factors. We extracted three factors from the correlation matrix and applied the oblique rotation called "promax", as recommended in Biber (1988). We ditched out the loadings smaller than 0.30 (a common practice). Loadings are correlations with the unobserved factors. Normally, each of the identified factors should have at least two or three variables with high factor loadings, and each variable should load highly only on one factor.

The 3-factor solution explained 0.22 variance, which is, admittedly, a relatively small proportion of the overall variance. However, this in not uncommon with natural language data, because the linguistic data that we find in texts can be very idiosyncratic and ambiguous and this elusiveness is reflected in the factor solution.

3.2.3. Grammatical Breakdown of the Factor Solution

The results of the 3-factor solution was interpreted grammatically and functionally in terms of textual dimensions (Biber, 1988). The functional interpretation of the textual dimensions is described in Santini and Jönsson (2020). Here we list the grammatical makeup of each dimension. Since each dimension has a positive (+) and a negative side (-), that normally are mutually exclusive, we interpreted each side of each dimension as a facet characterising an aspect of text complexity (we ditched out Dim2- because its loadings were below 0.30).

Dim1+ represents the Pronominal-Adverbial Facet. Features that tend to co-occur in Dim1+ are: pronouns, adverbs, interjections, attitude adverbials, question marks, common Swedish words, exclamation marks, negation adverbials, possessive pronouns and comparative adverbials.

Dim1- represents the Nominal Facet. This dimension has two loadings, both quite high, namely on prepositions and nouns, that both indicate the nominal character of the dimension.

Dim2+ represents the Adjectival Facet. This dimension has an adjectival nature since premodifiers, postmodifier and adjectives have the highest loading on this dimension. They are all grammatical devices that elaborate and specify the exact nature of nominals and nouns.

Dim3+ represents the Verbal Facet. The features that characterise Dim3+ are verbs, subordinators and infinitival markers and basic vocabulary.

Dim3- represents the Appositional Facet. The features that characterise this facet are appositions, the verb arity and commas. Appositions are "a maximally abbreviated form of postmodifier, and they include no verbs" (Biber et al., 1999). Commas are a common punctuation device to specify apposition. Verb arity indicates the number of arguments a verb may have. A high average indicates that a high amount of nominal information is glued to verbs.

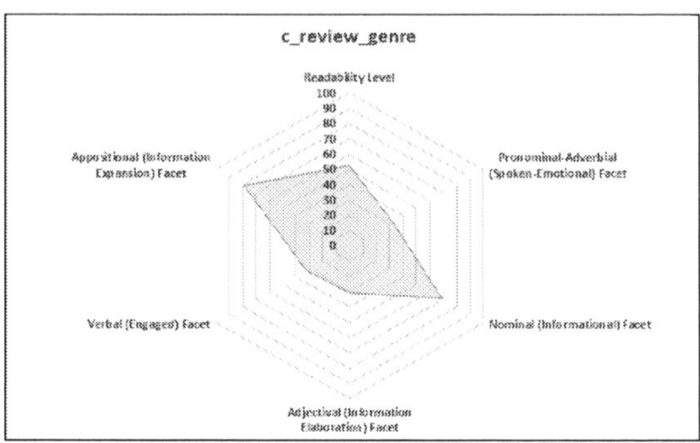

Figure 2: Review

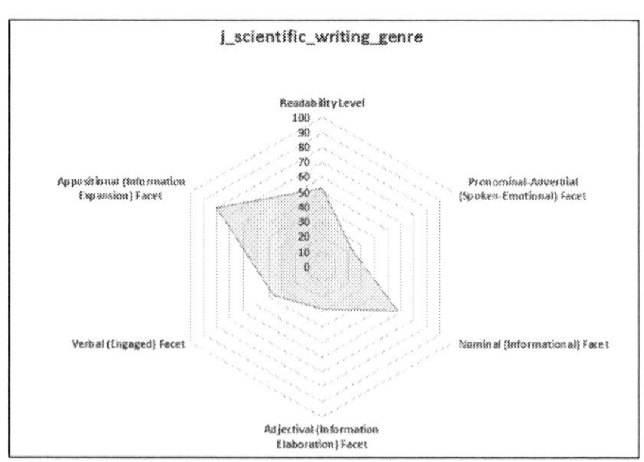

Figure 3: Scientific writing

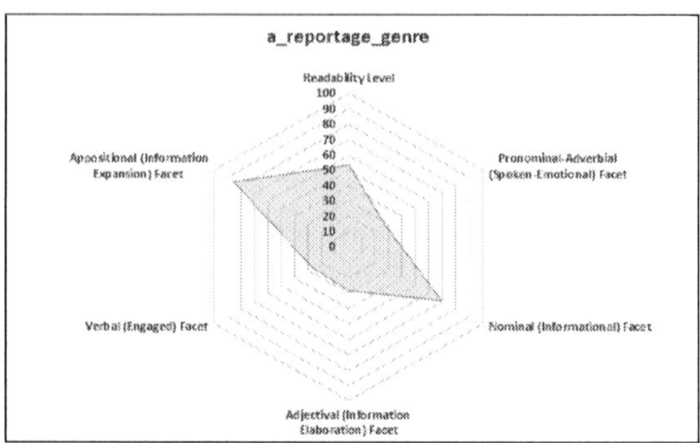

Figure 4: Reportage

3.2.4. Table and Bar Chart

We normalised the positive and negative values of the dimensions on a 0-100 scale in order to have a more accurate picture of how the text complexity facets and readability levels (Björnsson, 1968) vary across the SUC registers. Table 1 shows the SUC registers with normalised values plotted in Figure 1. The chart in Figure 1 is neat and provide interesting insights. For instance, we can observe that the readability level is rather uniform across the registers. When we map these readability values with those in Table 1, we can see that six SUC registers (the majority) have a readability level >50 (Very difficult), two registers are between 41 and 50 (difficult). Therefore all the registers in the SUC are rather difficult with the exception of popular lore (38.7), which appears to be easier to read than other registers. We can also observe that the nominal facet is often strong when also the appositional facet is pronounced.

We realised that the interpretation of the results with this type of visualization was indeed possible but required some cognitive effort and time, even for specialised people like linguists.

4. Visualizing Text Complexity in "Shapes"

To get a more intuitive understanding of the differences and similarities across the registers, we plotted each register as a radar chart and analyzed the a polygonal shape.

We could then observe that the faceted makeup of reviews (Figure 2), scientific writing (Figure 3) and reportage (Figure 4) is very similar. These three registers have a strong nominal facet associated with a pronounced appositional facet. The pronominal-adverbial facet is very flat, and the verbal and adjectival facets are weak. These characteristics are exemplified in the excerpts shown in Tables 2, 3 and 4. Bio-essay and imaginative prose have similar shapes (see Figures 5 and 6). The bio-essay and imaginative prose registers are characterized by strong pronominal-adverbial, adjectival and appositional facets. These characteristics are exemplified in the excerpts shown in Tables 5 and 6.

The hobby and miscellaneous registers (see Figures 7 and 8) are strong on the nominal-appositional facet (a similarities with the reportage, review and scientific writing registers) but they are also characterised by some prominence of the verbal facet, while the pronominal-adverbial facet and the adjectival facet are rather flat. These characteristics are exemplified in the excerpts shown in Tables 7 and 8.

The editorial and popular lore registers are two singletons (see Figures 9 and 10). They have a shape that is not similar to other registers in the SUC. Editorials have a strong nominal facet, but quite weak appositional facet. The texts in this register are difficult to read and they show a pronounced verbal facet that arguably implies more complex syntax. The adjectival facet is weak, so is the pronominal-adverbial facet. These characteristics are exemplified in the excerpts shown in Tables 9 and 10.

5. Discussion

We used radar charts to profile the registers of the SUC corpus with five text complexity facets and with readability levels. Figures 2-10 visually show the shape of the similarities and dissimilarities across the registers. The similarity between bio-essay and imaginative writing is striking and also quite intuitive if we think of the shared narration techniques that are normally used in these two registers. Similarly, the commonalities between reportage, review and academic writing is also unsurprising given the factual nature of these registers. Editorials and popular lore stick out for their dissimilarity with the other registers.

But what does a text complexity facet tell us? Essentially, a text complexity facet breaks down the linguistic nature

Excerpt	LIX score	Text ID	SUC Register
	39.05	cb05i	c_review_genre

Swedish	English Translation
Revoltens år, omstörtande och chockerande för många äldre, en optimistisk kamp för framtiden för de unga.	The year of the revolt, destructive and shocking for many elderly people, an optimistic struggle for the future of the young.

Table 2: Excerpt from a review

Excerpt	LIX score	Text ID	SUC Register
	54.24	ja05	j_scientific_writing_genre

Swedish	English Translation
Om kungamaktens tillbakagång under perioden 1906-1918 se Axel Brusewitz' klassiska Kungamakt, herremakt, folkmakt (1951).	On the decline of the king's power during the period 1906-1918, see Axel Brusewitz's seminal book "Kungamakt, herremakt, folkmakt" (1951).

Table 3: Excerpt of scientific writing

Excerpt	LIX score	Text ID	SUC Register
	41.08	af06j	a_reportage_genre

Swedish	English Translation
Man i Älvkarleö anhållen för hot En 33-årig man vid flyktingförläggningen i Älvkarleö greps på måndagskvällen av Tierpspolisen. Mannen är misstänkt för olaga hot och misshandel av sin hustru.	Man in Älvkarleö arrested for threats A 33-year-old man at the refugee camp in Älvkarleö was arrested by the Tierp's police on Monday evening. The man is suspected of unlawful threats and mistreatment of his wife.

Table 4: Excerpt from a reportage

Excerpt	LIX score	Text ID	SUC Register
	43.03	gb02	g_bio_essay_genre

Swedish	English Translation
Vi anpassade oss till omständigheterna och valde en läsart, vilken koncentrerade sig på karaktärerna och deras utveckling snarare än på scentekniska mirakel.	We adapted to the circumstances and chose a type of reader, which focused on the characters and their development rather than on the technical miracles.

Table 5: Excerpt from a text in the Bio-Essay register

Excerpt	LIX score	Text ID	SUC Register
	25.63	kl10	k_imaginative_prose_genre

Swedish	English Translation
Men det är mer en journal. Och inte fick jag laga maskinen heller. Då blev han dyster igen. Men att dom är sorgsna är alldeles klart. Allt du behöver göra för att vinna henne tillbaka är att visa att du älskar henne , mer än du älskar hundarna.	But it's more of a journal. And I couldn't fix the machine either. Then he became gloomy again. But that they are sad is perfectly clear. All you have to do to win her back is to show that you love her more than you love the dogs.

Table 6: Excerpt from a text of imaginative prose

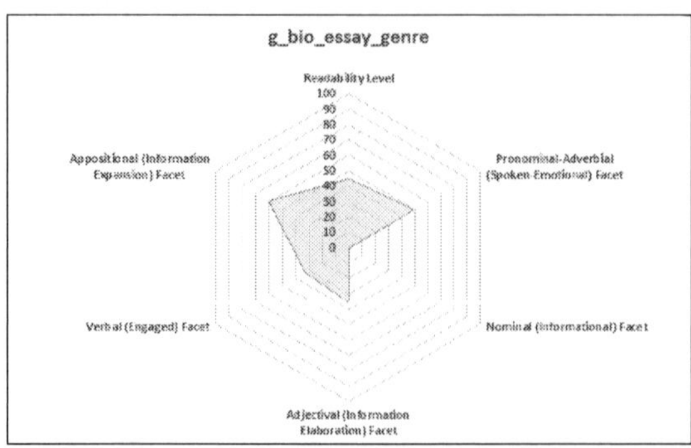

Figure 5: Bio-Essay

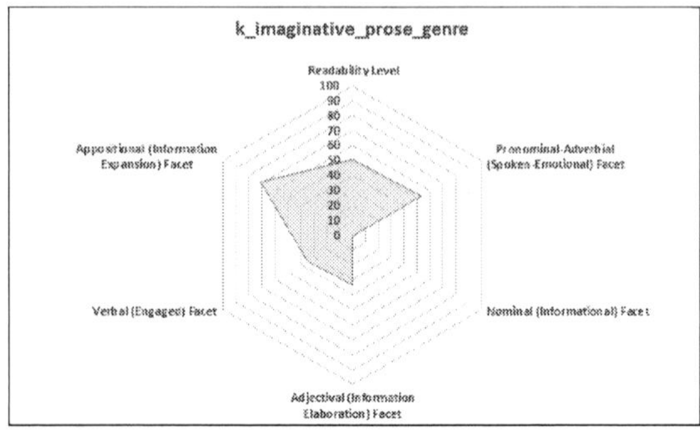

Figure 6: Imaginative prose

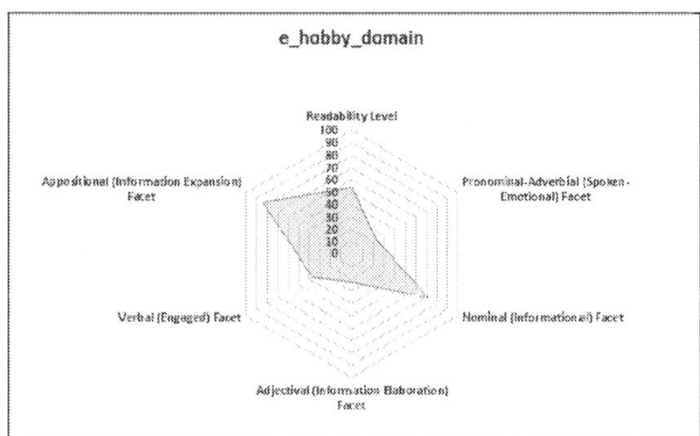

Figure 7: Hobby

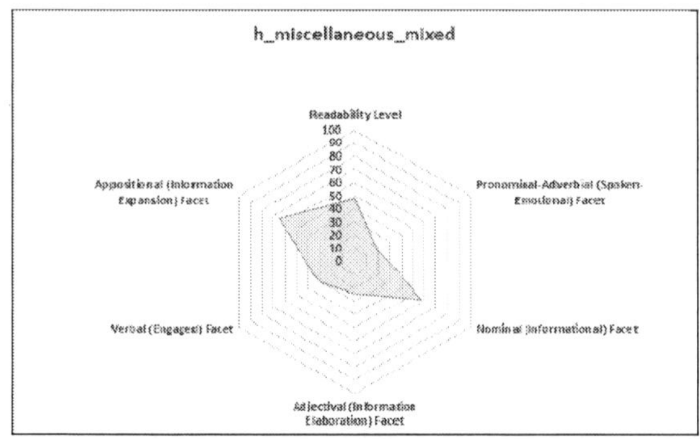

Figure 8: Miscellaneous

Excerpt	LIX score	Text ID	SUC Register
	50.06	ec02d	e_hobby_domain

Swedish	English Translation
Samtidigt varnar han för att Tyskland kan utmålas som syndabock om man inför den europeiska rymdorganisationen Esas ministermöte i november förklarar att landet ensidigt skall dra ned på sitt engagemang.	At the same time, he warns that Germany could be painted as a scapegoat if faced with the European Space Agency ESA's ministerial meeting in November declares that the country should unilaterally reduce its commitment.

Table 7: Excerpt from a text of the Hobby register

Excerpt	LIX score	Text ID	SUC Register
	43.09	he09c	h_miscellaneous_mixed

Swedish	English Translation
När journaler överförs per telefax finns risk för att obehöriga kan ta del av dem , inte minst om den som faxar råkar knappa in fel nummer.	When journals are transmitted by fax, there is a risk that unauthorized persons can access them, not least if the person who faxes accidentally dials the wrong number.

Table 8: Excerpt from a text in the Miscellaneous register

Excerpt	LIX score	Text ID	SUC Register
	59.07	ba05d	b_editorial_genre

Swedish	English Translation
Detta har förstärkt de farhågor som vuxit fram på den franska sidan av den omskrivna samarbetsaxeln för att man skall få en obunden tysk stormakt som svårhanterlig granne.	This has reinforced the fears that have emerged on the French side of the rewritten axis of cooperation in order to gain an unbounded German great power as a difficult-to-manage neighbor.

Table 9: Excerpt from an editorial

Excerpt	LIX score	Text ID	SUC Register
	46.53	fh03b	f_popular_lore_domain

Swedish	English Translation
Metoden gör att man på ett enkelt sätt kan minska risken för uppkomst av sprickor, förhindra tillväxt av defekter och ge skydd mot plötsliga rörbrott.	The method allows you to easily reduce the risk of cracking, prevent the growth of defects and provide protection against sudden pipe failure.

Table 10: Excerpt from a text in the Popular lore register

of text complexity and show how influential that facet is with respect to other facets that have a different linguistic makeup. It is, however, the combination of text complexity facets, and not the single facet, that gives us the characterisation of the texts in a register.

6. Conclusion and Future Work

In this paper, we argue that radar charts give an added value to the visualization of the results of MDA by producing "shapes" that help pin down more intuitively linguistic similarities across registers. In the study, we visualized the results of MDA applied to text complexity. From a 3-factor solution, we derived five text complexity facets. These facets highlight combinations of several linguistic aspects. The visualization of text complexity facets with radar charts indicates that there is correspondence between linguistic similarity and similarity of shape across registers. This is the main take away of this paper and it opens up new directions for future research. For instance, it could be possible to automatically compute shape similarity or poly-

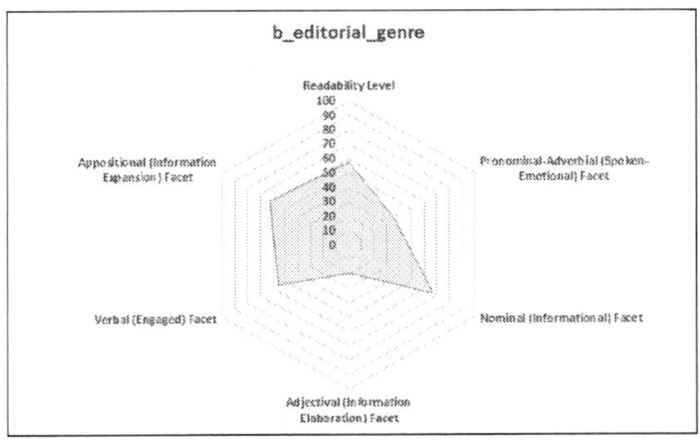

Figure 9: Editorial

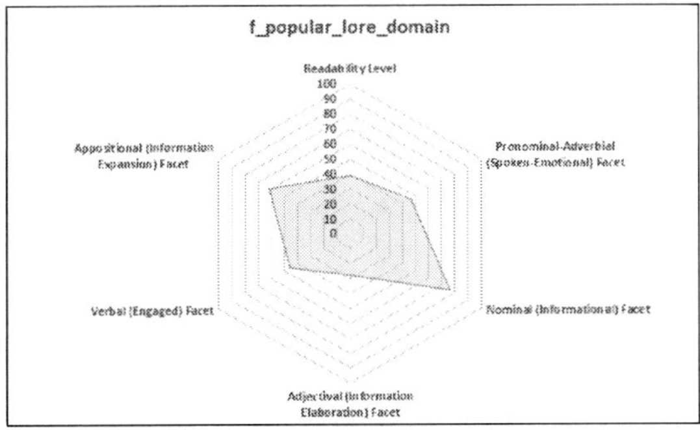

Figure 10: Popular lore

gon matching, which have a long tradition in geometry, to classify text complexity. What is more, the visualization of text complexity in different shapes could help people with cognitive impairments, such as people with dyslexia who have difficulties in detecting words (especially small function words) but have strong visual and spatial reasoning skills. Last but not least, shapes generated by automatic linguistic analysis could be used to as a "hallmark" of the different levels of text complexity and readability and used to guide the reader.

Acknowledgements

This research was supported by E-care@home, a "SIDUS – Strong Distributed Research Environment" project, funded by the Swedish Knowledge Foundation and RISE, Research Institutes of Sweden AB.

Companion Website

The study described in this paper if fully reproducible. Datasets, radar charts and R code are available here: http://santini.se/registerstudies2020/

Appendix: 45 Linguistic Features

3 lexical features
Namely: ratioSweVocC, ratioSweVocD, ratioSweVocH
SweVocC: lemmas fundamental for communication.
SweVocD: lemmas for everyday use.
SweVocH: other highly frequent lemmas.
A high ratio of SweVoc words should indicate a more easy-to-read text.

20 Morpho-syntactic features
Namely: pos_JJ (adjective), pos_DT (determiner), pos_HS (whPossessive), pos_HP (whPronoun), pos_RO (ordinalNum), pos_NN (noun), pos_VB (verb), pos_IE (infinitavalMarker), pos_HD (whDeterminer), pos_IN (interjection), pos_UO (foreignWord), pos_KN (coordinatingConj), pos_HA (whAdverb), pos_SN (subodinatingConj), pos_PM (properNoun), pos_PN (pronoun), pos_AB (adverb), pos_PP (preposition), pos_PS (possessivePronoun), and pos_PC (participle).

Unigram probabilities for 20 different parts-of-speech in the document, that is, the ratio of each part-of-speech, on a per token basis, as individual attributes. Such a unigram language model based on part-of-speech, and similar metrics, has shown to be a relevant feature for readability assessment for English (Heilman et al., 2007; Petersen, 2007).

18 Syntactic features
Namely: dep_AN (apposition), dep_AT (premodifier), dep_CA (contrastiveAdverbial), dep_EF (relativeClauseCleft), dep_I? (questionMark), dep_IK (comma), dep_IP (period), dep_IQ (colon), dep_IS (semicolon), dep_IU (exclamationMark), dep_KA (comparativeAdverbial), dep_MA (attitudeAdverbial), dep_NA (negationAdverbial), dep_PT (predicativeAttribute), dep_RA (placeAdverbial), dep_TA (timeAdverbial), dep_XA (sotospeak), dep_XT (socalled).

The presence of syntactic features is the most evident proof of textual complexity. The more syntactically complex a text is, the more difficult to read. These features are estimable after syntactic parsing of the text. The syntactic feature set is extracted after dependency parsing using the Maltparser (Nivre et al., 2006).

4 Averages
Namely: avgSentenceDepth, avgVerbalArity, avgNominalPremodifiers, avgNominalPostmodifiers
avgSentenceDepth: The average sentence depth. Sentences with deeper dependency trees could be indicative of a more complex text in the same way as phrase grammar trees has been shown to be.
Arity indicates number of arguments of a verb. The average arity of verbs in the document, calculated as the average number of dependents per verb
avgNominalPremodifiers. The average number of nominal pre-modifiers per sentence.
avgNominalPostmodifiers: The average number of nominal post-modifiers per sentence.

7.   Bibliographical References

Biber, D. and Conrad, S. (2009). *Register, genre, and style.* Cambridge University Press.

Biber, D., Johansson, S., Leech, G., Conrad, S., and Finegan, E. (1999). Longman grammar of written and spoken english. *Harlow: Longman.*

Biber, D. (1988). *Variation across speech and writing.* Cambridge: Cambridge Univ. Press, 1988.

Björnsson, C. H. (1968). *Läsbarhet.* Liber.

Branco, A., Rodrigues, J., Costa, F., Silva, J., and Vaz, R. (2014). Rolling out text categorization for language learning assessment supported by language technology. In *International Conference on Computational Processing of the Portuguese Language*, pages 256–261. Springer.

Dahl, Ö. (2004). *The growth and maintenance of linguistic complexity*, volume 71. John Benjamins Publishing.

Dale, E. and Chall, J. S. (1949). The concept of readability. *Elementary English*, 26(23).

Egbert, J. and Biber, D. (2018). Do all roads lead to rome?: Modeling register variation with factor analysis and discriminant analysis. *Corpus Linguistics and Linguistic Theory*, 14(2):233–273.

Fahlborg, D. and Rennes, E. (2016). Introducing SAPIS - an API service for text analysis and simplification. In *The second national Swe-Clarin workshop: Research collaborations for the digital age, Umeå, Sweden*.

Falkenjack, J., Heimann Mühlenbock, K., and Jönsson, A. (2013). Features indicating readability in Swedish text. In *Proceedings of the 19th Nordic Conference of Computational Linguistics (NoDaLiDa-2013), Oslo, Norway*, number 085 in NEALT Proceedings Series 16, pages 27–40. Linköping University Electronic Press.

Falkenjack, J. (2018). *Towards a model of general text complexity for swedish*. Ph.D. thesis, Linköping University Electronic Press.

Fang, Z. (2016). Text complexity in the us common core state standards: A linguistic critique. *Australian Journal of Language & Literacy*, 39(3).

Feng, L. (2010). *Automatic Readability Assessment*. Ph.D. thesis, City University of New York.

Gustafson-Capková, S. and Hartmann, B. (2006). Manual of the stockholm umeå corpus version 2.0. Technical report, Stockholm University.

Hayton, J. C., Allen, D. G., and Scarpello, V. (2004). Factor retention decisions in exploratory factor analysis: A tutorial on parallel analysis. *Organizational research methods*, 7(2):191–205.

Heilman, M. J., Collins-Thompson, K., Callan, J., and Eskenazi, M. (2007). Combining Lexical and Grammatical Features to Improve Readability Measures for First and Second Language Texts. In *Proceedings of NAACL HLT 2007*, pages 460–467.

Hiebert, E. H. (2012). Readability and the common core's staircase of text complexity. *Santa Cruz, CA: TextProject Inc*.

Housen, A., De Clercq, B., Kuiken, F., and Vedder, I. (2019). Multiple approaches to complexity in second language research. *Second Language Research*, 35(1):3–21.

Jelen, B. (2013). *Excel 2013 charts and graphs*. Que Publishing Company.

Jönsson, S., Rennes, E., Falkenjack, J., and Jönsson, A. (2018). A component based approach to measuring text complexity. In *Proceedings of The Seventh Swedish Language Technology Conference 2018 (SLTC-18)*.

Lu, X. (2010). Automatic analysis of syntactic complex-ity in second language writing. *International journal of corpus linguistics*, 15(4):474–496.

Nivre, J., Hall, J., and Nilsson, J. (2006). MaltParser: A Data-Driven Parser-Generator for Dependency Parsing. In *Proceedings of the fifth international conference on Language Resources and Evaluation (LREC2006)*, pages 2216–2219, May.

Pallotti, G. (2015). A simple view of linguistic complexity. *Second Language Research*, 31(1):117–134.

Petersen, S. (2007). *Natural language processing tools for reading level assessment and text simplification for bilingual education*. Ph.D. thesis, University of Washington, Seattle, WA.

Rello, L., Baeza-Yates, R., Bott, S., and Saggion, H. (2013a). Simplify or help? text simplification strategies for people with dyslexia. In *Proceedings of the 10th International Cross-Disciplinary Conference on Web Accessibility*, pages 1–10.

Rello, L., Baeza-Yates, R., Dempere-Marco, L., and Saggion, H. (2013b). Frequent words improve readability and short words improve understandability for people with dyslexia. In *IFIP Conference on Human-Computer Interaction*, pages 203–219. Springer.

Saggion, H. (2017). Automatic text simplification. *Synthesis Lectures on Human Language Technologies*, 10(1):1–137.

Santini, M. and Jönsson, A. (2020). Readability revisited? the implications of text complexity. *Register Studies*, 2:2.

Vega, B., Feng, S., Lehman, B., Graesser, A., and D'Mello, S. (2013). Reading into the text: Investigating the influence of text complexity on cognitive engagement. In *Educational Data Mining 2013*.

Wray, D. and Janan, D. (2013). Readability revisited? the implications of text complexity. *The Curriculum Journal*.

1st Workshop on Tools and Resources to Empower People with REAding DIfficulties (READI2020), pages 57–62
Language Resources and Evaluation Conference (LREC 2020), Marseille, 11–16 May 2020
© European Language Resources Association (ELRA), licensed under CC-BY-NC

CompLex: A New Corpus for Lexical Complexity Predicition from Likert Scale Data

Matthew Shardlow[1], Michael Cooper[1], Marcos Zampieri[2]
[1]Manchester Metropolitan University, UK
[2]Rochester Institute of Technology, USA
M.Shardlow@mmu.ac.uk, mikejcooper90@gmail.com, Marcos.Zampieri@rit.edu

Abstract

Predicting which words are considered hard to understand for a given target population is a vital step in many NLP applications such as text simplification. This task is commonly referred to as Complex Word Identification (CWI). With a few exceptions, previous studies have approached the task as a binary classification task in which systems predict a complexity value (complex vs. non-complex) for a set of target words in a text. This choice is motivated by the fact that all CWI datasets compiled so far have been annotated using a binary annotation scheme. Our paper addresses this limitation by presenting the first English dataset for continuous lexical complexity prediction. We use a 5-point Likert scale scheme to annotate complex words in texts from three sources/domains: the Bible, Europarl, and biomedical texts. This resulted in a corpus of 9,476 sentences each annotated by around 7 annotators.

Keywords: Complex Word Identification, Text Simplification, Lexical Complexity Prediction

1. Introduction

In many readability applications, it is useful to know the complexity of a given word. In early approaches to the readability task, simple metrics such as whether a word had more than 3 syllables (Mc Laughlin, 1969) or was on a given list or not (Dale and Chall, 1948) were used to identify complex words. More recently, automated methods for detecting complex words have also been used such as using a threshold on the word's frequency (Shardlow, 2013), or attempting to use a machine learning classifier to determine whether a word is complex or not (Paetzold and Specia, 2016; Yimam et al., 2018).

These approaches make the fundamental assumption that lexical complexity is binary. That words fall into one of two categories: difficult, or not. Previous approaches to Complex Word Identification (CWI), such as the one used in the CWI shared task (SemEval-2016 Task 11) (Paetzold and Specia, 2016), therefore typically refer to binary identification of complex words. A word close to the decision boundary is assumed to be just as complex as one further away. In our work, we move away from this assumption. We theorise that all words are in fact on a continuous scale of complexity and that lexical complexity should be identified accordingly. Binary Complex Word Identification effectively puts an arbitrary threshold on this scale, designating words above or below as complex or simple respectively. In this work, we have foregone the old acronym of CWI, in favour of a new acronym LCP (Lexical Complexity Prediction) which better suits our task of predicting how complex a given word may be.

Many factors can be considered to affect lexical complexity prediction. We may consider that the context in which a word is found will affect its understandability. If a word is found in the context of known words, then it may be possible to intuit the meaning from the context. Conversely, a word found in the context of other unknown words may be more difficult to comprehend. Similarly, a reader's familiarity with the genre of the text may affect the perceived complexity of a word. A Biologist reading a Physics journal may struggle with the specialist terms, as would a Physicist reading a Biology journal, but they would each be comfortable with reading material from their own field.

The role of the individual user cannot be overlooked when considering LCP and it is important to consider that although we aim to identify a complexity value for each word, this may need to be adapted for each reader, or group. It may be the case that some words have a high variability (i.e., some readers find them easy and some find them hard), whereas the complexity value of other words is more stable (i.e., all users give the word the same score).

Finally, we may wish to consider the effect of multi word expressions on lexical complexity. For example, if I know the complexity value of the constituent words in a multi word expression, can I combine these to give the complexity value of the MWE itself? In some cases, this may be possible (red car is a composition of 'red' and 'car'), whereas in others it may be more difficult ('European Union' has a deeper meaning than 'European' and 'Union' combined).

In our present work, we introduce CompLex [1], a new corpus for lexical complexity prediction. we have used crowd sourcing to annotate a new corpus of 8,979 instances covering 3 genres with lexical complexity scores using a 5-point Likert scale (Section 3.) We have performed baseline experiments to demonstrate the efficacy of a classifier in predicting lexical complexity, as well as further experiments to address some of the open questions as described above (Section 4.) We report our results and discuss our findings throughout (Section 5.)

2. Related Work

2.1. Lexical Complexity

Given the interest of the community in CWI, two shared tasks on this topic have been organized so far. The first edition of the CWI shared task was the aforementioned SemEval-2016 Task 11 (Paetzold and Specia, 2016). In CWI 2016, complexity was defined as whether or not

---

[1]`https://github.com/MMU-TDMLab/CompLex`

a word is difficult to understand for non-native English speakers. In the CWI 2016 dataset, the annotation followed the binary approach described in the Introduction, where English words in context were tagged as complex or non-complex. The organizers labeled a word as complex in the dataset if the word has been assigned by at least one of the annotators as complex. All words that have not been assigned by at least one annotator as complex have been labeled as non-complex. The task was to use this dataset to train classifiers to predict lexical complexity assigning a label 0 to non-complex words and 1 to complex ones. The dataset made available by the CWI 2016 organizers comprised a training set of 2,237 instances and a much larger test set of 88,221 instances, an unusual setting in most NLP shared tasks where most often the training set is much larger than the test set.

In Zampieri et al. (2017) oracle and ensemble methods have been used to investigate the performance of the participating systems. The study showed that most systems performed poorly due to the way the data was annotated and also due to the fact that lexical complexity was modelled as a binary task, a shortcoming addressed by CompLex.

Finally, a second iteration of the CWI shared task was organized at the BEA workshop 2018 (Yimam et al., 2018). In CWI 2018, a multilingual dataset was made available containing English, German, and Spanish training and testing data for monolingual tracks, and a French test set for multilingual predictions. It featured two sub-tasks: a binary classification task, similar to the CWI 2016 setup, where participants were asked to label the target words in context as complex (1) or simple (0); and a probabilistic classification task where participants were asked to assign the probability that an annotator would find a word complex. The element of regression in the probabilistic classification task was an interesting addition to CWI 2018. However, the continuous complexity value for each word was calculated as the proportion of annotators that found a word complex (i.e., if 5 out of 10 annotators marked a word as complex then the word was given a score of 0.5), a measure which is difficult to interpret as it relies on an aggregation of an arbitrary number of absolute binary judgements of complexity to give a continuous value.

2.2. Text Simplification

Text simplification evaluation is an active area of research, with recent efforts focussing on evaluating the whole process of text simplification in the style of machine translation evaluation. Whilst BLEU score (Papineni et al., 2002) has been used for text simplification evaluation, this is not necessarily an informative measure, as it inly measures similarity to the target. It does not help a researcher to understand whether the resultant text preserves meaning, or is grammatical.

To overcome some of these shortcomings, Xu et al. (2016) introduced the SARI method of evaluating text simplification systems. SARI comprises parallel simplified-unsimplified sentences and measures additions, deletions and those words that are kept by a system. IT does this by comparing input sentences to reference sentences to determine the appropriateness of a simplification. However,

SARI is still an automated measure and optimising systems to get a good SARI score may lead to systems that do well on the metric, but not in human evaluations. Recently, EASSE (Alva-Manchego et al., 2019) has been released to attempt to standardise simplification evaluation by providing a common reference implementation of several text simplification benchmarks.

Our work does not attempt to simplify a whole sentence through paraphrasing or machine translation, but instead looks at the possibility of identifying which words in a sentence are complex and specifically, how complex those words are. This is a task intrinsically linked to the evaluation of text simplification as the ultimate goal of the task is to reduce the overall complexity of a text. Therefore, by properly understanding and predicting the complexity of words and phrases in a text, we can measure whether it has reduced in complexity after simplification.

3. Dataset

3.1. Data Collection

In the first instance, we set about gathering data which we would later annotate with lexical complexity values. We felt it was important to preserve the context in which a word appeared to allow us to understand how the usage of the word affected its complexity. We also allowed multiple instances of each word (up to 5) to allow for cases in our corpus where one word is annotated with different complexity values given different contexts.

To add further variation to our data, three corpora were selected as follows:

Bible: We selected the World English Bible translation from Christodouloupoulos and Steedman (2015). This is a modern translation, so does not contain archaic words (thee, thou, etc.), but still contains religious language that may be complex.

Europarl: We used the English portion of the European Pariliament proceedings selected from europarl (Koehn, 2005). This is a very varied corpus talking about all manner of matters related to european policy. As this is speech transcription, it is often dialogical in nature.

Biomedical: We also selected articles from the CRAFT corpus (Bada et al., 2012), which are all in the biomedical domain. These present a very specialised type of language that will be unfamiliar to non-domain experts.

Each corpus has its own unique language features and styles. Predicting the lexical complexity of diverse sources further distinguishes our work from previous attempts, which have traditionally focused on Wikipedia and News texts.

In addition to single words, we also selected targets containing two tokens (henceforth referred to as multi word expressions). We used syntactic patterns to identify the multi word expressions, selecting for adjective-noun or noun-noun patterns. We discounted any syntactic pattern that was followed by a further noun to avoid splitting complex noun

	Contexts	Unique Words	Median Annotators	Mean Complexity	STD Complexity
All	9476 / 7974 / 1500	5166 / 3903 / 1263	7 / 7 / 7	0.394 / 0.385 / 0.442	0.110 / 0.108 / 0.105
Europarl	3496 / 2896 / 600	2194 / 1693 / 501	7 / 7 / 7.5	0.390 / 0.381 / 0.433	0.101 / 0.100 / 0.091
Biomed	2960 / 2480 / 480	1670 / 1250 / 420	7 / 7 / 7	0.407 / 0.395 / 0.470	0.115 / 0.112 / 0.109
Bible	3020 / 2600 / 420	1705 / 1362 / 343	7 / 7 / 8	0.385 / 0.379 / 0.422	0.112 / 0.111 / 0.112

Table 1: The statistics for CompLex. Each cell shows three values, which are split according to the statistics for 'All' / 'Single Words' / 'Multi Words'

phrases (e.g., noun-noun-noun, or adjective-noun-noun). Clearly this approach does not capture the full variation of multi word expressions. It limits the length of each expression to 2 tokens and only identifies compound or described nouns. We consider this a positive point as it allows us to make a focused investigation on these common types of MWEs, whilst discounting other less frequent types. The investigation of other types of MWEs may be addressed in a wider study.

We have not analysed the distribution of compositional vs. non-compositional constructions in our dataset, however we expect both to be present. It would be interesting to further analyse these to distinguish whether the complexity of an MWE can be inferred from tokens in the compositional case, and to what degree this holds for the non-compositional case.

For each corpus we selected words using predetermined frequency bands, ensuring that words in our corpus were distributed across the range of low to high frequency. As frequency is correlated to complexity, this allows us to be certain that our final corpus will have a range of high and low complexity targets. We chose to select 3000 single words and 600 MWEs from each corpus to give a total of 10,800 instances in our pre-annotated corpus. We automatically annotated each sentence with POS tags and only selected nouns as our targets. Again, this limits the field of study, but allows us to make a more focused contribution on the nature of lexical complexity. We have included examples of the contexts, target words and average complexity values in Table 2.

3.2. Data Labelling

As has been previously mentioned, prior datasets have focused on either (a) binary complexity or (b) probabilistic complexity. Neither of which give a true representation of the complexity of a word. In our annotation we chose to annotate each word on a 5-point Likert scale, where each point was given the following descriptor:

1. **Very Easy:** Words which were very familiar to an annotator.

2. **Easy:** Words with which an annotator was aware of the meaning.

3. **Neutral:** A word which was neither difficult nor easy.

4. **Difficult:** Words which an annotator was unclear of the meaning, but may have been able to infer the meaning from the sentence.

5. **Very Difficult:** Words that an annotator had never seen before, or were very unclear.

We used the following key to transform the numerical labels to a 0-1 range when aggregating the annotations: $1 \rightarrow 0$, $2 \rightarrow 0.25$, $3 \rightarrow 0.5$, $4 \rightarrow 0.75$, $5 \rightarrow 1$. This allowed us to ensure that our complexity labels were normalised in the range 0—1.

We employed crowd workers through the figure eight platform, requesting 20 annotations per data instance, paying around 3 cents per annotation. We selected for annotators from English speaking countries (UK, USA and Australia) and selected to disable the use of the Google Translate browser plug-in to ensure that annotators were reading the original source texts and not translated versions of them. In addition, we used the annotation platform's in-built quality control metrics to filter out annotators who failed preset test questions, or who answered a set of questions too quickly.

Our job completed within 3 hours, with over 1500 annotators. The annotators were able to fill in a post-hoc annotation survey, with average satisfaction being around 3 out of 5, the scores typically lower on the 'ease of job' metric.

After we had collected our results, we further analysed the data to detect instances where annotators had not fully participated in the task. We specifically analysed instances where an annotator had given the exact same annotation for all instances (usually these were all 'Neutral') and discarded these from our data. We retained any data instance that had at least 4 valid annotations in our final dataset.

3.3. Statistics

We have provided comprehensive statistics on our corpus in Table 1. These show that the average complexity for words in our corpus is 0.395, with a standard deviation of 0.115. A complexity score of 0.5 would be neutral and 0.25 would be easy, so this indicates that on average the words in our corpus fell towards the easier end of the scale. There are however words distributed across the full range of possible complexity annotations as shown by the ridgeline plot in Figure 1. This plot shows the density of complexity annotations in our corpus. It indicates that, whilst the majority of the probability mass is found to the left of the mid-point, there are still many annotations either side of the mid-point for each sub-corpus and for the corpus as a whole.

Table 1 shows that there was a median of 7 annotators per instance. We requested a total of 20 annotations per instance, but discarded individual annotations that did not meet our inclusion criteria. We discarded any data instances with fewer than 4 annotations. Accordingly, the lowest number of annotations was 4, and the highest was 20.

Analysing the sub-genres in our corpus shows some subtle, but meaningful differences between the genres. We used the same inclusion criteria to select words across genres,

Corpus	Context	Complexity
Bible	This was the **length** of Sarah's life.	0.125
Biomed	[...] cell **growth** rates were reported to be 50% lower [...]	0.125
Europarl	Could you tell me under which rule they were enabled to extend this item to have four rather than three **debates**?	0.208
Europarl	These agencies have gradually become very important in the **financial world**, for a variety of reasons.	0.438
Biomed	[...] leads to the **hallmark loss** of striatal neurons [...]	0.531
Bible	The **idols** of Egypt will tremble at his presence [...]	0.575
Bible	This is the law of the **trespass offering**.	0.639
Europarl	They do hold elections, but candidates have to be endorsed by the conservative clergy, so **dissenters** are by definition excluded.	0.688
Biomed	[..] due to a reduction in **adipose** tissue.	0.813

Table 2: Examples from out corpus, the target word is highlighted in bold text.

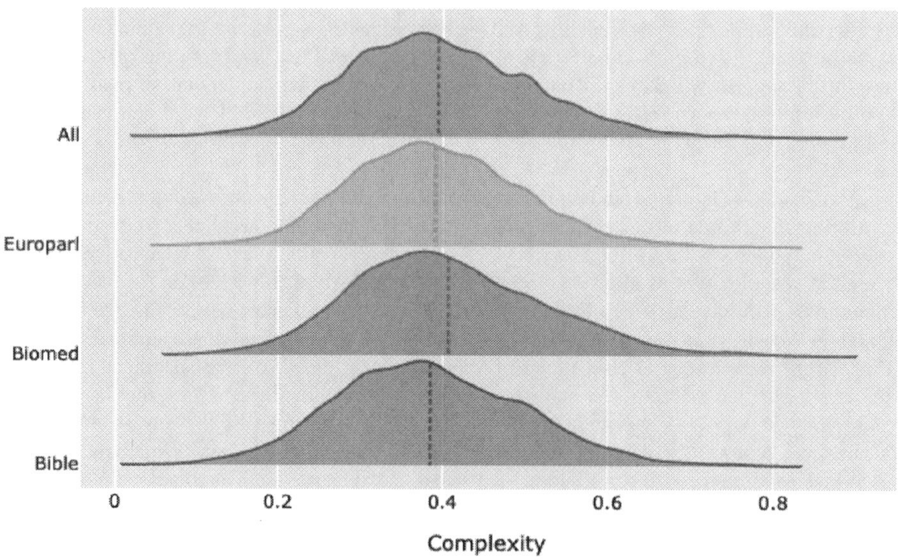

Figure 1: A ridge line plot showing the probability density function of the full dataset (all) as well as each of the genres contained within the full dataset. The vertical dashed line indicates the median in each case.

so as not to bias our results. Bible text and Europarl have very similar average complexity values (0.387 and 0.390), whereas Biomed is higher at 0.407. The biomedical texts are written for a technical audience and can be expected to contain more technical terminology. The bible and europarl may contain genre specific terminology, but will in general reference topics of common knowledge, which will result in higher familiarity and lower complexity.

We can also see that there is a difference in the complexity level of the annotations between multi word expressions and single words. In the aggregated corpus, single words have an average complexity score of 0.385, whereas multi-words have a higher score of 0.444. This is reflected across each genre, with the largest difference being in biomedical (0.395 / 0.470) and the smallest change being in the Bible (0.380 / 0.428).

4. Baseline System

We developed a baseline for predicting the complexity of a word using our data. We used a linear regression with embedding features for the word and context as well as three hand crafted features, which are known to be strong predictors of lexical complexity. Specifically, the feature sets we used are as follows:

Glove Embeddings: We captured the 300-dimensional Glove embedding (Pennington et al., 2014) for each token in our corpus. This was encoded as 300 separate features (one for each dimension of the embedding).

InferSent Embeddings: We captured the 4,096-dimensional embeddings produced by the InferSent library (Conneau et al., 2017) for each context. These were encoded as 4,096 separate features, one for each dimension of the embedding.

Hand Crafted Features: We recorded features which are typically known to be strong predictors of lexical complexity. Specifically, we looked at (1) word frequency according to the GoogleWeb1T resource (Brants and Franz, 2006), (2) Word length (as number of characters) and (3) syllable count[2].

We trained a linear regression using all of these features. We used a held-out test set of 10% of the data, stratified across corpus type and complexity labels. In addition to this, we also examined the effect of each feature subset. We examined this for the corpus as a whole, as well as for each sub-corpus. These results are presented in Table 3.

	All	HC	Glove	Sent
All	0.1238	**0.0853**	0.0875	0.1207
Bible	0.6648	**0.0888**	0.0911	—
Biomed	0.2954	**0.0908**	0.0939	—
Europarl	0.1982	**0.0801**	0.0879	—

Table 3: The results of our linear regression with different feature subsets. We have only reported the sentence embeddings for the whole corpus as the linear regression for the sub-corpora failed to provide a reliable model. All results are reported as mean absolute error. The column headers are as follows: 'All' refers to all features concatenated. 'HC' refers to hand crafted features, 'Glove' refers to the Glove Embeddings (at the target word level) and 'Sent' refers to the InferSent embeddings of the contexts.

5. Discussion

Our results show promise for future systems trying to predict lexical complexity by training on continuous data. In the best case, using hand crafted word features such as length, frequency and syllable count, we are able to predict complexity with a mean absolute error of 0.0853. Our values range from 0 (very easy) to 1 (very difficult), so this implies that we would be able to predict complexity with a good degree of accuracy. Features such as length and frequency have long been known to be good predictors of lexical complexity and so it is unsurprising that these ranked highly.

It is interesting to note that the word embeddings performed at a similar level of accuracy (0.0875) to the hand crafted word features. Word embeddings model the context of a word. It may have been the case that certain dimensions of the (300 dimensional) embeddings were more useful for predicting the complexity of a word than others. It would be interesting to further analyse this and to see what contextual information is encoded in the dimensions of these embeddings. It may be that some dimensions encode contexts that rely solely on less frequent, or more frequent words and are therefore better indicators of complexity than others.

Conversely however, the sentence embeddings did not turn out to be good predictors of lexical complexity. These embeddings (4,096 dimensions) were much larger than the

word embeddings, which may have made them less suitable for the linear regression. It may be the case that lower dimensional representations of the context would be have more predictive power in our corpus. Although this result implies that context is not important for lexical complexity, we may yet see that future experiments find new ways of integrating the context of the word to better understand it's complexity.

As a classifier, we chose a linear regression. We also used Glove embeddings and infersent. We may find that using embeddings which adapt to the context, such as in BERT and a neural network for prediction would yield stronger results. However, in this work we have only aimed to give an understanding of what types of features can be useful for predicting the values in our corpus, not to produce a state of the art system for the prediction of lexical complexity.

We can see that there are significant differences in the mean absolute error for each sub-corpus. Whereas the mean absolute error was lower for Europarl (0.0801), it was higher for the Bible and Biomed, indicating that the type of language in these two corpora was more difficult to model. This is reflected across different feature subsets, indicating it is a feature of the dataset and not a random fluctuation of our model.

We did not calculate an inter-annotator agreement as part of this work. This is difficult to do in a crowd sourcing setting as we have many annotators and there is no guarantee (or indeed a method to control) whether the same annotators see a common subset of the annotation data. Instead we used the following principles: (1) We selected for annotators who were known to the platform to provide high quality work. (2) We paid annotators well, encouraging them to take more time over the annotations. (3) We filtered out annotators who had not participated in the task properly. We do not necessarily expect annotators to completely agree on the complexity of a word as one annotator may be more familiar with a word than another and hence find it easier. We have taken the average values of all annotations for each instance in our corpus, with the hope that this will further smooth out any outliers. In Figure 2, we have shown a few words and their individual distributions. It is clear that whilst annotators generally agreed on some words, they differed greatly on others. This is reflective of the subjectivity that is present in complexity annotations and warrants further investigation.

6. Conclusion and Future Work

In this paper we presented CompLex, a new dataset for lexical complexity prediction. We propose a new 5-point Likert scale annotation scheme to annotate complex words in texts from three sources: the Bible, Europarl, and biomedical texts. The result is a dataset of 9,476 which opens new perspectives in lexical complexity research. We presented multiple baseline experiments using this data and report the best result of 0.0853 mean absolute error.

Our work leaves many open questions to be answered, and we intend to continue our research to further explore the remaining challenges facing the field of lexical complexity prediction. We have not explored the relationship between the multi-word expressions and single words in our corpus,

---

[2] https://pypi.org/project/syllables/

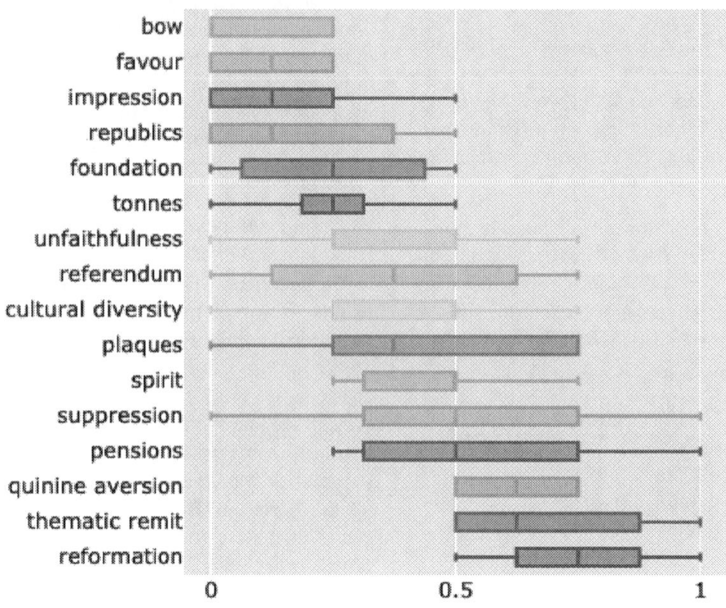

Figure 2: Box plot showing the distribution of annotation scores for different words in CompLex.

nor have we explored the transferability of complexity values between corpora. We have also not fully explored the range of classifiers and deep learning architectures that are available from the machine learning community. Again, we expect to cover these in future work.

Acknowledgements

We would like to thank the anonymous reviewers for their valuable feedback. We would also like to thank Richard Evans for insightful discussions on lexical complexity and data annotation.

Bibliographical References

Alva-Manchego, F., Martin, L., Scarton, C., and Specia, L. (2019). EASSE: Easier automatic sentence simplification evaluation. In *Proceedings of EMNLP-IJCNLP*.

Bada, M., Eckert, M., Evans, D., Garcia, K., Shipley, K., Sitnikov, D., Baumgartner, W. A., Cohen, K. B., Verspoor, K., Blake, J. A., et al. (2012). Concept annotation in the craft corpus. *BMC bioinformatics*, 13(1):161.

Brants, T. and Franz, A. (2006). The google web 1t 5-gram corpus version 1.1. *LDC2006T13*.

Christodouloupoulos, C. and Steedman, M. (2015). A massively parallel corpus: the bible in 100 languages. *Language Resources and Evaluation*, 49(2):375–395, Jun.

Conneau, A., Kiela, D., Schwenk, H., Barrault, L., and Bordes, A. (2017). Supervised learning of universal sentence representations from natural language inference data. In *Proceedings of EMNLP*.

Dale, E. and Chall, J. S. (1948). A formula for predicting readability: Instructions. *Educational research bulletin*, pages 37–54.

Koehn, P. (2005). Europarl: A parallel corpus for statistical machine translation. In *Proceedings of MT Summit*.

Mc Laughlin, G. H. (1969). Smog grading-a new readability formula. *Journal of reading*, 12(8):639–646.

Paetzold, G. H. and Specia, L. (2016). SemEval 2016 Task 11: Complex Word Identification. In *Proceedings of SemEval*.

Papineni, K., Roukos, S., Ward, T., and Zhu, W.-J. (2002). Bleu: a method for automatic evaluation of machine translation. In *Proceedings of ACL*.

Pennington, J., Socher, R., and Manning, C. D. (2014). Glove: Global vectors for word representation. In *Proceedings of EMNLP*.

Shardlow, M. (2013). A Comparison of Techniques to Automatically Identify Complex Words. In *Proceedings of the ACL Student Research Workshop*.

Xu, W., Napoles, C., Pavlick, E., Chen, Q., and Callison-Burch, C. (2016). Optimizing statistical machine translation for text simplification. *Transactions of the Association for Computational Linguistics*, 4:401–415.

Yimam, S. M., Biemann, C., Malmasi, S., Paetzold, G., Specia, L., Štajner, S., Tack, A., and Zampieri, M. (2018). A report on the complex word identification shared task 2018. In *Proceedings of BEA*.

Zampieri, M., Malmasi, S., Paetzold, G., and Specia, L. (2017). Complex word identification: Challenges in data annotation and system performance. In *Proceedings of NLP-TEA*.

1st Workshop on Tools and Resources to Empower People with REAding DIfficulties (READI2020), pages 63–69
Language Resources and Evaluation Conference (LREC 2020), Marseille, 11–16 May 2020
© European Language Resources Association (ELRA), licensed under CC-BY-NC

LagunTest: A NLP Based Application to Enhance Reading Comprehension

Itziar Gonzalez-Dios, Kepa Bengoetxea, Amaia Aguirregoitia
University of the Basque Country (UPV/EHU)
Rafael Moreno *Pitxitxi*, 2. 48013 Bilbao (Bizkaia)
{itziar.gonzalezd, kepa.bengoetxea, amaia.aguirregoitia}@ehu.eus

Abstract

The ability to read and understand written texts plays an important role in education, above all in the last years of primary education. This is especially pertinent in language immersion educational programmes, where some students have low linguistic competence in the languages of instruction. In this context, adapting the texts to the individual needs of each student requires a considerable effort by education professionals. However, language technologies can facilitate the laborious adaptation of materials in order to enhance reading comprehension. In this paper, we present *LagunTest*, a NLP based application that takes as input a text in Basque or English, and offers synonyms, definitions, examples of the words in different contexts and presents some linguistic characteristics as well as visualizations. *LagunTest* is based on reusable and open multilingual and multimodal tools, and it is also distributed with an open license. *LagunTest* is intended to ease the burden of education professionals in the task of adapting materials, and the output should always be supervised by them.

Keywords: language technologies for education, reading comprehension, multilingual and multimodal applications

1. Introduction

In the Basque Autonomous Community, Basque and Spanish are used as official languages for teaching, whereas English is introduced at an early age. In this education system, most of the students study in Basque, but for a majority it is not their native language (immersion programme). Furthermore, there is an increasing number of schools teaching some of the subjects through English, which is a foreign language for most of the students.

On the other hand, one of the challenges for nowadays schools is to integrate children from different countries and with different native languages in a trilingual education system. At school, these incoming students are expected to read and understand contents in Basque and Spanish, which are foreign languages for them.

In the last years of primary education and in secondary education, students must deal with a large amount of written information in a second language (L2), and it is not easy for education professionals to offer the individual support that is ideally required. Besides, evaluations have proved that the reading comprehension ability has been decreasing during the last years in the three languages used at school, above all in the forth degree of primary (ISEI-IVEI, 2016a; ISEI-IVEI, 2016b; ISEI-IVEI, 2016c). Therefore, it is crucial to provide teachers and education professionals with tools that facilitate the adaptation of written texts to maximize learning.

In this context, language technologies and natural language processing (NLP) tools can support personalization and adaptation of written contents to promote understanding. Similarly, automatic text adaptation can ease the burden on the education professionals and boost their efficiency to teach contents.

In this paper we present *LagunTest*[1], a web application based on open source language technologies that aims to help education professionals to enhance the comprehension of texts written in Basque or English to assist students with different linguistic competence. Specifically, *LagunTest* i) identifies the most frequent words to ease global understanding using a word cloud; ii) offers additional information through images representing the meanings, definitions and synonyms adapted to the student's level; iii) displays the different PoS (part of speech) using colors and iv) represents the dependency tree of the sentence to highlight the morphosyntactic characteristics. *LagunTest* is based on multilingual, multimodal, open source and reusable NLP tools and resources. Its code is available at `https://github.com/kepaxabier/LagunTest` under GNU General Public License v3.0.

This paper is structured as follows: In Section 2 we present the related work; in Section 3, we detail the design criteria and technical resources used to develop *LagunTest* and we explain its functionalities in Section 4. We discuss the limitations of the application in Section 5 and we conclude and outline the future work in Section 6. The text we use as example is shown in Appendix A.

2. Related work

Adapting educational material and building educational applications have directed the attention of many researchers in NLP. Examples of their outcomes are for instance the works presented in main NLP conferences, journals and in the series of BEA workshops organized by ACL SIGEDU[2]. Besides, works on inclusive and adaptive technologies and in automatic text simplification have also been presented in the specialised workshops such as PITR (Predicting and Improving Text Readability for target reader populations) organised in 2012, 2013 and 2014; NLP4ITA (Natural Language Processing for Improving Textual Accessibility) in 2012 and 2013; ATS-MA (Automatic Text Simplification-Methods and Applications in the Multilingual Society) in 2014; ISI-NLP (Improving Social Inclusion using NLP: Tools and resources), QATS (Quality Assessment for Text

---

[1] `http://178.128.198.190:8080/`

[2] `https://sig-edu.org/`

Simplification) and Computational Linguistics for Linguistic Complexity (CL4LC) in 2016; and ATA (Workshop on Automatic Text Adaptation) in 2018.

In the educational domain, reading comprehension and reading strategies have been investigated, even from institutional perspectives (National Reading Panel (US), 2000; RAND Reading Study Group, 2002). Moreover, in the last years, the use of technologies at schools in order to assist students with reading difficulties has also been a research line of interest e.g. (Gasparini and Culén, 2012; Haßler et al., 2016; Crossley et al., 2017).

Regarding the educational technologies, most of the works have focused on English and major languages. For example, R-A Reading (resource assisted reading)[3] offers additional contexts and definition for the words e but, it is only available for French and English. Multidict [4] offers a definition adapted to two levels of difficulty, different languages and different dictionaries. Wordlink [5] makes web pages more accessible by linking the words to Multidict.

But less spoken languages such as Basque have plenty of prototypes and tools in this area e.g. question-answering for education (Aldabe et al., 2006; Aldabe et al., 2013), auto-evaluation of essays (Castro-Castro et al., 2008), readability assessment (Gonzalez-Dios et al., 2014) and automatic text simplification (Gonzalez-Dios, 2016). The creation of multilingual vocabulary exercises by means of NLP tools has also been explored (Agirrezabal et al., 2019).

Regarding levelled materials, Clilstore[6] offers learning materials in different languages (including Basque, but limited) which are organised in levels according to the CEFR. Moreover, these materials include links to definitions from dictionaries of the presented vocabulary.

3.   Design criteria and resources

In this section we present the resources and language technologies that we have been used to build the application. All the resources we use are open sourced or open licensed. Moreover, we have decided to use multilingual and multimodal resources, so that the application can be easily adapted to other languages.

3.1.   Determining vocabulary level

In order to obtain an application adaptable to the different language levels and literacy skills of the students, we have included a feature to select among three vocabulary levels: beginner, intermediate and advanced. This level selection allows to adjust the performance and the results to the level of the student and it determines which words will be adapted and which will be displayed. By adjusting the output to the selected level we avoid oversimplification of the text but also the difficulties of too demanding words for the student. To define the levels, we have followed two strategies: a tool-based strategy and a corpus-based strategy.

In the case of English, we have followed a tool-based strategy: we have used the Wordfreq tool (Speer et al., 2018),

which provides estimations on how often a word is used in 36 languages, for example in Spanish and English. This tool returns the word frequency of a word in a corpus of 10^9 words as the logarithm in base 10 of the number of times a word appears per billion words in different sources such as Wikipedia, Subtitles, News, Books, Web Texts, Twitter, Reddit and others. In Table 1 we show examples for each scale of values that Zipf returns. Following van Heuven et al. (2014), a Zipf value equal to 3 means that the word appears 10^3 times for every 10^9 words, that is, 1 per million. So, using wordfreq and based on Begoetxea et al. (2020), where different values have been tested for educational purposes, we have determined the following values for the vocabulary levels:

- **Beginner level:** words with a Zipf value less than or equal to 8

- **Intermediate level:** words with a Zipf value less than or equal to 5

- **Advanced level:** words with a Zipf value less than or equal to 3

In the case of Basque, as Wordfreq does not provide frequencies for this language, we have followed a corpus-based strategy. Specifically, we have performed a corpus analysis to determine the vocabulary levels. The resource we have used is the frequency list of the corpus *Lexikoaren Behatokia* [7] from *Euskaltzaindia*, the Academy of the Basque Language. This list was created on the 2014 version of the corpus that had 41,773,391 words and it has been used before in automatic text simplification studies for Basque (Gonzalez-Dios, 2016). Based on the values of the list and the distributions of the frequencies, we have stipulated three levels of words:

- **Beginner level:** words whose lemma appears 100,000 or less than 100,000 times in the corpus

- **Intermediate level:** words whose lemma appears 34 or less than 34 times in corpus

- **Advanced level:** words whose lemma appears 6 or less than 6 times in the corpus

3.2.   Choosing the NLP tools

For the automatic analysis of the text, LagunTest can be easily adapted to any model which is the state-of-the-art in segmentation (tokenization and sentence-splitting), lemmatization, POS tagging and dependency parsing task for over 50 languages. In this paper, we have tested NLP-Cube (0.1.0.7) and StanfordNLP (0.2.0) (Qi et al., 2019), that were the best systems in English on CoNLL 2018 Shared Task: Multilingual Parsing from Raw Text to Universal Dependencies (Zeman and Hajič, 2018) but we have decided to use the StanfordNLP 0.2.0 tool[8] that was trained

---

Zipf value	fpmw	Examples
1	0.01	antifungal, bioengineering, farsighted, harelip, proofread
2	0.1	airstream, doorkeeper, neckwear, outsized, sunshade
3	1	beanstalk, cornerstone, dumpling, insatiable, perpetrator
4	10	dirt, fantasy, muffin, offensive, transition, widespread
5	100	basically, bedroom, drive, issues, period, spot, worse
6	1,000	day, great, other, should, something, work, years
7	10,000	and, for, have, I, on, the, this, that, you

Table 1: Examples based on the SUBTLEX-UK word frequencies. fpmw= frequency per million words.

on 70 languages using the Universal Dependencies framework (Nivre et al., 2016). We have limited the analysis to the following processes: tokenisation, sentence splitting, PoS tagging, NER and syntactic parsing.

As a semantic resource, we have used WordNet (Miller, 1995). Exactly, for the texts in English we have used the version included in the NLTK (Bird et al., 2009) and for the texts in Basque the version of the MCR (Gonzalez-Agirre et al., 2012).

In order to perform Word Sense Disambiguation (WSD), we have used UKB, which is available for several languages. UKB applies the so-called Personalized PageRank on a Lexical Knowledge Base (LKB) such as WordNet or Basque WordNet (Pociello et al., 2011) to rank the vertices of the LKB and, thus, disambiguate the words (Agirre et al., 2014).

3.3. Obtaining the images

To make the information in written texts as visual as possible, we have decided to provide images of the words. To obtain the images, we have used three resources: ImageNet (Deng et al., 2009), Wikidata and Wikipedia. ImageNet is a collection of images mapped to WordNet. There are images for 21,841 synsets. Wikidata is a free, collaborative and multilingual database which currently contains 475 images mapped to WordNet. And, finally, Wikipedia is a collaborative encyclopedia from which you can directly obtain images of the names or entities that appear in the raw text, but, in this case, in an ambiguous manner.

To display the images, we have determined that the application selects the image first by means of the WordNet sense identifier (the output of the WSD tool). If there is no image in ImageNet or Wikidata for that sense, the application selects image from WIkipedia with the wordform in the text (without disambiguiation).

4. Functionalities

In this section we describe the functionalities provided by *LagunTest* (Figure 1) to assist teachers on adapting the content. Guided by usability principles, *LagunTest*:

- allows the user to insert text manually or import the text in a document by uploading files in any of the following formats: .txt, .doc, .docx and .odt.

- allows texts in two languages: English or Basque. The user can select the language from a dropdown list on the initial screen.

- computes and displays the results according to the selected level of vocabulary (beginner, intermediate or advanced) in the selected language.

- offers an overall visual representation of the content of the texts by organizing the most important content words of the text as a wordcloud.

- integrates visual and textual information to assist in grasping the meaning of words of less frequent words.

The available options are accessible and visible at the top on the initial screen. The user only needs to set the language and level from the options at the bottom of the initial screen and submit the text to get the results.

Figure 1: Main Page of LagunTest Web Tool

LagunTest is organized into seven tabs which are described in detail in the following subsections. The first two tabs (*Analyze Text* and *Analyze File*) are used to insert the text and the following five to access the visualizations and the rest of lexico-semantic and syntactic information available after submitting the text. To illustrate the functionalities, we will use as example throughout the following subsections the first paragraph of the article *Milk* in Simple Wikipedia,[9] which is also presented in Appendix 1, targeted at a learner with basic level of English.

4.1. Analyze Text and Analyze File tabs: Inserting text

The *LagunTest* application allows to insert the text in two ways: 1) in the *Analyze Text* tab, the user can enter the text by typing it into a text box; 2) in the *Analyze File* tab the user can upload a document in one of the following formats:

---

[9] https://simple.wikipedia.org/wiki/Main_Page

.txt, .doc, .docx and .odt. This avoids the need of converting the text to a specific format.

Once the text has been inserted, the user needs to select the language of the text (Basque or English). Additionally, the user needs to choose a level (basic, intermediate or advanced). Based on the language level, the application adapts the output as presented in Section 3. Finally, the user must click on the submit button, and automatically, the user can check the available information using one of the following tabs: *WordCloud*, *Pictures*, *Definitions*, *Synonym List* and *Syntax*.

4.2. WordCloud tab: overall representation of the text as a wordcloud

Wordclouds are visualization tools that highlight the relative frequency of words in a text. Wordclouds are very useful to quickly identify the more frequent words in the text, since they will appear bigger and bolder. This is a way to pull out the most pertinent parts of textual data. If a student can easily identify the words that appear most frequently in the text, he probably knows effortlessly which are the most pertinent parts, and therefore, the ones he should focus on because they are critical to understand the ideas. Additionally, this visual representation offers a different perspective on the text. Some students will probably have a more visual learning style, and may benefit from observing this global representation. Teachers can use the resulting wordcloud to stimulate reflection on the contents, and open a dialogue with the students intended to relate the words and link the concepts represented by the words.

In Figure 2 we show the wordcloud created by *LagunTest* for the example, where *milk*, *mammals* and *babies* appear in a bigger font.

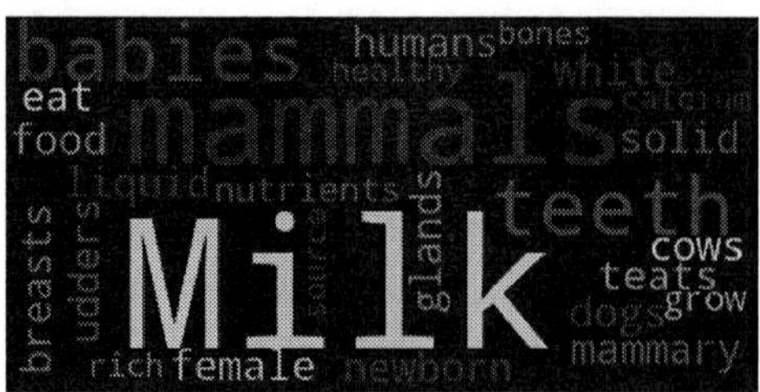

Figure 2: Wordcloud of the example sentence

4.3. Pictures tab: Images of some of the most difficult words from the text

The *Pictures* tab shows the images of the words in the text. In educative contexts, images can be useful to evoke the words. In the current example, the application has returned 9 Wikipedia images for the words *liquid*, *glands*, *breasts*, *udders*, *teats*, *babies*, *teeth*, *calcium* and *bones* and 6 ImageNet image for the words *Milk*, *mammal*, *cow*, *dog*, *humans* and *food*.

In Figure 3 we show the image returned for *udders*, where that part of the body of the cow is shown. The rest of the returned images can be accessed through the urls of Table 2. We also show where they come from.

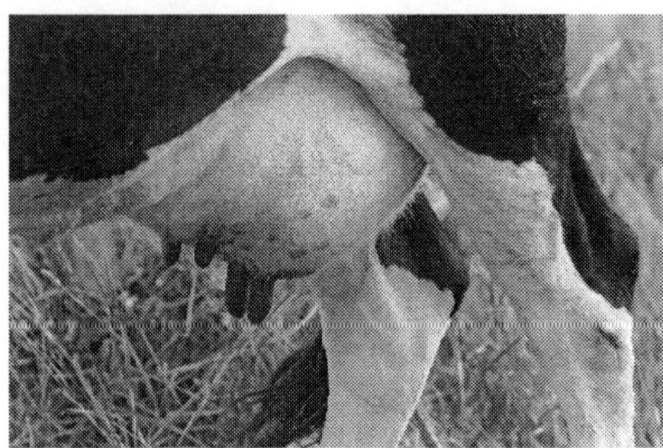

Figure 3: Image returned for the word *udders*

4.4. Definitions tab: definitions and examples

The *Definitions* tab shows the definitions of the nouns and verbs if they are in the respective wordnets. Definitions and examples can be useful to help understanding the concepts in the texts.

In the case of the beginner level, the application offers the definitions and examples for the following words: *milk, liquid, made, mammals, cows, dogs, humans, glands, breasts, udders, teats, babies, have, teeth, given, eat, food, nutrients, help, grow, source, calcium* and *bones*. As an example, we show the definition "any warm-blooded vertebrate having the skin more or less covered with hair" and the example "young are born alive except for the small subclass of monotremes and nourished with milk" for the word *mammals*.

In addition, both in the *Definitions* and *Synonyms* tabs, the words of the text entered are colored according to their PoS: nouns in light green, verbs in red, adjectives in dark blue, proper names in pink, pronouns in dark green, particles in yellow and finally adverbs in orange.

4.5. Synonym List tab: Synonyms

The *Synonym List* tab shows the synonyms of the nouns and verbs that appear in the respective wordnets for the beginner level. Synonyms can be suitable when introducing new vocabulary.

Below, we show the synonyms that were obtained from the example for some of the words (for brevity, we do not include the whole list).

- **made:** 'get'

- **cows:** 'moo-cow'

- **humans:** 'homo', 'man', 'human_being'

- **breasts:** 'titty', 'boob', 'knocker', 'tit', 'bosom'

- **babies:** 'infant', 'babe'

- **have:** 'hold', 'have_got'

- **food:** 'nutrient'

- **help:** 'aid', 'assist'

- **source:** 'origin', 'beginning', 'rootage', 'root'

- **calcium:** 'ca', 'atomic_number_20'

Word	Source	Url
milk	ImageNet	`http://farm4.static.flickr.com/3618/3479565830_54ec716835.jpg`
liquid	Wikipedia	`https://upload.wikimedia.org/wikipedia/commons/4/43/2006-01-14_Surface_waves.jpg`
mammal	ImageNet	`http://static.flickr.com/1250/1487336553_f99ee15b0a.jpg`
cow	ImageNet	`http://farm3.static.flickr.com/2145/2150559343_8de1c310e3.jpg`
dog	ImageNet	`http://farm3.static.flickr.com/2325/1891011832_cb5d5098c2.jpg`
humans	ImageNet	`http://farm3.static.flickr.com/2358/1797858275_bbff0e1b73.jpg`
glands	Wikipedia	`https://upload.wikimedia.org/wikipedia/commons/3/37/405_Modes_of_Secretion_by_Glands_updated.svg`
breasts	Wikipedia	`https://upload.wikimedia.org/wikipedia/commons/b/bd/Bare_breasts_are_our_weapons_crop.jpg`
udders	Wikipedia	`https://upload.wikimedia.org/wikipedia/commons/6/61/Cow_udders02.jpg`
teats	Wikipedia	`https://upload.wikimedia.org/wikipedia/commons/9/91/Bundesarchiv_Bild_183-17369-0004%2C_Barby%2C_Bauer_eine_Melkmaschine_pr%C3%A4sentierend.jpg`
babies	Wikipedia	`https://upload.wikimedia.org/wikipedia/commons/8/84/Baby_%28126372492%29.jpg`
teeth	Wikipedia	`https://upload.wikimedia.org/wikipedia/commons/c/cb/Close_up_-_chimpanzee_teeth.png`
food	ImageNet	`http://farm4.static.flickr.com/3079/2852414223_0d0fa765a0.jpg`
calcium	Wikipedia	`https://upload.wikimedia.org/wikipedia/commons/5/51/Ca%28aq%296_improved_image.tif`
bones	Wikipedia	`https://upload.wikimedia.org/wikipedia/commons/2/23/603_Anatomy_of_Long_Bone.jpg`

Table 2: Url of the images returned by the application

4.6. Syntax tab: dependency tree

Finally, in the *Syntax* tab, the application shows the syntactic dependencies of sentence, based on the framework of Universal Dependencies. This can be practical when teachers aim at practicing or focusing on a particular syntactic structure.

In Figure 4 we can see the generated syntax tree of the fourth sentence: "Milk has many nutrients to help babies grow and be healthy".

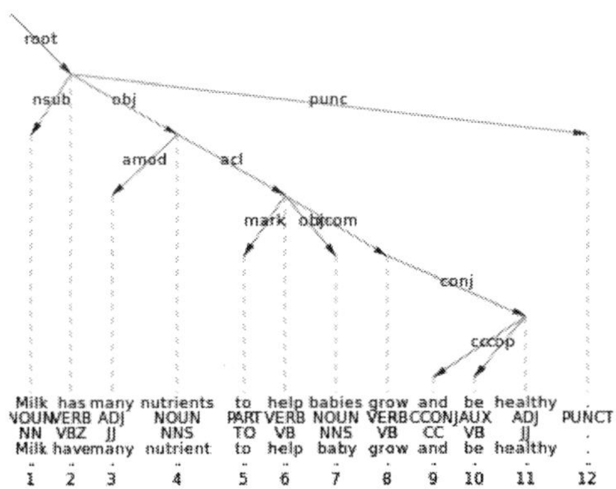

Figure 4: The syntax tree obtained using the StanfordNLP parser

5. Discussion

According to Stanovich (1986), children who read slowly and do not enjoy it, develop the vocabulary knowledge slower, while children who read well learn more words and, therefore read better. This is known as the Matthew effects in reading, which was first introduced in education by Walberg and Tsai (1983).

That is why we claim that using this tool to assist in acquiring vocabulary, particularly at early stages, can promote comprehension and can be used as a facilitator of further reading. However, since the process used by *LagunTest* is fully automatic, there are some limitations to the results.

Regarding the recall, *LagunTest* is limited by the words that are covered in the referenced resources. For example, in the case of the Basque version, not all the nouns have definitions in Basque WordNet. Moreover, regarding the word frequencies, the tools and corpora are general purpose tools containing above all journalist texts for adults and words that can be usual for children such as *milk* can be detected as ow frequency words.

Regarding synonyms, we may encounter register issues. For example, for the word *calcium* the application shows synonyms *ca* and *'atomic_number_20*. As a general resource has been used, these words may be counterproductive for schoolchildren and they may not be very suitable for users with a low level of English. In order to overcome this problem, a possibility is to get frequencies by crawling a corpus from websites for children, or to use the Oxford Children's Corpus (Wild et al., 2012) and filter the results. Moreover, in relation, to the definitions, some of them can be difficult for children.

Regarding the images obtained by the tool, in the image returned for *breast*, a woman is protesting by showing her bare breast. This image may not be the most adequate for children. Besides, in the case of the images obtained from Wikipedia, the tool may offer incorrect images since it has not been disambiguated. On the other hand, web images can also have biases (Crawford and Paglen, 2019). Obtaining suitable images is an open problem in machine learning and Artificial Intelligence.

Summing up, we certainly recommend that the teachers supervise the output of the tool and validate the results for each particular case before using it in the classroom. They know best their students and should decide, for instance, if it is better to work with definitions or with synonyms depending on the task. *LagunTest* is a resource that may offer valuable information to the professionals, but it is worth noting that this type of automatic assistance can never take the role of a professional educator.

6.   Conclusion and future work

In this article we have presented the application *LagunTest*, its design criteria and possible shortcomings. *LagunTest* aims at enhancing reading comprehension by showing images, definitions and synonyms according to the level of knowledge. Through this application we attempt to assist education professionals in adapting materials.

At the moment, *LagunTest* is available to work on vocabulary of English and Basque, but we are working to adapt it to other languages such as Spanish, Galician and Catalan. We also plan to improve its output by adapting it as possible to children by including computational resources for children. Furthermore, the evaluation of the usability of the application and the appropriateness of the contents by education professionals is our main future goals.

7.   Acknowledgments

We acknowledge following projects: DL4NLP (KK-2019/00045), DeepReading RTI2018-096846-B-C21 (MCIU/AEI/FEDER, UE), Ixa Group: consolidated group type A by the Basque Government (IT1343-19) and BigKnowledge for Text Mining, BBVA.

8.   Bibliographical References

Agirre, E., López de Lacalle, O., and Soroa, A. (2014). Random walks for knowledge-based word sense disambiguation. *Computational Linguistics*, 40(1):57–84.

Agirrezabal, M., Altuna, B., Gil-Vallejo, L., Goikoetxea, J., and Gonzalez-Dios, I. (2019). Creating vocabulary exercises through NLP. *Proceedings of the Digital Humanities in the Nordic Countries 4th Conference, CEUR-WS*, pages 18–32.

Aldabe, I., Lopez De Lacalle, M., Maritxalar, M., Martinez, E., and Uria, L. (2006). Arikiturri: an automatic question generator based on corpora and nlp techniques. In *International Conference on Intelligent Tutoring Systems*, pages 584–594. Springer.

Aldabe, I., Gonzalez-Dios, I., Lopez-Gazpio, I., Madrazo, I., and Maritxalar, M. (2013). Two approaches to generate questions in basque. *Procesamiento del lenguaje natural*, 51:101–108.

Bengoetxea, K., Gonzalez-Dios, I., and Aguirregoitia, A. (2020). AzterTest: Open Source Linguistic and Stylistic Analysis Tool. *Procesamiento del Lenguaje Natural*, 64:61–68.

Bird, S., Klein, E., and Loper, E. (2009). *Natural language processing with Python: analyzing text with the natural language toolkit.* " O'Reilly Media, Inc.".

Castro-Castro, D., Lannes-Losada, R., Maritxalar, M., Niebla, I., Pérez-Marqués, C., Álamo-Suárez, N., and Pons-Porrata, A. (2008). A multilingual application for automated essay scoring. In *Ibero-American Conference on Artificial Intelligence*, pages 243–251. Springer.

Crawford, K. and Paglen, T. (2019). Excavating AI: The Politics of Images in Machine Learning Training Sets. `https://www.excavating.ai/`.

Crossley, S. A., McNamara, D. S., et al. (2017). *Adaptive educational technologies for literacy instruction.* Routledge.

Deng, J., Dong, W., Socher, R., Li, L., Kai Li, and Li Fei-Fei. (2009). Imagenet: A large-scale image database. In *2009 IEEE Conference on Computer Vision and Pattern Recognition*, pages 248–255, June.

Gasparini, A. A. and Culén, A. L. (2012). Tablet pcs– an assistive technology for students with reading difficulties. In *ACHI 2012: The Fifth International Conference on Advances in Computer-Human Interactions*, pages 28–34.

Gonzalez-Agirre, A., Laparra, E., and Rigau, G. (2012). Multilingual central repository version 3.0. In *LREC*, pages 2525–2529.

Gonzalez-Dios, I., Aranzabe, M. J., Díaz de Ilarraza, A., and Salaberri, H. (2014). Simple or complex? assessing the readability of basque texts. In *Proceedings of COLING 2014, the 25th international conference on computational linguistics: Technical papers*, pages 334–344.

Gonzalez-Dios, I. (2016). *Euskarazko egitura sintaktiko konplexuen analisirako eta testuen sinplifikazio automatikorako proposamena / Readability Assessment and Automatic Text Simplification. The Analysis of Basque Complex Structures.* Ph.D. thesis, University of the Basque Country (UPV/EHU).

Haßler, B., Major, L., and Hennessy, S. (2016). Tablet use in schools: A critical review of the evidence for learning outcomes. *Journal of Computer Assisted Learning*, 32(2):139–156.

ISEI-IVEI. (2016a). *Rs1.2.1 Curriculum konpetentzia LHko 4. mailan: Euskara.* Instituto Vasco de Evaluación e Investigación Educativa.

ISEI-IVEI. (2016b). *Rs1.2.2 Curriculum konpetentzia LHko 4. mailan: Gaztelania.* Instituto Vasco de Evaluación e Investigación Educativa.

ISEI-IVEI. (2016c). *Rs1.2.4. Nivel de competencia curricular en 4 curso de Educación Primaria: Inglés.* Instituto Vasco de Evaluación e Investigación Educativa.

Miller, G. A. (1995). Wordnet: a lexical database for english. *Communications of the ACM*, 38(11):39–41.

National Reading Panel (US). (2000). Teaching children to read: Reports of the subgroups. The Panel.

Nivre, J., De Marneffe, M.-C., Ginter, F., Goldberg, Y., Hajic, J., Manning, C. D., McDonald, R., Petrov, S., Pyysalo, S., Silveira, N., et al. (2016). Universal dependencies v1: A multilingual treebank collection. In *Proceedings of the Tenth International Conference on Language Resources and Evaluation (LREC'16)*, pages 1659–1666.

Pociello, E., Agirre, E., and Aldezabal, I. (2011). Methodology and Construction of the Basque WordNet. *Language resources and evaluation*, 45(2):121–142.

Qi, P., Dozat, T., Zhang, Y., and Manning, C. D. (2019). Universal dependency parsing from scratch. *arXiv preprint arXiv:1901.10457*.

RAND Reading Study Group. (2002). *Reading for understanding: Toward an R&D program in reading comprehension.* Santa Monica, CA: Rand.

Speer, R., Chin, J., Lin, A., Jewett, S., and Nathan, L. (2018). Luminosoinsight/wordfreq: v2.2, October.

Stanovich, K. E. (1986). Matthew Effects in Reading: Some Consequences of Individual Differences in the Acquisition of Literacy. *Reading Research Quarterly*, 21(4):360–407.

van Heuven, W., Mandera, P., Keuleers, E., and Brysbaert, M. (2014). SUBTLEX-UK: a new and improved word frequency database for British English. *Quarterly journal of experimental psychology*, 67:1176–1190.

Walberg, H. J. and Tsai, S.-L. (1983). Matthew Effects in Education. *American Educational Research Journal*, 20(3):359–373.

Wild, K., Kilgarriff, A., and Tugwell, D. (2012). The Oxford Children's Corpus: Using a Children's Corpus in Lexicography. *International Journal of Lexicography*, 26(2):190–218, 09.

Daniel Zeman et al., editors. (2018). *Proceedings of the CoNLL 2018 Shared Task: Multilingual Parsing from Raw Text to Universal Dependencies*. ACL, Brussels, Belgium, October.

Appendix A: Example text

Milk is a white liquid made by mammals, like cows, dogs, and humans. It is made in the mammary glands (breasts, udders, or teats) of female mammals. Because newborn babies have no teeth, they must be given milk before they can eat solid food. Milk has many nutrients to help babies grow and be healthy. It is also a rich source of calcium which is good for your bones and teeth.

1st Workshop on Tools and Resources to Empower People with REAding DIfficulties (READI2020), pages 70–76
Language Resources and Evaluation Conference (LREC 2020), Marseille, 11–16 May 2020
© European Language Resources Association (ELRA), licensed under CC-BY-NC

A Lexical Simplification Tool for Promoting Health Literacy

Leonardo Zilio[1], Liana Braga Paraguassu[2], Luis Antonio Leiva Hercules[3],
Gabriel L. Ponomarenko[2], Laura P. Berwanger[2], Maria José Bocorny Finatto[2]
[1] Centre for Translation Studies, University of Surrey, United Kingdom, l.zilio@surrey.ac.uk
[2] PPG-LETRAS, Federal University of Rio Grande do Sul, Brazil,
liana@linguatraducoes.com, mariafinatto@gmail.com
[3] Automatic Data Processing, Brazil

Abstract

This paper presents MedSimples, an authoring tool that combines Natural Language Processing, Corpus Linguistics and Terminology to help writers to convert health-related information into a more accessible version for people with low literacy skills. MedSimples applies parsing methods associated with lexical resources to automatically evaluate a text and present simplification suggestions that are more suitable for the target audience. Using the suggestions provided by the tool, the author can adapt the original text and make it more accessible. The focus of MedSimples lies on texts for special purposes, so that it not only deals with general vocabulary, but also with specialized terms. The tool is currently under development, but an online working prototype exists and can be tested freely. An assessment of MedSimples was carried out aiming at evaluating its current performance with some promising results, especially for informing the future developments that are planned for the tool.

Keywords: Healthcare, Health Literacy, Lexical Simplification, Natural Language Processing, Corpus Linguistics, Terminology

1. Introduction

Most health professionals in Brazil have no specific or even complementary training in the area of communication. However, when it comes to health-related information, as Cambricoli (2019) points out, based on a study made by Google, 26% of Brazilians have the Internet as their first source to look for information about their own or their relatives' illnesses, which puts Brazil in the number one position in health-related searches on Google and the YouTube. In a scenario like that, it is important to have support for improving health communication and patient understanding, and this is directly related to health literacy. Health literacy is about communication and understanding; it affects how people understand wellness and illness, and participate in health promotion and prevention activities (Osborne, 2005).

Adding to the question of health literacy, Brazil presents a panorama where functional illiteracy[1] rates are critical. According to a recent INAF[2] report (Lima and Catelli Jr, 2018) published by the Paulo Montenegro Institute, 29% of Brazilians (38 million people) with ages ranging from 15 to 64 years old are considered functional illiterates. Also according to this INAF report, only 12% of the Brazilian population at working age can be considered proficient.

Even though literacy skills are low on the country, Brazil has perceived a significant increase of Internet access in the past years, and information has become available to a much larger number of people. According to the Brazilian Institute of Geography and Statistics (IBGE)[3], in 2017, 67% of the Brazilian population have access to the Internet, as opposed to less than half of the population in 2013.

As it is now, the Brazilian scenario shows a considerable number of people looking for health-related information on the Internet, while only a small percentage of the population can be considered proficient. Adding to that, health professionals don't usually receive the necessary training for providing information that matches the literacy level of a large number of people. In this scenario, a tool that aims at making information more accessible to different audience profiles and that respects the choices of a specialized writer can provide a relevant service both for professionals in charge of communication and for the society in general. MedSimples[4] was conceived for supporting the involvement of health professionals and health communication professionals and for helping them to write information that can be understood by a large part of the population. It is a tool that was designed to help professionals in the task of improving the communication of health-related information to lay people that have low literacy skills. In that way, MedSimples works as a text simplification tool that highlights lexical items and offers suggestions that could improve the accessibility of a health-related text for the Brazilian population. The project is currently focused on the Parkinson's disease domain, and in this paper our aim is to conduct an initial evaluation of the tool, so that we can draw some considerations for its future improvements, especially bearing in mind that the current working structure of MedSimples will be later adjusted for other topics from the Health Sciences.

This paper is divided as follows: Section 2 presents information about text simplification in general and about the PorSimples project, which deals with text simplification for Portuguese; in Section 3, we present how MedSimples was

---

[1] People are considered functionally illiterate when they cannot use reading, writing, and calculation skills for their own and the community's development.

[2] INAF is a Brazilian literacy indicator. More information about INAF can be found at: `http://www.ipm.org.br/inaf`

[3] `https://bit.ly/2HBwmND`

[4] Freely available at: `http://www.ufrgs.br/textecc/acessibilidade/page/cartilha/`.

build, how it works and what are its main features and resources; Section 4 discusses the methodology we applied for evaluating MedSimples and presents its results; in Section 5 we further discuss the evaluation by presenting some data from an error analysis; finally, Section 6 reports on the main findings of this paper and discusses future improvements and changes to the online tool.

2. Related Work

There are several studies regarding text simplification in general and regarding areas that are directly related to text simplification, such as readability assessment (e.g. Vajjala and Meurers (2014), complex word identification (e.g. Wilkens et al. (2014)), intralingual translation (e.g. Rossetti (2019)). However, in this section, we will first focus on briefly introducing the task of text simplification in general, presenting different levels of simplification, and proceed to describe some more applied related work that was developed in the form of a tool that deals with the task of simplifying texts written in Portuguese.

2.1. Text Simplification

In Natural Language Processing, the text simplification task focuses on rewriting a text, adding complementary information (e.g. definitions), and/or discarding irrelevant information for minimizing the text's complexity, but all the while trying to assure that the meaning of the simplified text be not greatly altered, and that the new, rewritten version seem natural and fluid for the reader (Siddharthan, 2002; Siddharthan, 2014; Paetzold and Specia, 2015). This simplification usually occurs by replacing complex words or phrases with simpler ones, in what is called lexical simplification, and/or by modifying the text syntactical structure to render it more simple, which is called a syntactical simplification.

Different types of simplification architectures have been proposed (e.g. Siddharthan (2002; Gasperin et al. (2009; Coster and Kauchak (2011; Paetzold and Specia (2015)), dealing with either or both levels of simplification, generally going from the syntactical level to the lexical level. In this paper, we are focusing on the lexical level, following the bases described by Saggion (2017). MedSimples addresses words, phrases and terms that may be complex for people with low literacy and presents simpler suggestions or term explanations. However, it is important to point out that MedSimples does not focus on trying to automatically replace complex phrases. It is designed to help communicators of health-related information to write more simplified texts. As such, it only presents suggestions of changes, in the form of simpler words or term explanations, that may or may not be accepted by the author of the text.

2.2. Simplification for Portuguese

For Portuguese, there are studies focusing on the classification of complex texts, such as Wagner Filho et al. (2016), and Gazzola et al. (2019), and others that aim at evaluating sentence complexity, such as Leal et al. (2019). However, for the purposes of text simplification, i.e., identifying complex structures of a text and suggesting simpler replacement structures, in the way that we are looking for in Med-

Simples, project PorSimples (Aluísio et al., 2008; Aluísio and Gasperin, 2010) is the one that currently exists with the most similarities.

The project PorSimples deals with the challenges of text simplification and has an online tool called Simplifica (Scarton et al., 2010) that helps authors to write simpler texts. Simplifica uses lexical resources allied with automatically extracted features to identify complex parts of a text and make suggestions on how to make it more readable for people with low literacy. It presents a module for lexical simplification and another module for syntactical simplification, allowing for some customization in terms of which resources are used and which types of syntactical structures are target of the simplification.

While Simplifica serves as an interesting model as a simplification authoring tool, it focuses on the general language, and, as such, it usually cannot suggest befitting simplifications for specialized terms, and this is where the main strength of MedSimples lies. By drawing on specialized resources, MedSimples aims at focusing on different areas of the human knowledge for providing more suitable suggestions for simplifications, and, by aiming at health-related texts, it addresses a widely recognized issue for text simplification (Rossetti, 2019).

3. System Description

MedSimples relies on different corpora and lexical resources, and uses a parsing system at its core. By combining these resources, it can identify complex words and present suggestions for lexical simplification. In this section, we first discuss the lexical resources that were created for MedSimples and then present the pipeline.

3.1. Simple Corpus and Lexical Resources

One of the challenges of text simplification is to identify what kind of vocabulary could be complex to the target audience and try to suggest simpler replacement words or definitions. At this stage of the project, MedSimples deals with the specialized, health-related area of Parkinson's disease[5], so it has to identify not only phrases that are complex from the point of view of the general language, but also terms. It also has to treat complex phrases and terms differently, because offering a simpler lexical suggestion for a term may not help for preserving approximately the same semantic content for the reader, which could lead to serious consequences in a text with information about a health-related subject. For instance, it is possible to substitute the word *involuntário* [involuntary] with *inconsciente* [unconscious] without much semantic difference. However, substituting the term *dopamina* [dopamine] with a simplified version would render the information much less precise, and this could have serious, life-impacting consequences. Considering this different treatment for complex phrases and terms, MedSimples relies on two lexical resources: a list with simpler suggestions for complex phrases from the general language, and a list of simpler definitions for terms (and, when possible, simpler lexical variants).

---

[5]The inclusion of other health-related areas are already in development.

Resource	Source	# of Items
List of simple words	CorPop	6,881
List of complex words	TeP	15,427
List of terms	Handcrafted + Validation	439

Table 1: Lexical resources used by MedSimples for identifying complex lexical items and suggesting simpler alternatives.

For deciding what should be considered as a complex phrase, we decided to look at the problem from a different perspective. By relying on CorPop (Pasqualini, 2018; Pasqualini and Finatto, 2018), a corpus composed of texts that were written for and/or by people with low literacy skills, we were able to estimate which words could be considered simple for our target audience. The corpus was tagged using the PassPort parser (Zilio et al., 2018), and a frequency-ranked word list was generated considering both lemma and part of speech. From this word list, we selected all words with frequency of five or more to be part of our list of simple words. CorPop is a small corpus, containing around 740k tokens and 24k lemmas associated to different word classes, but it was positively evaluated in terms of adequacy for people with low literacy, so we considered that even a low frequency such as five would be enough to warrant the status of simple word to a lemma that is present in this corpus, this led to a list of almost 7k lemmas (associated to the respective word class).

We used this list from CorPop to then filter the Thesaurus of Portuguese (TeP) 2.0 (Maziero and Pardo, 2008) and generate a list of complex words with simpler synonyms. TeP is a language resource that contains WordNet-like synsets for Portuguese. We automatically analyzed each synset and set complex words (i.e. those which were not in the CorPop list of simple words) as entries, while the other words in the synset that were present in our list of simple words were set as simpler synonyms. This list of complex words with simpler synonyms contains more than 15k entries, and also includes some multiword structures, such as *a favor* [in favor], *abóbada celeste* [celestial dome], *curriculum vitae*, *de súbito* [suddenly].

In addition to the list of complex words with simpler synonyms generated from TeP and the list of simple words extracted from CorPop, MedSimples also relies on a list of terms related to Parkinson's disease. This list is still in the process of being completed and simplified, for achieving definitions that are suitable for our target audience. It is being manually built by linguists and also manually validated by a specialist in Medicine[6].

These three lexical resources are used for the automatic process of complex word identification and suggestion of simplifications, as we explain in the next subsection. Table 1 shows the precise numbers of items in each of them.

3.2. Identification and Suggestions

The MedSimples online tool uses automatic text processing and relies on the PassPort parser (Zilio et al., 2018) for

first tagging the text that is used as input by the user. It then analyses each sentence by matching the items first to the list of terms, then to the list of simple words and, finally, to the list of complex words. For matching the list of terms, MedSimples uses the surface forms of words, based on the terminological principle that terms can differentiate themselves by their surface realization (Krieger and Finatto, 2004). Then, it uses the lemma forms to either ignore the word (if it is present in the list of simple words), or to identify it as complex and present a simpler suggestion (if it is present in the complex word list).

MedSimples is still under development, but all the steps mentioned above were already implemented, and the system can visually highlight terms and complex words with suggestions in different colors (depending on whether it is a term or complex word). As it is now, the system is only visually flagging words as complex if there are simpler suggestions in our lexical resources, otherwise, they are ignored. This can be modified, and the idea in the future is to be able to annotate as complex also some types of words that are not in the list of complex words, so as to at least indicate their complexity to the user. Here, for the purpose of this evaluation, we wanted the system to only identify complex words for which we have suggestions, so that we could more easily verify how our suggestions were fitting the context. However, this decision also means we are not currently presenting all the info that we can, and this is reflected in the evaluation process, as will be seen in the next section. This same approach was not used for terms, which we are marking as recognized even if we don't yet have a definition for them. We took this different approach for each type of automatic annotation because the list of terms is much smaller than the number of out-of-vocabulary words, and we expect to have definitions in place for them in the foreseeable future. Figure 1 shows how the system is currently presenting the information about terms and complex phrases. As explained above, this presentation was chosen to speed up the current evaluation, but, in the future, the suggestions will be shown in a different way, in order to not pollute the text for the user.

4. Evaluation

In this paper, one of our aims is to measure how MedSimples is performing in its current state, and what areas should be the focus of our next efforts. To that end, we designed a strict evaluation using a gold standard that was created using authentic online material. In the next subsections, we discuss the creation of the gold standard, then explain the evaluation methodology and, finally, present the results.

4.1. Gold Standard

The first step for creating a gold standard for the evaluation of MedSimples was to create a corpus with texts related to the Parkinson's disease domain. To achieve this, we crawled the web using trigram-combinations of 7 terms related to the target domain: "doença de Parkinson" [Parkinson's disease], "Parkinson", "mal de Parkinson" [alternative denomination for Parkinson's disease[7]], "cuidador"

---

[6]Ricardo Eizerik Machado, M.D., CRMRJ 52-0110079-3.

[7]"Mal de Parkinson" is an alternative denomination for which the use is currently not recommended by the World Health Orga-

Simplificação sugerida

A doença de Parkinson (DP) é uma doença degenerativa (tipo de doença em que a condição da pessoa vai piorando aos poucos) crónica do sistema nervoso central (sistema formado pelo cérebro, medula espinhal e nervos) que afeta principalmente a coordenação motora (capacidade do nosso corpo de realizar e controlar os movimentos). [1] Os sintomas (termo, pesquisar) vão se manifestando de forma lenta e gradual ao longo do tempo. [1] Na fase inicial da doença, os sintomas (termo, pesquisar) mais óbvios (evidente) são tremores (termo, pesquisar), rigidez (endurecimento), lentidão (demora, preguiça, vagar) de movimentos e dificuldade em caminhar. [1] Podem também ocorrer problemas de raciocínio e comportamentais. [2] Nos estádios avançados da doença é comum a presença de demência (perda de capacidades do cérebro, como capacidade intelectual, memória, raciocínio). [2] Cerca de 30 % de as pessoas manifestam depressão (doença que causa tristeza e desânimo constante, entre outros sintomas) e ansiedade. [2] Entre outros possíveis sintomas (termo, pesquisar) estão problemas sensoriais, emocionais e perturbações de o sono. [1] [2] O conjunto de os principais sintomas (termo, pesquisar) a nível motor denominam (chamar, classificar, designar, nomear) se "Parkinsonismo ", ou "síndrome de Parkinson ". [4] [8]

Embora se desconheça a causa exata de a doença, acredita se que envolva tanto fatores genéticos (termo, pesquisar) como fatores ambientais. [4] As pessoas com antecedentes familiares de a doença apresentam um risco superior de vir a desenvolver Parkinson. [4] Existe também um risco superior em pessoas expostas a determinados pesticidas e entre pessoas com antecedentes de lesões em a cabeça. Por outro lado, o risco é menor entre fumadores e consumidores de café e chá. [4] [9] Os sintomas (termo, pesquisar) da doença a nível motor resultam da morte de células na substância negra (termo, pesquisar), uma região do mesencéfalo (parte do cérebro responsável pela visão, audição). [1] A morte leva a uma diminuição da produção de dopamina (hormônio muito importante naturalmente produzido no cérebro que ajuda a realizar uma série de funções, como controlar os movimentos, sentir cheiros, lembrar das coisas etc.) nessas regiões. [1] As causas desta morte celular ainda são mal compreendidas, mas envolvem a acumulação (aumento) de proteínas nos corpos de Lewy (agrupamento anormal de proteínas dentro de células nervosas) nos neurónios. [4] O diagnostico de um caso comum é baseado nos sintomas (termo, pesquisar), podendo ser acompanhado de exames neuroimagiológicos para descartar outras possíveis doenças. [1]

✎ EDITAR   ⎙ COPIAR   ⬇ EXPORTAR TXT

Figure 1: Suggestions of simplifications for a text excerpt about the Parkinson's disease on MedSimples. Source: `https://pt.wikipedia.org/wiki/Doen%C3%A7a_de_Parkinson`

[caretaker], "DP" [acronym for Parkinson's disease], "sintoma motor" [motor symptom], and "qualidade de vida" [quality of life]. These terms were manually selected based on word and n-grams lists extracted from the book *Entendendo a Doença de Parkinson* [Understanding Parkinson's Disease] (Rieder et al., 2016). We used slate3k[8] to scrape PDF documents and jusText[9] to exclude boilerplate and non-interesting content. We also made sure to only scrape content from different Websites, by not repeating previously scraped URLs.

From the resulting crawled corpus, we created 8 random samples of 120 medium-to-long sentences[10] each and distributed them to 8 annotators[11]. Each sample had 30 sentences that were annotated by all annotators and 90 sentences that were annotated only by each individual annotator, totaling 750 sentences. Annotators were asked to annotate any word, phrase or term that they deemed to be complex or terminological, making an explicit distinction between terms and complex phrases.

The result of the annotation was then analysed in terms of a pairwise Cohen's kappa inter-annotator agreement (Cohen, 1960) by using the agreement verified on the 30 sentences that were annotated by all. Since it was a free-flow annotation, in which any part of a sentence could be selected for annotation and there was also a classification task (complex phrase or term) on top of it, this can be considered a very complicated task, so we did not expect to achieve high levels of kappa, but we set .20 as a bare minimum. After calculating the agreement (Table 2), two annotated samples were excluded from the gold standard for not achieving a minimum mean kappa score of 0.20. The final Fleiss' kappa score (Fleiss, 1971) for the remaining annotators' samples was 0.25. This filtering process generated a final gold standard with 570 annotated sentences, and 2080 annotated instances. These final instances were thoroughly checked for inconsistencies (errors resulting from the manual annotation) by one of the authors.

4.2. Methodology

Having a gold standard for the evaluation, we randomized the sentences in it and divided all the instances among the authors for evaluation. Since the evaluation was a somewhat more straightforward process, we did not duplicate sentences for calculating the agreement on the evaluation process (as we did for the generation of the gold standard). Some of the gold standard annotators worked as evaluators as well.

For the evaluation, we asked evaluators to check three aspects of the automatic annotation: first, if the word or

---

nization, because it can cause discrimination or prejudice. Still it can easily appear in online texts about the subject of Parkinson's disease, so we decided to include it as well.

[8] `https://pypi.org/project/slate3k/`

[9] `http://corpus.tools/wiki/Justext`

[10] Each sentence in the gold standard has a minimum of 15 space-separated tokens.

[11] All annotators are linguists or undergraduate students of Linguistics. Some of the authors also contributed as annotators.

	A1	A2	A3	A4	A5	A6	A7	A8
A1	1.0000	0.3828	0.4292	0.3823	0.3355	0.4725	0.2259	0.0765
A2	0.3828	1.0000	0.3568	0.2982	0.2290	0.3534	0.2389	0.1667
A3	0.4292	0.3568	1.0000	0.2625	0.3232	0.5775	0.2946	0.0480
A4	0.3823	0.2982	0.2625	1.0000	0.3854	0.2165	0.1121	0.0465
A5	0.3355	0.2290	0.3232	0.3854	1.0000	0.2090	0.1390	0.0237
A6	0.4725	0.3534	0.5775	0.2165	0.2090	1.0000	0.2235	0.1284
A7	0.2259	0.2389	0.2946	0.1121	0.1390	0.2235	1.0000	0.0734
A8	0.0765	0.1667	0.0480	0.0465	0.0237	0.1284	0.0734	1.0000
Mean	0.3292	0.2894	0.3274	0.2433	0.2350	0.3115	0.1868	0.0805

Table 2: Cohen's kappa pairwise agreement among all annotators. The mean scores ignore the lines where annotators are paired with themselves.

phrase was recognized as complex or as a term; second, if it was correctly recognized as either term or difficult phrase; and, third, to check if the suggestion semantically fitted the context[12]. For the evaluation of the semantic and the recognition task, there was an option for a partial match[13]. In order to simplify the process for the human evaluators, we did not further divide the classification of the partially recognized instances into mismatch for term or complex phrases. In addition to the recognition and the semantic evaluation, in cases where MedSimples failed to recognize the target phrase (either no recognition or only partial recognition), evaluators were asked to proceed with an error analysis, by checking if there were no typos (such as numbers attached at the beginning or end of an instance, spelling errors, etc.), foreign words[14] or unrelated terms[15]. The phrases on the gold standard were also compared with the words on the list of simple words to see if there were any matches.

4.3. Results

As we explained in the previous sections, we used a hard test to see how MedSimples is currently performing, especially because the aim of this study was to look for points in which we need to improve in the future. As shown on Table 3, one of the negative results that we got from this evaluation is that MedSimples currently does not achieve a good coverage. From all the instances, 67.88% were not taken into account for simplification in any way. However, there is also positive information coming from these results: for all the instances that were correctly recognized, MedSimples provided the correct meaning on 67.04% of the cases (with a slightly better performance for terms, as expected, which have their suggestions coming from a handcrafted

glossary).

When there was a partial recognition of an instance (which could only happen for multiword instances) or a mismatch, we see that MedSimples struggles to provide a suggestion that fits the context. This is especially true in the case of mismatches, where the number of suggestions that do not fit the context (bad suggestions) is 3.5 times higher than the number of good suggestions. By further analyzing the partially recognized instances, we see that the vast majority of unfitting suggestions come from our list of complex words (the one that was automatically created using TeP (Maziero and Pardo, 2008) and CorPop (Pasqualini, 2018)).

5. Discussion

After looking at the results, especially the ones from unrecognized and partially recognized instances, we can look at an error analysis to better understand what was missing.

Table 4 shows information about out-of-scope terms (i.e. terms that do not belong to the area of Parkinson's Disease), foreign words present on the target instances, and typos. The number of out-of-scope terms accounted for 13.05% of the terms that were not recognized by the tool (counting also the ones that were partially recognized or mismatch). The number of foreign words and typos, on the other hand, are almost negligible, accounting for only 4.67% of the unrecognized instances.

As a second part of this error analysis, we looked at our own list of words that are assumed to be simple (this is the list of words that was extracted from CorPop, which was already tested by Pasqualini (2018) in terms of complexity) and matched it against instances that were considered as complex phrases by the annotators. In total, we found out that 393 instances that were not recognized in any form contained words that were in our list of simple words, this accounts for 55.11% of the unrecognized complex phrases in the evaluation.

This comparison revealed a complicated, but expected (as pointed out by Cabré (1993), Krieger and Finatto (2004)), aspect of the lexical simplification: there are words or phrases with a generally simple meaning that can have a complex meaning in specific contexts (for instance, "administração" [administration] in general has a fairly simple meaning, but in the context of "administration of medicines to patients", it takes a more complex meaning). However, by looking further into this comparison, it also

---

[12]In those cases where the suggestion was a whole synset, only one of the suggested replacement words should fit to be considered a good suggestion. This decision take into consideration that we rely on the user to decide which one of the suggested replacement words would fit the context.

[13]For instance, if only part of a term was identified or if a suggestion of simplification would only partially fit in the context.

[14]Since we are using lexical resources for the Brazilian Portuguese variant, the evaluators were instructed to mark European Portuguese variants as foreign words as well.

[15]Since the corpus was crawled from the internet, there is always the possibility of having sentences that do not belong to the Parkinson's disease domain, even if the keywords used were heavily linked to the domain.

	Recognized			Partially Recognized			Mismatch			Unrecognized	Total
	Good	Bad	Partial	Good	Bad	Partial	Good	Bad	Partial		
Terms	125	47	0	47	87	22	10	35	4	699	1076
Complex phrases	172	73	26	5	11	4	0	0	0	713	1004
Total	297	120	26	52	98	26	10	35	4	1412	2080

Table 3: Evaluation results. The labels "Good", "Bad" and "Partial" reflect the evaluation of the meaning of MedSimples' suggestions in the given context.

	Out-of-Scope Terms	Foreign Words	Typos	Total
Terms	118	19	22	159
Complex phrases	0	19	6	25
Total	118	38	28	184

Table 4: Error Analysis

revealed that the number of complex instances in the evaluation may as well have been overestimated (for instance, words like "demonstrar" [demonstrate], "interferir" [to interfere], and "promover" [to promote] were annotated as complex, even if the context in which they appear does not imply a more complex meaning). This observation requires some further analyses that we haven't yet carried out, to better estimate what could be considered to be included in our current lexical resources and what can be viewed as an overestimation of complexity from the annotation.

The case of words that assume a more complex meaning in context is the one that poses an interesting challenge for MedSimples. Since we are currently not using any type of disambiguation, we have no way of distinguishing between the "administration of a business" and the "administration of medicines", and this should be a matter to take into account for the future steps of the tool.

6.   Final Thoughts and Future Work

In this paper we presented MedSimples, an authoring tool that is mainly focused on helping producers of content from the healthcare industry to provide more accessible texts to Brazilian people with low literacy. MedSimples is currently under development, but has a working online prototype for testing. By accessing the Website, a user can input a text and, after having selected the domain and type of target reader and submitting it for processing, receive suggestions of simpler words or definitions for terms that could be taken into consideration for formulating a more accessible text.

In order to expand MedSimples, an evaluation was developed to assess the current state of the system and to provide useful information for the steps going forward. One of the results of the evaluation was that MedSimples is still lacking in terms of good suggestions that would fit the context of a text dealing with Parkinson's disease. That is one of the reason's why the list of complex words and simple suggestions is going to be target of a major review, that intends on checking for entries that are not very helpful and trying to provide suggestions that would potentially present a better fit for the specialized context, considering meanings that would be more in line with the domain. This evaluation also presented some interesting information for expanding MedSimples' term base, which currently contains almost 450 terms, but that could be expanded to have a broader coverage of the area, possibly including terms that are not directly linked to the Parkinson's disease, but that deals with more general terminology of the healthcare area.

Going forward, we have several improvements planned for the tool. Along with the changes planned for the lists of terms and of complex words explained above, we are also studying, for instance, the possibility of expanding the identification of complex words to some of those for which we currently don't have a simpler suggestion, for it might help the user to identify possible challenges for their target audience. The changes are not only planned for the backend, but also for the interface. By presenting a more visually appealing interface (for instance, without the presentation of suggestions within the text), the tool can be made more suitable for helping health professionals and communicators of the health industry in their tasks of writing texts for people with low literacy.

7.   Acknowledgments

The authors would like to thank these funding sources that contributed to this research: Expanding Excellence in England (E3), Google LARA Award 2019, PIBIC-PROPESQ-UFRGS, CNPq, and CAPES.

8.   Bibliographical References

Aluísio, S. M. and Gasperin, C. (2010). Fostering digital inclusion and accessibility: the porsimples project for simplification of portuguese texts. In *Proceedings of the NAACL HLT 2010 Young Investigators Workshop on Computational Approaches to Languages of the Americas*, pages 46–53. Association for Computational Linguistics.

Aluísio, S. M., Specia, L., Pardo, T. A., Maziero, E. G., and Fortes, R. P. (2008). Towards brazilian portuguese automatic text simplification systems. In *Proceedings of the eighth ACM symposium on Document engineering*, pages 240–248.

Cabré, M. T. (1993). *La terminología: teoría, metodología, aplicaciones*. Antártida/Empúries.

Cambricoli, F. (2019). Brasil lidera aumento das pesquisas por temas de sa[ude no google.

Cohen, J. (1960). A coefficient of agreement for nominal scales. *Educational and psychological measurement*, 20(1):37–46.

Coster, W. and Kauchak, D. (2011). Learning to Simplify Sentences Using Wikipedia. In *Proceedings of Text-To-Text Generation, ACL Workshop*.

Fleiss, J. L. (1971). Measuring nominal scale agreement among many raters. *Psychological bulletin*, 76(5):378.

Gasperin, C., Maziero, E., Specia, L., Pardo, T. A., and Aluísio, S. M. (2009). Natural language processing for social inclusion: a text simplification architecture for different literacy levels. *Proc. of SEMISH-XXXVI Seminário Integrado de Software e Hardware*, pages 387–401.

Gazzola, M., Leal, S. E., and Aluisio, S. M. (2019). Prediç ao da complexidade textual de recursos educacionais abertos em português.

Krieger, M. d. G. and Finatto, M. J. B. (2004). *Introdução à terminologia: teoria e prática*. Editora Contexto.

Leal, S. E., de MAGALHAES, V., Duran, M. S., and Aluísio, S. M. (2019). Avaliação automática da complexidade de sentenças do português brasileiro para o domínio rural. In *Embrapa Gado de Leite-Artigo em anais de congresso (ALICE)*.

Lima, A. and Catelli Jr, R. (2018). Inaf brasil 2018: Resultados preliminares. ação educativa/instituto paulo montenegro, 2018.

Osborne, H. (2005). *Health Literacy from A to Z. Practical Ways to Communicate Your Health Message*. Jones and Bartlett Publishers.

Paetzold, G. H. and Specia, L. (2015). Lexenstein: A framework for lexical simplification. *ACL-IJCNLP 2015*, 1(1):85.

Rieder, C. R. M., Chardosim, N., Terra, N., and Gonzatti, V. (2016). Entendendo a doença de parkinson: Informações para pacientes, familiares e cuidadores. *Aspectos Cognitivos na Doença de Parkinson. Porto Alegre, RS: EDIPU-CRS*, 2016:97–104.

Rossetti, A. (2019). Intralingual translation and cascading crises. *Translation in Cascading Crises*.

Saggion, H. (2017). Automatic text simplification: Synthesis lectures on human language technologies, vol. 10 (1). *California, Morgan & Claypool Publishers*.

Scarton, C., Oliveira, M., Candido Jr, A., Gasperin, C., and Aluísio, S. (2010). Simplifica: a tool for authoring simplified texts in brazilian portuguese guided by readability assessments. In *Proceedings of the NAACL HLT 2010 Demonstration Session*, pages 41–44.

Siddharthan, A. (2002). An architecture for a text simplification system. In *Language Engineering Conference*, pages 64–71.

Siddharthan, A. (2014). A survey of research on text simplification. *ITL-International Journal of Applied Linguistics. Special Issue on Readability and Text Simplification. Peeters Publishers, Belgium*.

Vajjala, S. and Meurers, D. (2014). Exploring measures of "readability" for spoken language: Analyzing linguistic features of subtitles to identify age-specific tv programs. In *Proceedings of the 3rd Workshop on Predicting and Improving Text Readability for Target Reader Populations (PITR) at EACL*, volume 14.

Wagner Filho, J. A., Wilkens, R., Zilio, L., Idiart, M., and Villavicencio, A. (2016). Crawling by readability level. In *International Conference on Computational Processing of the Portuguese Language*, pages 306–318. Springer.

Wilkens, R., Dalla Vecchia, A., Boito, M. Z., Padró, M., and Villavicencio, A. (2014). Size does not matter. frequency does. a study of features for measuring lexical complexity. In *Advances in Artificial Intelligence–IBERAMIA 2014*, pages 129–140. Springer.

Zilio, L., Wilkens, R., and Fairon, C. (2018). Passport: A dependency parsing model for portuguese. In *International Conference on Computational Processing of the Portuguese Language*, pages 479–489. Springer.

9. Language Resource References

Maziero, E. and Pardo, T. (2008). Interface de acesso ao tep 2.0–thesaurus para o português do brasil. *Relatório técnico. University of Sao Paulo*.

Pasqualini, B. and Finatto, M. J. B. (2018). Corpop: a corpus of popular brazilian portuguese. In *Latin American and Iberian Languages Open Corpora Forum - OpenCor*.

Pasqualini, B. F. (2018). *CorPop: um corpus de referência do português popular escrito do Brasil*. Ph.D. thesis, Universidade Federal do Rio Grande do Sul.

1st Workshop on Tools and Resources to Empower People with REAding DIfficulties (READI2020), pages 77–84
Language Resources and Evaluation Conference (LREC 2020), Marseille, 11–16 May 2020
© European Language Resources Association (ELRA), licensed under CC-BY-NC

A multi-lingual and cross-domain analysis of features for text simplification

Regina Stodden and Laura Kallmeyer
Heinrich Heine University
Düsseldorf, Germany
{stodden, kallmeyer}phil.hhu.de

Abstract

In text simplification and readability research, several features have been proposed to estimate or simplify a complex text, e.g., readability scores, sentence length, or proportion of POS tags. These features are however mainly developed for English. In this paper, we investigate their relevance for Czech, German, English, Spanish, and Italian text simplification corpora. Our multi-lingual and multi-domain corpus analysis shows that the relevance of different features for text simplification is different per corpora, language, and domain. For example, the relevance of the lexical complexity is different across all languages, the BLEU score across all domains, and 14 features within the web domain corpora. Overall, the negative statistical tests regarding the other features across and within domains and languages lead to the assumption that text simplification models may be transferable between different domains or different languages.

Keywords: text simplification, corpus study, multi-lingual, multi-domain

1. Introduction

In research regarding readability and text simplification, several features are mentioned which identify easy-to-read sentences or help to transform complex to simplified texts. However, features such as readability metrics are highly criticized because they only consider surface characteristics, e.g., word and sentence length, ignore other relevant factors, such as infrequent words (Collins-Thompson, 2014), and are optimized only for English. Therefore, Collins-Thompson (2014) proposes more sophisticated features, e.g., parse tree height or word frequency, which might be applicable to non-English-languages too.

Similar to the research in text readability, most text simplification research is concerned with English, with some exceptions, e.g., Italian (Brunato et al., 2016) or Czech (Barančíková and Bojar, 2019), or multi-lingual approaches, e.g., Scarton et al. (2017). Text simplification or readability measurement models with the same feature set for all corpora have been shown to perform well on cross-lingual (Scarton et al., 2017), multi-lingual (Yimam et al., 2017), and cross-domain (Gasperin et al., 2009) corpora. However, due to language or domain characteristics, distinct features, e.g., parse tree height, proportion of added lemmas, or usage of passive voice, might be more or less relevant during the simplification process and also during its evaluation. So far, it has not been investigated whether the relevance of distinct text simplification features differs across languages and domains. We therefore address the following research questions (RQ) in this paper:

1. Do complex texts and its simplified version differ significantly regarding linguistic features? Can language-independent linguistic features explain at least partially the simplification process?

2. Is the simplification process consistent between corpora across and within domains?

3. Is the simplification process consistent between corpora within and across languages?

Concretely, we analyze the relevance of features named in readability and text simplification research on aligned sentence simplification pairs in five languages, i.e., Czech, German, English, Spanish, and Italian, and in three domains, i.e., web data, Wikipedia articles, and news articles. This automated multi-lingual text simplification corpus analysis is implemented based on the analysis proposed in Martin et al. (2018). For re-use on other corpora, our code is available on github[1].

The paper is structured as follows: Section 2 gives an overview of related work, the next section describes our methods for addressing the above mentioned research questions, including corpora, features, and evaluation methods. Section 4 discusses our results, and Section 5 concludes.

2. Related Works

Several studies of text readability/simplification analyze or compare texts or sentence pairs with different complexity levels, e.g., Collins-Thompson (2014) or Kauchak et al. (2014) in English, Hancke et al. (2012) in German, Gasperin et al. (2009) or Aluisio et al. (2010) in Portuguese, Pilán and Volodina (2018) in Swedish, and Scarton et al. (2017) in English, Italian, and Spanish. However, in contrast to the paper in hand, they focus on building either complexity level assessment models using and comparing grouped features sets or on the theoretical justification of these features (Collins-Thompson, 2014) rather than on a comparison of the relevance and statistical significance of the distinct features (see RQ1). Most of the text level features proposed in these studies, e.g., parse tree height, passive voice, length of verb phrases, are also considered in our work. Unfortunately, we could not include discourse-level features, e.g., coherence, idea density, or logical argumentation, because of the lack of alignments at that level.

In the context of text simplification, several related corpus studies exist either to analyze the quality of a new corpus,

---

[1] https://github.com/rstodden/TS_corpora_analysis

e.g., (Xu et al., 2015) or Scarton et al. (2018), or to build an evaluation metric, e.g., Martin et al. (2018). Martin et al. (2018) implemented several features regarding English text simplification and test whether they correlate with human judgments in order to build an evaluation metric which does not require gold simplifications. Their work is the most similar to ours, but in comparison to them, we will analyze simplification features from another perspective: Instead of comparing with human judgments, we will evaluate the features at their simplification level, language, and domain. The analysis proposed here is based on their implementation, but it extends it with more features and enables the analysis of other languages than English.

Gasperin et al. (2009) built a classifier that predicts whether a sentence needs to be split in the context of Portuguese text simplification. Their basic feature set, including, e.g., word length, sentence length, and number of clauses, achieved good results on the news-article domain (F-score of 73.40), the science articles domain (72.50) but performs best cross-domain (77.68). We use similar features but analyze them separately and evaluate them regarding other domains, i.e., web data and Wikipedia (see RQ2).

The topic of multi-lingual text simplification is also related to this paper. For complex word identification, a sub-task of text simplification, a data set in German, English, and Spanish exists (Yimam et al., 2017). On this data set, Finnimore et al. (2019) tested language-independent features as to whether they generalize in a cross-lingual setting. Their ablation tests identified the number of syllables, number of tokens, ratio of punctuation, and word probability as the best performing features. In contrast, Scarton et al. (2017) focus on syntactical multi-lingual simplification. They proposed a multi-lingual classifier for deciding whether a sentence needs to be simplified or not for English, Italian, and Spanish, using the same features for all languages. For each language, the system achieved an F1-score of roughly 61% using the same feature set. In our study, we investigate whether their findings also hold for both syntactic and lexical simplifications and not only one of them (see RQ3).

3. Method

In order to compare text simplification corpora in different languages and domains, we have chosen eight corpora in five languages and three domains (see Section 3.1). For the analysis, we use in sum 104 language-independent features (see Section 3.2). In order to analyze relevance of the features per corpus, language, and domain, we conduct several statistical tests (see Section 3.3).

3.1. Data

Most text simplification research focuses on English, but also research in other languages exist, e.g., Bulgarian, French, Danish, Japanese, Korean. However, due to limited access, now-defunct links, non-parallel-versions, or a missing statement regarding availability, we focus on the following four non-English text simplification corpora:

- German (DE) web data corpus (Klaper et al., 2013),
- Spanish (ES) news corpus Newsela (Xu et al., 2015)[2],

- Czech (CS) newspaper corpus COSTRA (Barančíková and Bojar, 2019)[3], and
- Italian (IT) web data corpus PaCCSS (Brunato et al., 2016)[4].

In contrast, several freely available corpora for English text simplification exist. We decided to use the following four:

- TurkCorpus (Xu et al., 2016)[5],
- QATS corpus (Štajner et al., 2016)[6], and
- two current used versions of the Newsela corpus (Xu et al., 2015)[7].

The first version of Newsela (2015-03-02) (Xu et al., 2015) is already sentence-wise aligned whereas the second version (2016-01-29) is not aligned. Therefore, the alignment is computed on all adjacent simplification levels (e.g., 0-1, 1-2, .., 4-5) with the alignment algorithm MASSAlign proposed in Paetzold et al. (2017)[8] using a similarity value α of 0.2 for the paragraph as well as for the sentence aligner. In addition to the language variation, the corpora chosen for this purpose differ in their domains, i.e., newspaper articles, web data, and Wikipedia data. An overview, including the license, domain, size, and alignment type of the corpora, is provided in Table 1.

As illustrated in Table 1, the corpora largely differ in their size of pairs (CS-Costra: 293, EN-Newsela-15: 141,582) as well as in the distribution of simplification transformations (see Table 1), e.g., 15% of only syntactic simplifications in EN-QATS but only 0.03% in EN-Newsela-15.

3.2. Features

For the analysis, overall, 104 language-independent features are measured per corpus, domain, or language. 43 features, further called *single features*, are measured per item in the complex-simplified pair. For the domain and language comparison, the difference of each of the same 43 features between the complex and simplified text is measured, further called *difference features*. The remaining 18 features, *paired features*, describe respectively one feature per complex-simplified pair. The implementation of the features is in Python 3 and is based on the code provided by Martin et al. (2018). In contrast to them, we are offering the usage of SpaCy[9] and Stanza[10] instead of NLTK for pre-processing. In comparison to SpaCy, Stanza is slower but has a higher accuracy and supports more languages. In the following, the results using SpaCy are presented.

---

[3]https://lindat.mff.cuni.cz/repository/xmlui/handle/11234/1-3123

[4]http://www.italianlp.it/resources/paccss-it-parallel-corpus-of-complex-simple-sentences-for-italian/

[5]https://github.com/cocoxu/simplification

[6]http://qats2016.github.io/shared.html

[7]https://newsela.com/data/

[8]The code of the tool is originally published in Python 2. The tool was used in Python 3 following the code published at https://github.com/samuelstevens/massalign.

[9]https://spacy.io/

[10]https://stanfordnlp.github.io/stanza/

---

[2]https://newsela.com/data/

		Domain	Size	License	Sentence length		Word length		S	L	L&S	-L&-S	I
					comp	simp	comp	simp					
CS-COSTRA		News Headlines	293	CC BY 4.0	11.47	9.65	5.43	5.29	1.02	58.02	40.61	0.34	0
DE-Klaper		Web Data	1,888	Available Upon Request	12.79	12.45	6.98	6.34	1.06	20.71	57.20	21.03	20.60
EN-Newsela_15		News Articles	141,582	Scientific Usage	26.27	17.25	5.32	5.15	0.03	37.21	62.75	0.01	0
EN-Newsela_16	0-1	News Articles	69,185	Scientific Usage	25.50	24.63	4.99	4.96	2.87	24.60	27.73	44.81	41.54
	1-2		76,533		21.35	20.41	4.99	4.94	3.35	26.67	29.48	40.50	36.85
	2-3		69,229		18.18	16.94	4.93	4.84	3.78	29.53	34.60	32.10	28.80
	3-4		61,383		15.17	14.05	4.84	4.76	4.13	28.60	34.82	32.45	29.15
	4-5		966		12.36	10.87	4.64	4.52	4.14	32.40	39.75	23.71	21.12
EN-QATS		Wikipedia + Encyclopedia	505	Free Usage	28.20	23.53	5.35	5.32	15.45	29.70	30.50	24.36	18.61
EN-Turk		Wikipedia	18,872	GNU General Public License	22.35	21.37	5.38	5.20	3.50	47.50	28.05	20.96	15.96
ES-Newsela	0-1	News Articles	7,529	Scientific Usage	31.31	28.96	5.28	5.25	2.36	38.23	37.06	22.35	19.83
	1-2		8,235		25.87	23.77	5.26	5.22	3.05	33.71	34.73	28.51	24.53
	2-3		6,783		21.36	18.81	5.21	5.13	3.07	35.03	40.31	21.60	19.08
	3-4		5,707		16.35	14.43	5.13	5.07	3.31	33.70	39.41	23.59	20.90
	4-5		101		14.39	11.84	4.98	4.97	0.99	34.65	57.43	6.93	4.95
IT-PaCCSS		Web Data	63,012	Scientific Usage	9.26	8.29	4.62	4.64	1.50	68.8	25.53	4.15	0

Table 1: An overview of the used corpora including domain, corpus size, license, sentence length per complex (comp) and simple (simp) text, word length per complex and simple text, and the proportion of simplification transactions per corpus in percent (S=syntactic, L=lexical, L&S=lexical and syntactical, -L&-S=no lexical nor syntactical, I=identical). A complex-simplified text pair is considered as lexical simplification if new tokens are added to the simplified text or tokens are rewritten in the simplified text. A pair is considered as syntactic simplification if the text is split or joined.

The pre-processing with SpaCy includes sentence-splitting, tokenization, lemmatizing, POS-tagging, dependency parsing, named entity recognition, and generating word embeddings. The SpaCy word embeddings are replaced in this study by pre-trained word embeddings of FastText (Grave et al., 2018) to achieve a higher quality[11]. Unless otherwise stated, this data is used to measure the used features.

3.2.1. Single Features

The single features are grouped into *proportion of part of speech (POS) tags*, *proportion of clauses & phrases*, *length of phrases*, *syntactical*, *lexical*, *word frequency*, *word length*, *sentence length*, and *readability features*. An overview is provided in Table 2.

Proportion of POS Tags Features. Gasperin et al. (2009) and Kauchak et al. (2014) name the proportion of POS tags per sentence as a relevant feature for text simplification. According to Kercher (2013), a higher proportion of verbs in German indicates for instance a simpler text because it might be more colloquial. POS tag counts are normalized by dividing them by the number of tokens per text, as in Kauchak et al. (2014). A list of all used POS tags features is provided in Table 2.

Proportion of Clauses and Phrases Features. Gasperin et al. (2009) and recommend using the proportion of clauses and phrases. The clauses and phrases extend and complex a sentence, so they are often split (Gasperin et al., 2009). The proportion of the clauses and phrases is measured using the dependency tree of the texts and differentiated, as shown in Table 2.

Length of Phrases Features. In a study regarding sentence splitting prediction (Gasperin et al., 2009), the length of noun, verb, and prepositional phrases are used as features because the longer a phrase, the more complex the sentence and the higher the amount of processing.

Syntactic Features. We use six syntactic features, computed based on the SpaCy dependency trees and POS tags. Inspired by Niklaus et al. (2019), we measure whether the head of the text is a verb (Feature 1). If the text contains more than one sentence, at least one root must be a verb. Following Universal Dependencies[12], a verb is most likely to be the head of a sentence in several languages. So, sentences whose heads are not verbs might be ungrammatical or hard to read due to their uncommon structure. Therefore, the feature of whether the head of the sentence is a noun is added (2).

Niklaus et al. (2019) also state that a sentence is more likely to be ungrammatical and, hence, more difficult to read if no child of the root is a subject (3).

According to Collins-Thompson (2014), a sentence with a higher parse tree is more difficult to read, we therefore add the parse tree height as well (4).

Feature (5) indicates whether the parse tree is projective; a parse is non-projective if dependency arcs cross each other or, put differently, if the yield of a subtree is discontinuous in the sentence. In some languages, e.g., German and Czech, non-projective dependency trees are rather frequent, but we hypothesize that they decrease readability.

Gasperin et al. (2009) suggest passive voice (6) as a further feature because text simplification often includes transforming passive to active, as recommended in easy-to-read

---

[11]This has the disadvantage that the here proposed corpus analysis is only available for languages supported by SpaCy and FastText.

[12]https://universaldependencies.org/docs/en/dep/root.html

text guidelines, because the agent of the sentence might get clearer. Due to different dependency label sets in SpaCy for some languages, this feature is only implemented for German and English.

Lexical Features. Further, six features are grouped into lexical features. The lexical complexity (Feature 1) might be a relevant feature because a word might be more familiar for a reader the more often it occurs in texts. In order to measure the lexical complexity of the input text, the third quartile of the log-ranks of each token in the frequency table is used (Alva-Manchego et al., 2019).

The lexical density –type-token-ratio– (2) is calculated using the ratio of lexical items to the total number of words in the input text (Martin et al., 2018; Collins-Thompson, 2014; Hancke et al., 2012; Scarton et al., 2018). It is assumed that a more complex text has a larger vocabulary than a simplified text (Collins-Thompson, 2014).

Following Collins-Thompson (2014), the proportion of function words is a relevant feature for readability and text simplification. In this study, function words (3) are defined using the universal dependency labels "aux", "cop", "mark" and "case".

Additionally, we added the proportion of multi-word expressions (MWE, 4) using the dependency labels "flat", "fixed", and "compound" because it might be difficult for non-native speakers to identify and understand the separated components of an MWE, especially when considering long dependencies between its components.

The ratio of referential expressions (5) is also added based on POS tags and dependency labels. The more referential expression, the more difficult the text because the reader has to connect previous or following tokens of the same or even another sentence. Lastly, the ratio of named entities (6) is examined because they might be difficult to understand for non-natives or non-experts of the topic.

Word Frequency Features. As another indication for lexical simplification, the word frequency can be used (Martin et al., 2018; Collins-Thompson, 2014). Complex words are often infrequent, so word frequency features may help to identify difficult sentences. The frequency of the words is based on the ranks in the FastText Embeddings (Grave et al., 2018). The average position of all tokens in the frequency table is measured as well as the position of the most infrequent word.

Word and Sentence Length Features. Word length and sentence length are well-established measurements used for readability measurement. Following Scarton et al. (2018), we distinguish word length in number of characters, and syllables and sentence length in number of characters, syllables, and words.

Readability Metric Features. Furthermore, as proposed by Martin et al. (2018), we use readability metrics. Readability metrics calculate based on sentence length and number of syllables the complexity of a text and estimates, for example, the minimum grade of understanding. We differentiate between Flesch-Kincaid Grade Level and Flesh Reading Ease (Kincaid et al., 1975).

3.2.2. Paired Features

The paired features (see Table 3) are grouped into *lexical*, *syntactic*, *simplification*, *word embeddings*, and *machine translation* features.

Lexical Features. Inspired by Martin et al. (2018) and Alva-Manchego et al. (2019), the following proportions relative to the simplified or complex texts are included as lexical features:

- **Added Lemmas:** Additional words can make the simplified sentence more precise and comprehensible by enriching it with, e.g., decorative adjectives or term definitions.
- **Deleted Lemmas:** Deleting complex words might contribute to ease of readability.
- **Kept Lemmas:** Keeping words, on the other hand, might contribute to preserving the meaning of the text (but also its complexity). Kept lemmas describe the words which occur in both texts but might be differently inflected.
- **Kept Words:** Kept Words are a portion of kept lemmas, they describe the proportion of words which occur exactly in the same inflection in both texts.
- **Rewritten Words:** Words which are differently inflected in the simplified text, compared to the complex one, but have the same lemma are called rewritten words. Granted that complex words are rewritten, a higher amount of rewritten words represents a more simplified text.

The compression ratio is similar to the Levenshtein Distance and measures how many characters are left in the simplified text compared to the complex text. The Levenshtein Similarity measures the difference between complex and simplified texts by insertions, substitutions, or deletions of characters in the texts.

Syntactic Features. The idea of the features of split and joined sentences are based on Gasperin et al. (2009), both show an applied simplification transaction. The sentence is counted as split if the number of sentences of the complex text is lower than of the simplified text. The sentence is counted as joined if the number of sentences of the complex text is higher than of the simplified text.

Simplification Features. In order to address more simplification transactions, we measure lexical, syntactical, and no changes. A complex-simplified-pair is considered as a lexical simplification if tokens are added or rewritten in the simplified text. A complex-simplified-pair is considered as a syntactic simplification if the text is split or joined. Also, a change from non-projective to projective, passive to active, and a reduction of the parse tree height are considered as syntactic simplifications. A complex-simplified-pair is considered as identical if both texts are the same, so no simplification has been applied. As each pair is solely analyzed, the standard text simplification evaluation metric SARI (Xu et al., 2016), which needs several gold references, cannot be considered in the analysis.

Word Embedding Features. The similarity between the complex and the simplified text (Martin et al., 2018) is measured using pre-trained FastText embeddings (Grave et al.,

2018). We consider cosine similarity, and also the dot product (Martin et al., 2018). The higher the value, the more similar the sentences, the more the meaning might be preserved and the higher the simplification quality might be.

Machine Translation (MT) Features. Lastly, three MT features are added to the feature set, i.e., BLEU, ROUGE-L, and METEOR. As text simplification is a monolingual machine translation task, evaluation metrics from MT, in particular the BLEU score, are often used in text simplification. Similar to the word embedding features, the higher the value the more meaning of the complex text is preserved in the simplified text. The BLEU score is a well-established measurement for MT based on n-grams. We use 12 different BLEU implementations, 8 from the Python package NLTK and 4 implemented in Sharma et al. (2017).

3.3. Evaluation

The research questions stated in Section 1 will be answered using non-parametric statistical tests using the previously described features on the eight corpora.

In order to answer the first research question regarding differences between the simplified and the complex text, the complexity level is the dependent variable (0: complex, 1: simple). The features previously named are the independent variables and the values per complex-simple pairs are the samples. To evaluate whether the feature values differ between the simplified and complex texts, we use non-parametric statistical hypothesis test for dependent samples, i.e., Wilcoxon signed-rank tests. Afterwards, we measure the effect size r, where $r>=0.4$ represents a strong effect, $0.25<=r<0.4$ a moderate effect and $0.1<=r<0.25$ a low effect.

For the analysis of the research questions 2 and 3 regarding differences between the corpora regarding domains or languages, Kruskal–Wallis one-way analyses of variance are conducted. Therefore, the dependent variables are the languages or domains and the independent variables are the paired and difference features. For the analysis within domains and languages, the tests are evaluated against all corpora of one domain or language, e.g., for Wikipedia data the values of EN-QATS and EN-TurkCorpus are analyzed. For the analysis within and across languages and domains, the tests are evaluated against stacked corpora. All corpora assigned to the same language or domain are stacked to one large corpus, e.g., the German corpus and IT-PaCCSS are stacked as web data corpus and are tested against the stacked Wikipedia corpus and the stacked news article corpus. If there is a significant difference between the groups, a Dunn-Bonferonni Post-hoc Test is applied to find the pair(s) of the difference. Afterwards, again, the effect size is measured using the same interpretation levels as for the Wilcoxon signed-rank tests.

4. Results and Discussion

The results of the analysis are reported on eight corpora, five languages, three domains, and 104 features using Wilcoxon signed-rank tests and Kruskal-Wallis tests[13].

---

[13]All statistical characteristics are provided as supplementary material in the linked github repository.

These results should be handled with caution because they might be biased due to errors in SpaCy's output, e.g., regarding dependency parsing and named entity recognition, or due to the unbalanced corpora.

4.1. Differences between Complex and Simplified Texts (RQ1)

The results concerning the question whether the feature values of complex texts and its simplified version differ significantly are summarized in Table 2.

For all three sentence length features, both readability features, and the parse tree height feature, Wilcoxon signed-rank tests indicate at least low but significant effects between the complex and simplified text pairs overall all corpora when analyzing the corpora solely.

The result is not surprising since sentence length has already been shown to be a relevant feature in different languages, e.g., in English Napoles and Dredze (2010) and Martin et al. (2018), in German Hancke et al. (2012), and in Portuguese Aluisio et al. (2010).

The parse tree height also differs significantly for all corpora in the complex and simplified texts. Pilán and Volodina (2018) and Napoles and Dredze (2010) also conclude in their studies regarding Swedish and English that the parse tree height is a relevant complexity measurement feature.

Considering differences between the proportion of verbs in complex and simplified texts, the Wilcoxon signed-rank tests indicate at least low but significant effects for each corpus except EN-QATS. So, the assumption of Kercher (2013), that a higher number of verbs simplifies a text can be generalized to other languages than German.

In contrast, several features are only relevant for a few corpora and differ even more in the effect size. For example, Wilcoxon signed-rank tests indicate a strong significant effect for the lexical density in EN-Newsela-2015 (M_{comp}=0.89±0.08, M_{simp}=0.93±0.07, n=141,582, t(141,581)=1329762920.5, $p<=.01$) but only indicate at most moderate effects on three other corpora and no effect on the remaining four corpora. Furthermore, for several features, the Wilcoxon signed-rank tests indicate no significant difference not even for one corpus, e.g., non-projectivity, proportion of symbols, or proportion of named entities (see Table 2).

Overall, the results show that some of the proposed features help to explain the simplification processes in the selected corpora even if the features might well not be sufficient to explain the simplification process at all. In the next Subsections, we will follow up on these assumptions by comparing the consistency of the simplification process regarding domains and languages.

4.2. Domain Simplification Consistency (RQ2)

Since the selected features are useful to explain the simplification process, the consistency or differences in the simplification process are measured using the difference version of these features as well as the paired features. The results regarding domains are separated into differences within and across domains.

Prop. POS Tags				Prop. Clauses & Phrases				Readability				Lexical Features		
Adjectives	♡■			All Clauses	♡♠■			FRE	♥♠			Lex. Complexity	♡♠■■	■
Adpositions	♡♠■			Coord. clauses	♡			FKGL	♥♠■			Lex. Density	♡	♣
Adverbs	♡♠■			Subord. clauses	♡			**Word Length in**				Prop. MWEs	♠■	
Auxiliary verbs	♡♠■			PPs	♡♠■			Characters	♥♠■	♣		Prop. Named Ent.	♠	
Conjunctions	♡♠■			Relative Phrases	♡♠■			Syllables	♥♠			Prop. Funct. Words	♡♠■	
Determiners	♡♠■			**Syntactic Features**				**Length of Phrases**				Prop. Ref. Expr.		
Interjections				Head is Noun				Noun Phrase	♡			**Word Frequency**		
Nouns	♡			Head is Verb				Verb Phrase		♣		Avg. Position	♡♠■	♣
Numerals	♡♠■			Subj. child of root				PPs				Max. Position	♡♠■	
Particles	♡			Parse Tree Height	♥♠■	♣		**Sent. Length in**						
Pronouns	♡♠■	♣		Non-Projectivity		♣		Characters	♥♠■	♣				
Punctuation	♡♠■	♣		Passive Voice				Syllables	♥♠■					
Symbols								Words	♥♠■					
Verbs	♥♠■													

Table 2: The single and difference features are presented sorted by groups. In the 2nd, 5th, 8th and 11th column, differences between the complex-simplified pairs are listed: ♥ symbolizes differences in the pairs per corpus (RQ1), ♣ in the pairs within domains, ♠ in the pairs across domains, ♦ in the pairs within languages, and ■ in the pairs across languages. In the 3rd, 6th, 9th and 12th column, the differences between the languages and the domains are shown in across and within settings using the same symbols. The color of the symbols indicates the distribution of the effects: Black illustrates an effect for all languages or domains, gray for most of them and lightgray/white for only a few.

Lexical	Effect		Simplification	Effect
Prop. Added Lemmas	♣		Lexical Simplification	
Prop. Deleted Lemmas			Syntactic Simplification	
Prop. Kept Lemmas	♣		Identical	
Prop. Kept Words	♣		**Machine Translation**	**Effect**
Prop. Rewritten Words			BLEU	♠ ♣
Compression Ratio			METEOR	
Levenshtein Similarity			ROUGE-L	♣
Levenshtein Distance			**Word Embeddings**	**Effect**
Syntactic	**Effect**		Cosine Similarity	
Sentence Split			Dot Product	
Sentences Joined				

Table 3: The paired features are presented sorted by their group label. The significant effects per features are highlighted using the following symbols per research question: The ♣ symbol represents within domain results, ♠ across domains, ♦ within languages, and ■ across languages. Black illustrates an effect for all languages or domains, gray for most of them and white for only a few.

Within Domains. When the features are analyzed regarding the consistency within a domain, significant differences are indicated only between the corpora of the web text domain. The German and Italian corpora of this domain differ significantly with a low effect for 14 features (see Table 2 and Table 3), e.g., parse tree height difference, difference of non-projectivity, characters per word, and BLEU score.

The parse tree height is significantly more reduced in German (Difference: M_{DE}=1.16±1.96, N_{DE}=1,888) than in Italian (M_{IT}=0.13±0.64, N_{IT}=63,012, $H(1)$=759.71, p <=.01, r=.11) which might be due to a higher average parse tree height in the German corpus (M_{comp}=4.74±2.41, M_{simple}=3.58±1.35) than in the Italian corpus (M_{comp}=3.14±0.97, M_{simp}=3.02±0.94).

Parse tree height and sentence length are reduced in both corpora in the simplified texts, but, surprisingly, the average word length in characters is slightly increased in Italian (M_{comp}=4.62±0.91, M_{simp}=4.64±0.89). So, this effect might explain the significant difference between both corpora and should be considered for following analysis.

Overall, the differences between the two web data corpora may tie to the high proportion of only lexical simplification in the IT corpus and high proportion of lexical and syntactic simplification in the DE corpus. The other corpora within one domain are more similar in their distribution, which may explain why they do not differ significantly.

Across Domains. The only significant difference across all domains is the BLEU score ($H(2)$=1429.0979, p <=.01, r=.12). A Dunn-Bonferonni Post-hoc Test indicates that the web (M=0.61±0.15, N=64,900) and Wikipedia data (M=0.67±0.22, N=19,377) are differing. This confirms the findings of Sulem et al. (2018) that BLEU is not suitable for measuring text simplification.

Furthermore, the domains differ also in more features even if not significantly between all domains. The following features show only a significant difference between complex and simplified texts in one of the domains.

- **web data:**
  - word frequency avg. position (r=.26, p <=.01),
  - word frequency max. position (r=.14, p <=.01),
  - prop. of adjectives (r=.22, p <=.01),
  - prop. of adverbs (r=.21, p <=.01),
  - prop. of determiners (r=.52, p <=.01),
  - prop. of function words (r=.31, p <=.01), and
  - prop. of numerals (r=.18, p <=.01)
- **newspaper articles:**
  - prop. of clauses (r=.15, p <=.01),
  - prop. of MWEs (r=.14, p <=.01),
  - prop. of adpositions (r=.12, p <=.01),
  - prop. of conjunctions (r=.2, p <=.01),
  - prop. of propositional phrases (r=.12, p <=.01),
  - prop. of relative phrases (r=.16, p <=.01).

In contrast, some features are relevant for text simplification in all domains, i.e., characters per sentence, syllables per sentence, words per sentence, parse tree height, proportions of auxiliary verbs and of verbs, FKGL, and FRE. Overall, these results show, also in combination with BLEU as the only significant difference across domains, that the simplification process seems to be consistent across the web, Wikipedia, and news article domain.

4.3. Language Simplification Consistency (RQ3)

The results of the differences in the simplification process regarding languages are separated into differences within and across languages.

Within Languages. The comparison within a single language is done only for English because this is the only language where we have more than one corpus. All English corpora[14] are combined into a large corpus of 230,144 complex-simplified pairs. Using a Kruskal–Wallis test, no significant difference is indicated between the English corpora, which led to the conclusion that the simplification process measured using several linguistic features in these corpora is consistent. However, this must be handled with particular caution because the size of the corpora is unbalanced and, furthermore, the simplification processes applied have different focuses, varying between lexical and syntactic simplification, e.g., EN-QATS has 15.45% of syntactically simplified text pairs whereas EN-Newsela-15 has only 0.03% (see Table 1).

Across Languages. The only significant difference between all languages is the lexical complexity difference ($H(4)$=425.1521, p <=.01, r=.12). A Dunn-Bonferonni Post-hoc Test indicates that only the German (M=0.33±1.07) and the Czech corpus (M=-0.09±1.19) are significantly differing. Surprisingly, the lexical complexity seems to increase in Czech during simplification. On the one hand, Wilcoxon signed-rank tests also indicate some features with a significant difference in the language-wise data regarding complex and simplified texts for only one or two languages:

- **DE:** lexical complexity (r=.31, p <=.01),

- **IT:** proportion of function words (r=.32, p <=.01), proportion of numerals (r=.19, p <=.01),

- **DE and IT:** proportion of pronouns (r_{DE}=.31, r_{IT}=.31, p <=.01),

- **EN and CS:** proportion of relative phrases (r_{CS}=.12, r_{EN}=.15, p <=.01).

On the other hand, the simplification processes of all languages are similar regarding the following 9 features: characters per sentence, syllables per sentence, words per sentence, parse tree height, proportion of adpositions, proportion of verbs, proportion of prepositional phrases, FKGL, and FRE. Following these results as well as the result of the lexical complexity as sole difference regarding languages, the simplification process seems to be more or less consistent across Czech, German, English, Spanish, and Italian.

---

¹⁴From EN-Newsela-2016 only level 0 to 1 is used.

5. Conclusion and Future Works

This study investigated whether text simplification processes differ within or across five languages (Czech, German, English, Italian, and Spanish) and three domains (newspaper articles, web texts, and Wikipedia texts). To this end, we first tested linguistic features as to their relevance for characterizing the differences in complex-simplified text pairs of eight corpora. Statistical tests indicate significant differences for some of the features, e.g., sentence length, parse tree height, or proportion of verbs. So, these features are used to measure the simplification process in this study. However, the selected features might well not be sufficient to explain the whole simplification process. Other features, such as morphological or grammatical features could improve it in future work.

Furthermore, our study shows differences in the relevance of features per corpus. This insight was further refined regarding differences within and across domains. For the newspaper and Wikipedia corpora, no differences were found within each of the two domains, the statistical tests indicated only differences for the web corpora. These results as well as the finding of only one differing feature across domains, led to the assumption that the simplification process is consistent across and within domains, such as similarly stated in Vajjala and Meurers (2014).

Our study regarding within and across language comparisons also supports the results of Scarton et al. (2017) and Finnimore et al. (2019): text simplification seems to be consistent across languages, which indicates that cross-lingual text simplification based on a single language-independent feature set is a viable approach. Nevertheless, features might be weighted differently per language.

Overall, the negative statistical tests regarding differences across and within domains and languages led to the assumption that the simplification process is robust across and within domains and languages. Especially the features of parse tree height, readability, and sentence length seem to be robust against domains and languages. In contrast, in the evaluation and designing of text simplification models, features such as lexical complexity, and BLEU score should be used with caution due to their found differences in the corpora. These findings might help to build a text simplification model or a text simplification metric that is aware of language or domain characteristics.

6. Acknowledgments

This research is part of the PhD-program "Online Participation", supported by the North Rhine-Westphalian funding scheme "Forschungskolleg".

7. Bibliographical References

Aluisio, S., Specia, L., Gasperin, C., and Scarton, C. (2010). Readability assessment for text simplification. In *Proceedings of the NAACL HLT 2010 5th Workshop on Innovative Use of NLP for Building Educational Applications*, pages 1–9, Los Angeles, California, June. ACL.

Alva-Manchego, F., Martin, L., Scarton, C., and Specia, L. (2019). EASSE: Easier automatic sentence simplification evaluation. In *Proceedings of the 2019 Conference* on *EMNLP and the 9th IJCNLP*, pages 49–54, Hong Kong, China, November. ACL.

Collins-Thompson, K. (2014). Computational assessment of text readability: A survey of current and future research. *ITL - International Journal of Applied Linguistics*, 165(2):97–135.

Finnimore, P., Fritzsch, E., King, D., Sneyd, A., Ur Rehman, A., Alva-Manchego, F., and Vlachos, A. (2019). Strong baselines for complex word identification across multiple languages. In *Proceedings of the NAACL HTL 2019*, pages 970–977, Minneapolis, Minnesota, June. ACL.

Gasperin, C., Specia, L., Pereira, T. F., and Aluisio, R. M. (2009). Learning when to simplify sentences for natural text simplification. In *Proceedings of ENIA*, pages 809–818.

Hancke, J., Vajjala, S., and Meurers, D. (2012). Readability classification for German using lexical, syntactic, and morphological features. In *Proceedings of COLING 2012*, pages 1063–1080, Mumbai, India, December. The COLING 2012 Organizing Committee.

Kauchak, D., Mouradi, O., Pentoney, C., and Leroy, G. (2014). Text simplification tools: Using machine learning to discover features that identify difficult text. In *2014 47th Hawaii International Conference on System Sciences*, pages 2616–2625, Jan.

Kercher, J. (2013). *Verstehen und Verständlichkeit von Politikersprache*. Springer Fachmedien Wiesbaden.

Kincaid, J. P., Fishburne Jr, R. P., Rogers, R. L., and Chissom, B. S. (1975). Derivation of new readability formulas (automated readability index, fog count and flesch reading ease formula) for navy enlisted personnel.

Martin, L., Humeau, S., Mazaré, P.-E., de La Clergerie, É., Bordes, A., and Sagot, B. (2018). Reference-less quality estimation of text simplification systems. In *Proceedings of the 1st Workshop on Automatic Text Adaptation*, pages 29–38, Tilburg, the Netherlands, November. ACL.

Napoles, C. and Dredze, M. (2010). Learning simple Wikipedia: A cogitation in ascertaining abecedarian language. In *Proceedings of the NAACL HLT 2010 Workshop on Computational Linguistics and Writing*, pages 42–50, Los Angeles, CA, USA, June. ACL.

Niklaus, C., Freitas, A., and Handschuh, S. (2019). MinWikiSplit: A sentence splitting corpus with minimal propositions. In *Proceedings of the 12th INLG*, pages 118–123, Tokyo, Japan, October–November. ACL.

Paetzold, G., Alva-Manchego, F., and Specia, L. (2017). MASSAlign: Alignment and annotation of comparable documents. In *Proceedings of the IJCNLP 2017*, pages 1–4, Tapei, Taiwan, November. ACL.

Pilán, I. and Volodina, E. (2018). Investigating the importance of linguistic complexity features across different datasets related to language learning. In *Proceedings of the Workshop on Linguistic Complexity and Natural Language Processing*, pages 49–58, Santa Fe, New-Mexico, August. ACL.

Scarton, C., Palmero Aprosio, A., Tonelli, S., Martín Wanton, T., and Specia, L. (2017). MUSST: A multilingual syntactic simplification tool. In *Proceedings of the IJCNLP 2017*, pages 25–28, Tapei, Taiwan, November. ACL.

Scarton, C., Paetzold, G., and Specia, L. (2018). Text simplification from professionally produced corpora. In *Proceedings of the 11th LREC*, Miyazaki, Japan, May. ELRA.

Sharma, S., El Asri, L., Schulz, H., and Zumer, J. (2017). Relevance of unsupervised metrics in task-oriented dialogue for evaluating natural language generation. *CoRR*, abs/1706.09799.

Sulem, E., Abend, O., and Rappoport, A. (2018). BLEU is not suitable for the evaluation of text simplification. In *Proceedings of the 2018 Conference on EMNLP*, pages 738–744, Brussels, Belgium, October-November. ACL.

Vajjala, S. and Meurers, D. (2014). Readability assessment for text simplification:from analyzing documents to identifying sentential simplifications. *International Journal of Applied Linguistics, Special Issue on Current Research in Readability and Text Simplification*.

Yimam, S. M., Štajner, S., Riedl, M., and Biemann, C. (2017). Multilingual and cross-lingual complex word identification. In *Proceedings of RANLP 2017*, pages 813–822, Varna, Bulgaria, September. INCOMA Ltd.

8. Language Resource References

Barančíková, P. and Bojar, O. (2019). COSTRA 1.0: A dataset of complex sentence transformations. LINDAT/CLARIN digital library at the Institute of Formal and Applied Linguistics (ÚFAL), Faculty of Mathematics and Physics, Charles University.

Brunato, D., Cimino, A., Dell'Orletta, F., and Venturi, G. (2016). PaCCSS-IT: A parallel corpus of complexsimple sentences for automatic text simplification. In *Proceedings of the 2016 Conference on EMNLP*, pages 351–361, Austin, Texas, November. ACL.

Grave, E., Bojanowski, P., Gupta, P., Joulin, A., and Mikolov, T. (2018). Learning word vectors for 157 languages. In *Proceedings of the 11th LREC*, Miyazaki, Japan, May. ELRA.

Klaper, D., Ebling, S., and Volk, M. (2013). Building a German/simple German parallel corpus for automatic text simplification. In *Proceedings of the 2nd Workshop on Predicting and Improving Text Readability for Target Reader Populations*, pages 11–19, Sofia, Bulgaria, August. ACL.

Štajner, S., Popović, M., Saggion, H., Specia, L., and Fishel, M. (2016). Shared task on quality assessment for text simplification. In *qats2016: LREC 2016 Workshop & Shared Task on Quality Assessment for Text Simplification (QATS), 28th May 2016, Portorož, Slovenia ; proceedings*, pages 22–31, Paris. ELRA-ERDA. Online-Ressource.

Xu, W., Callison-Burch, C., and Napoles, C. (2015). Problems in current text simplification research: New data can help. *Transactions of the ACL*, 3:283–297.

Xu, W., Napoles, C., Pavlick, E., Chen, Q., and Callison-Burch, C. (2016). Optimizing statistical machine translation for text simplification. *Transactions of the ACL*, 4:401–415.

1st Workshop on Tools and Resources to Empower People with REAding DIfficulties (READI2020), pages 85–92
Language Resources and Evaluation Conference (LREC 2020), Marseille, 11–16 May 2020
© European Language Resources Association (ELRA), licensed under CC-BY-NC

Combining Expert Knowledge with Frequency Information to Infer CEFR Levels for Words

Alice Pintard[1], Thomas François[2]
[1] Le Mans Université, Le Mans, France
[2]Cental, IL&C, University of Louvain, Louvain-la-Neuve, Belgique
Alice.Pintard.Etu@univ-lemans.fr, thomas.francois@uclouvain.be

Abstract

Traditional approaches to set goals in second language (L2) vocabulary acquisition relied either on word lists that were obtained from large L1 corpora or on collective knowledge and experience of L2 experts, teachers, and examiners. Both approaches are known to offer some advantages, but also to have some limitations. In this paper, we try to combine both sources of information, namely the official reference level description for French language and the FLElex lexical database. Our aim is to train a statistical model on the French RLD that would be able to turn the distributional information from FLElex into one of the six levels of the Common European Framework of Reference for languages (CEFR). We show that such approach yields a gain of 29% in accuracy compared to the method currently used in the CEFRLex project. Besides, our experiments also offer deeper insights into the advantages and shortcomings of the two traditional sources of information (frequency vs. expert knowledge).

Keywords: Lexical difficulty, French as a foreign language, NLP

1. Introduction

Second language acquisition (SLA) research established a strong relationship between the development of reading abilities and the knowledge of vocabulary (Laufer, 1992). For Grabe (2014, 13): "The real goal for more advanced L2 reading is an L2 recognition vocabulary level anywhere above 10,000 [words]". It is no surprise that vocabulary resources used by designers of L2 curricula, publishers of educational materials, and teachers to set vocabulary learning goals are close to such size. For French language, the popular "Français Fondamental" (Gougenheim et al., 1964), which was built from a corpus of authentic documents and influenced a whole generation of French teachers and SLA researchers, includes about 8800 words. Similarly, the currently most popular lexical resources are the Reference Level Descriptions (RLDs), based on the Common European Framework of Reference for languages (CEFR), and available in various languages. The French version, designed by a team of experts, also amounts to about 9,000 words and expressions. However, both type of lists - either built from language data or from the expertise of language and teaching experts - are faced with the issue of identifying the most important words to teach at each stage of the learning process.

The most common answers to that challenge have been (1) to use frequency lists obtained from a large corpus of texts intended for native readers and split the list into N frequency bands, each of which is related to one of the stage of the learning process; or (2) to rely on expert knowledge, such as teacher expertise or linguists' recommendations, to assign each word to a given level of reading proficiency. This classification of words in developmental stages is a delicate process whose reliability has hardly been assessed in a systematic manner on L2 learners. Besides, the two main sources of information to build vocabulary lists - word frequency in massive corpora or the knowledge of L2 teach-

ing experts - have hardly been exploited together[1].

Recently, an alternative research avenue was investigated within the framework of the CEFRLex project. It offers receptive vocabulary lists for 5 languages: English (Dürlich and François, 2018), French (François et al., 2014), Swedish (François et al., 2016), Dutch (Tack et al., 2018), and Spanish. Its innovative side resides in the fact that it does not provide a single frequency for each word, but rather a frequency distribution across the six levels of the CEFR. Moreover, frequencies have been estimated on documents intended for L2 learners, i.e. textbooks and simplified readers, instead of L1 texts. As a result, the resource provides further insights about the way a given word is used across the various development stages of the L2 curriculum. It is also possible to compare word frequency at a given level (e.g. A2) in order to define priorities in terms of vocabulary learning goals. Unfortunately, when it comes to assigning a CEFR level at which a given word should be learned, it is not obvious how the frequency distributions should be transformed in a single CEFR level.

In this paper, we aim to investigate two main issues. First, we will test whether we can leverage the knowledge from the French RLD to train a mathematical function, based on machine learning algorithms, able to transform any CEFR-Lex distribution into a CEFR level. Second, we will take advantage of these experiments to further characterize the linguistic and pedagogical differences between these two approaches - building a frequency list from a corpus vs. assigning words to proficiency levels based on expert knowledge - to set vocabulary learning goals. The paper is organized as follows: Section 2. provides more details about

---

[1]In the case of the English Vocabulary Profile (EVP), the designers have indeed combined lexicographical and pedagogical knowledge with word frequency information (Capel, 2010). However, the frequencies were estimated from a learner corpus and therefore are representative of productive skills rather than receptive ones.

the two approaches we will compare (frequency lists and RLD) and reports previous attempts to transform CEFR frequency distributions into a unique CEFR level. Section 3. introduces all methodological details related to our experiments: the three lexical resources used in the study (French RLD, Lexique3, and FLELex) and the process by which these resources were prepared for training machine learning algorithms. This section ends up with the description of the experiments carried out. In Section 4., we report the results of the various experiments before taking advantage of a manual error analysis to discuss the differences between expert knowledge and frequency-based lists at Section 5..

2. Previous work

The process of setting vocabulary goals for L2 learners generally relies on graded lexical resources in which words are assigned to one proficiency level. Such resources are usually built based on the two approaches we have previously outlined: leveraging word frequency information estimated on a corpus or using L2 teaching experts knowledge.

Frequency lists, built from a corpus, have been used since the seminal work of Thorndike (1921) who laboriously built the first significant vocabulary for English, including 20,000 words, without the help of any computer. The first computational list was obtained by Kučera and Francis (1967) from the Brown corpus and has a large influence in education and psychology. At the same time, Gougenheim et al. (1964) published the *Français Fondamental* that would impact a generation of L2 French teachers. More recently, other lists have been developed from larger corpora, such as the CELEX database (Baayen et al., 1993), the list based on the British National Corpus (Leech et al., 2001), or SUBTLEX (Brysbaert and New, 2009). The main shortcomings of such lists for L2 education are that (1) they represent the native distribution of words, which is not fully compatible with the distribution of words in books and textbooks intended for L2 learners; (2) they do not specify at which proficiency level a given word is supposed to be learned.

As regards expert knowledge, the most recent and influential resource is connected to the CEFR framework. Since 2001, this framework has been widely adopted within Europe to help standardizing L2 curricula, which involves defining a proficiency scale ranging from A1 (beginners) to C2 (mastery). However, textbook designers, assessment experts and language teachers have agreed that it lacks precision when it comes to describing the linguistic forms that should be learned at a given proficiency level. In a number of countries, efforts have been made to interpret the CEFR guidelines in the form of reference level descriptions[2]. These books describe the language competences expected from an L2 learner in each of the CEFR levels, including lists of words, syntactic structures, and expressions associated with specific communicative functions or themes.

Finally, a few papers specifically investigated methods to transform CEFRLex word distribution into a CEFR level

coherent from a pedagogical perspective. (Gala et al., 2013) suggested two approaches. The first one, to which we will refer as *First occ*, assigns to a given word the level of the textbook it was first observed in. In other words, the level of a word corresponds to the first CEFR level for which FLELex reports a non null frequency. Although simplistic, this rule appeared to be the most effective to predict unknown words reported by four Dutch learners of FFL (Tack et al., 2016) and was consequently used in the CEFRLex interface. The second approach was a variant of the *First occ* that yields continuous scores and prove to be inferior to the first one. More recently, Alfter et al. (2016) introduced the concept of *significant onset of use*, that consists in selecting the first level having a sufficiently large enough delta compared to its previous level. All of these studies used mathematical rules to transform distribution into CEFR levels and later use those level as gold-standard for further process. So far, no experiments were reported that tried to cross-validate such mathematical rules, for instance using learners data.

3. Methodology

Our approach consists in considering the French RLD as a gold standard regarding the assignment of words to a given CEFR level. We then infer, from this pedagogical information, a statistical model able to transform the word frequency distribution from FLELex into a CEFR level. To carry out this experiment, the following steps had to be realized. The acquisition and digitization of the French RLD word list is described at Section 3.1., which also briefly reminds the reader of the main characteristics of the two other lexical resources used in our study, namely Lexique3 (New et al., 2007) and FLELex (François et al., 2014). In the next section (Section 3.2.), we describe a preliminary step prior to the statistical modelling, which consists in delineating the intersection between the three resources. This stage aims at ensuring that missing words would not lead to results biased towards one of the resources. We also took advantage of this step to investigate the coverage discrepancies between the French RLD and FLELex as a first way to characterize the differences between the expert knowledge approach and the frequency-based one. Section 3.3. describes the design of two datasets used for our experiments, whereas Section 3.4. presents the different baselines and models tested.

3.1. Source Word Lists

3.1.1. The French RLD word list

The RLD for French language was created by Beacco and his collaborators between 2004 and 2016 (Beacco et al., 2008; Riba, 2016). Each level – corresponding to a distinct book – is split into 10 chapters representing various dimensions of the linguistic knowledge (e.g. vocabulary, syntactic structures, phonemes, graphemes, fonctional skills, etc.), except for C1 and C2 levels which share the same volume and have a different structure[3]. The classification of linguistic forms to a given level was performed based on crite-

---

[2]See the list of concerned languages at `http://www.coe.int/t/dg4/linguistic/dnr_EN.asp?`

---

[3]The RLD book for the C levels (Riba, 2016) was not used in this study, as it doesn't provide lists of lexical items, but rather describe more conceptual abilities, like managing and structuring

Level	# FLELex	# First occ	# Beacco
A1	4,097	4,097	827
A2	5,768	2,699	615
B1	9,074	3,980	1334
B2	6,309	1,299	2742
C1	7,267	1,665	x
C2	3,932	496	x

Table 1: Distribution of entries per CEFR level, including the total number of items per level in FLELex, the number of items per level calculated with *First occ*, and the number of words per level in Beacco.

ria selected by the authors for their relevance and objectivity: essentially the official descriptors from the CEFR, collective knowledge and experience of experts, teachers and examiners, and examples of learner productions deemed to be at a particular level (Beacco et al., 2008).

To our knowledge, the French RLD, also refered to as "Beacco" in this study, has not been used so far in any NLP approaches as it was published in paper format only and is not available in a digitized version. As a consequence, we had to digitize the two chapters relative to lexicon, namely chapter 4, focusing on general notions (e.g. quantity, space), and chapter 6 that focuses on specific notions (e.g. human body, feelings, sports). Those chapters share the same architecture across all levels, organizing words within semantic categories, then specifying the part-of-speech (POS) categories and sometimes providing a context. Polysemous words can therefore have up to 8 entries across the four levels (e.g. "être", *to be*). However, as FLELex and Lexique3 do not provide fine-grained semantic distinctions for forms (all meanings are gathered under the same orthographic form), we decided to drop the information on semantic category from the French RLD. When a form had several CEFR levels associated to it, we kept the lowest one, which is in line with the way polysemy is handled in FLELex. This process led us to drop about 2,968 entries, going from 8,486 to 5,518 entries. The number of entries per CEFR level is described in Table 1 (*#Beacco*).

3.1.2. The Lexique3 word list

As previous approaches relying on word frequencies to assign proficiency levels to words relied on a L1 corpus, we decided to compare the performance obtained with FLELex with a word list whose frequencies were estimated on a large L1 corpus. We used *Lexique3* (New et al., 2007) for this purpose, as it is a rather modern database. The lexicon includes about 50,000 lemmas and 125,000 inflected forms whose frequencies were obtained from movie subtitles.

3.1.3. FLELex

FLELex (François et al., 2014) is one of the resources being part of the CEFRLex project described above. Similarly to the other languages, it offers frequency distributions for French words across the six CEFR levels. There are

two versions of FLELex: one is based on the TreeTagger (FLELex-TT) and includes 14,236 entries, but no multi-word expressions as they cannot be detected by the Tree-Tagger; the second one is based on a conditional random field (CRF) tagger and amounts to 17,871 entries, including 2,037 multi-word expressions. However, the second version has not yet been manually checked and includes various problematic forms. This is why we decided to carry out our experiments based on the FLELex-TT version. Table 1 summarizes the total number of entries having a non null frequency per level (*#FLELex*), along with the number of new entries per level, currently used in the CEFRLex project to assign a unique level to a given word (*#First occ*).

3.2. Mapping the RLD to FLELex and Lexique3

As explained above, in order to ensure a comparability of results for each of the three word lists, we delineated their intersection. A prerequisite step was to arrange the POS tagsets compatibility. The main differences regarding those tagsets are that Beacco divides conjunctions in two categories (coordination and subordination), whereas FLELex and Lexique3 split determiners and prepositions (DET:ART vs. DET:POS and PRP vs. PRP:det). We merged all split categories, keeping the TreeTagger labels (Schmid, 1994). After standardization, nine POS remained: ADJ, ADV, KON, DET, INT, NOM, PRP, PRO, and VER.

Second, we identified words in common between Beacco and FLELex: their intersection contains 4,020 entries. This leaves 1,498 words from Beacco that do not appear in FLELex and 10,216 FLELex words absent from Beacco. Such figures were expected as the coverage of FLELex is larger due to its building principles. However, we were concerned by the fact that so many words from Beacco were not found in FLELex and carried out a manual investigation of these. Most missing words can be related to the following causes:

- Beacco includes 113 past participle forms of verbs that have not been lemmatized, whereas it is the case in FLELex (e.g. "assis" *sat*, "épicé" *seasoned*);

- Similarly, Beacco also includes 103 feminine or plural forms which are lemmatized in FLELex (e.g. "vacances" *holiday*, "lunettes" *glasses*, "serveuse" *waitress*, etc.);

- Words were sometimes shared by both resources, but were assigned a different POS-tag, preventing automatic matching (e.g. "bonjour" *hi !* or "vite" *be quick* are interjections in Beacco, but are tagged as nouns or adverbs in FLELex);

- 61 entries were kept with capital letters in Beacco as a way to provide information about the word in use (e.g. "Attention" *Look up !*, "Courage" *Cheer up !*);

- Unlike Beacco, FLELex does not include acronyms (e.g.: "CD", "DVD", "CV", etc.);

- Some words were not captured in FLELex despite their presence in FFL textbooks, because they appear in the instructions, grammatical boxes, maps, or calendars rather than in texts related to comprehension

---

discourse in terms of rhetorical effectiveness, natural sequencing or adherence to collaborative principles.

tasks (e.g. "fois" *time*, "adjectif" *adjective*, "virgule" *comma*, "Asie" *Asia*, etc.);

- Other words refer to very salient objects in the real world that are poorly represented in corpora. Since Michéa (1953), they are known as available words and, as was expected, some of them were not found in the corpus used to build FLELex (e.g. "cuisinière" *cooker*, "sèche-cheveux" *hair-dryer*, etc.);

- Finally, a few words in Beacco were extremely specific (e.g. "humagne", a type of grape or "escrimeur" *fencer*).

This manual investigation was, to some extent, reassuring, as a fair amount of missing words from Beacco were due to discrepancies in the lemmatization process between a systematic tool and a human. Lexical availability was also an issue, but a predictable one as it concerns all frequency-based approaches. Finally, it appears that restricting the selection of textbook materials to texts related to receptive tasks might help to better model receptive knowledge of L2 learners, but also comes at a cost as regards coverage.

We manually solved some of these issues by lemmatizing the entries; converting the POS of all interjections that were nouns or adverbs in FLELex, and replacing capital letters by lowercase letters. In this process, we lost precious information from the RLD about the function of some linguistic forms, but were able to reintroduce 314 words that were not considered as shared by both lexicons before. As a result, the intersection between both resources amounts to 4,334 words. Finally, in order to compare FLELex with Lexique3, we computed the intersection between all three lexicons. Lexique3 having the larger coverage (51,100), there were only 38 words missing from it. The final intersection therefore includes 4,296 entries.

3.3. Preparing datasets for experiments

Based on this intersection between the three resources, we defined two datasets that will be used for our experiments.

3.3.1. BeaccoFLELexAtoB

This first dataset corresponds to the intersection between FLELex, Lexique3 and Beacco as defined at Section 3.2.. It contains 4,296 entries, shared by the three lexicons, and classified from A1 to B2 according to Beacco. In this dataset, each entry (word + POS-tag) is related to its CEFR reference level from Beacco and is described with 8 frequency variables, as shown in Table 2. The frequency variables includes the 7 frequencies provided by FLELex along with the frequency from Lexique3. The latter will however be used only for the computation of the Lexique3 baseline (see Section 4.).

3.3.2. BeaccoFLELexC

The main application of this study is to develop a more accurate mathematical model to transform FLELex frequencies into a single CEFR level, with the purpose of integrating this model within the web interface of the CEFR-Lex project instead of the *First occ* heuristic currently used. Therefore, training our model on the intersection described above has a main shortcoming: it is not able to classify any

entries beyond B2 level, since it would not have seen any word from the C levels. In the FLELex interface, we nevertheless want to be able to classify words at those levels, as FLELex likely contains more difficult words than Beacco. To create this second dataset (*BeaccoFLELexC*), we first assumed that the 9,903 FLELex entries missing from Beacco can be considered as C level. However, before adding these entries to the 4,296 word intersection, we manually investigated them and noticed that about 2% present high frequencies in A levels textbooks, which is not expected for C words. We thus considered these cases as anomalies. Some causes of these anomalies were already discussed previously, but new issues also arose:

- Function words appearing in Beacco's chapter 5, i.e. the grammar section, were not digitized, but they were logically captured in FLELex. They include personal pronouns ("je", "tu", "toi"), interrogative pronouns ("combien", "où", "comment", "quand"), determiners ("la"), prepositions ("en", "sur"), conjunctions ("après", "pour", "que"), modals ("devoir", "pouvoir"), and negative particles ("non", "ne", "pas");

- We also identified a few words appearing in chapter 3, linked to particular communicative functions, that were also excluded from our digitizing process (e.g. "cher" *dear*, "bise" *kiss*, "peut-être" *maybe*, "d'accord" *all right*, etc.);

- Other words are very likely part of the A levels even if they are not included in Beacco's chapters we digitized (e.g. "joli" *pretty*, "dormir" *to sleep*, "anglais" *English*, or "espagnol" *Spanish*);

- Finally, we identified a few remaining tagging problems in FLELex that escaped the manual cleaning process (e.g. "étudiant" *student*, "ami" *friend* were found as adjectives in FLELex instead of nouns).

To resolve some of these issues, we manually corrected tagging problems in FLELex and added the missing words appearing in chapters 3 and 5, assigning them their correct Beacco level. In total, 87 words were thus corrected, but some problems remain for a few entries.

The last step in the preparation of this dataset *BeaccoFLELexC* consisted in creating a balanced dataset. Adding 9,903 C entries obviously produced a class-imbalanced issue within the data, which we rebalanced using undersampling of overrepresented categories (C and B2). We used a random undersampling technique based on the number of entries in B1, reducing the size of this dataset from 14,236 to 4,878 words.

3.4. Experiments

For our experiments, we decided to use three standard machine learning algorithms, namely tree classification, boosting, and support vector machine (SVM). Neural networks were not considered due to the limited amount of data. We also defined four baselines to compare with, that are described below.

All experiments were conducted following the same methodology. We first split each dataset into a training

word	pos	beacco	freqA1	freqA2	freqB1	freqB2	freqC1	freqC2	freqtotal	lex3
plier	VER	B2	0.00	2.14	5.15	13.73	3.44	12.83	8.37	14.37
chanteur	NOM	A2	46.75	42.96	21.32	18.26	3.44	50.42	36.12	21.17
humide	ADJ	A1	0.00	0.00	13.94	0.00	18.00	0.00	5.36	11.23
entre	PRP	B1	601.22	995.40	1023.06	774.83	1599.32	2023.56	1032.37	372.72

Table 2: Examples of entries for "plier" *to fold*, "chanteur" *singer*, "humide" *humid* and "entre" *between* from the first dataset, illustrating the variables used in our experiments.

(and validation) set including 80% of the entries and a test set including 20% of the entries. We then applied a grid search on the training set using a stratified 10-fold cross-validation setup to estimate the performance of each set of meta-parameters tested. Once the best set of meta-parameters was chosen, we estimated the classification accuracy of the model on the test set. This procedure is more reliable than a standard 10-fold cross-validation setup as the meta-parameters and the parameters are not optimized on the same data.

3.4.1. Baselines

Four baselines were used in this study. The first one (*Maj class*) assigns to all words the level of the majority class. It is a common baseline for all classification tasks. The second baseline (*First occ*) assigns to a given word the level of the textbook it was first observed in. The third baseline (*Most freq*), used for instance in Todirascu et al. (Todirascu et al., 2019), assigns to each word the level with the highest frequency. For the fourth baseline, we trained three models (SVM, tree, and boosting) based only on Lexique3 frequencies, as a way to assess whether the L2-specific and more fine-grained frequency information from FLELex would lead to some improvements on the task.

3.4.2. The models

We applied the three above-mentioned algorithms to both our datasets: *BeaccoFLELexAtoB* and *BeaccoFLELexC*.

- On the former, the optimal meta-parameters found by the grid search for Lexique 3 were: Tree (max_depth = 4, min_sample_leaf = 40, and min_sample_split = 50); SVM (RBF kernel with C = 0.01 and γ = 0.001); Boosting with 5 iterations.

- The meta-parameters found for FLELex frequencies were: Tree (max_depth = 3, min_sample_leaf = 20, and min_sample_split = 50); SVM (RBF kernel with C = 1 and γ = 0.0001); Boosting with 5 iterations.

- On the latter, *BeaccoFLELexC*, the optimal meta-parameters found using the grid search were: Tree (max_depth = 3, min_sample_leaf = 20, and min_sample_split = 50); SVM (RBF kernel with C = 1 and γ = 0.001); Boosting with 5 iterations.

4. Results

In this study, we aim to predict L2 expert knowledge based on word frequencies and thus obtain a machine learning algorithm able to transform a given word's frequency into a unique CEFR level. First, our systematic evaluation on the *BeaccoFLELexAtoB* dataset, whose results are reported in

BeaccoFLELexAtoB				
	Acc	Prec	F1	MAE
First occ	0.25	0.45	0.21	1.25
Most freq	0.18	0.35	0.23	1.62
Maj class	0.40	0.16	0.23	1.13
Lexique3 frequency				
Tree	0.47	0.46	0.46	0.76
SVM	0.49	0.44	0.43	0.76
Boosting	0.49	0.38	0.39	0.80
FLELex frequencies				
Tree	0.52	0.52	0.52	0.68
SVM	0.53	0.48	0.46	0.68
Boosting	0.54	0.51	0.48	0.66
BeaccoFLELexC				
	Acc	Prec	F1	MAE
First occ	0.27	0.33	0.23	1.35
Most freq	0.19	0.23	0.20	1.69
Maj class	0.22	0.05	0.08	1.19
Tree	0.47	0.46	0.46	0.76
SVM	0.44	0.41	0.40	0.87
Boosting	0.48	0.45	0.45	0.75

Table 3: Test results on both datasets.

Table 3, reveals that the *First occ* rule, currently used in the CEFRLex interface, yields poor performance. Its accuracy is as low as 25%, which is actually lower than the accuracy reached by a majority class classifier (40%) and its mean absolute error is 1.25, which means that this classification rule can miss targeted levels by even more than one level on average. Similarly, the *Most freq* rule, sometimes used as a simple and intuitive solution by some researchers, appears to be quite disappointing: its accuracy of 18% reveals that it is actually biased towards wrong answers. Using a machine learning algorithm to train a non-linear and more complex mathematical rule to transform FLELex distributions into CEFR levels seems to be a better path. We were able to reach 54% for the Boosting classifier and a mean absolute error of 0.66. The SVM model is more than twice as good as the *First occ* rule, and it outperforms the majority class classifier by 13%.

On the second dataset, that corresponds better to the pragmatic problem we want to solve, it is interesting to notice that *First occ* outperforms the dummy baseline using majority class by 5%. The *Most freq* rule remains the worst option, whereas machine learning remains the best with the boosting algorithm reaching 48% of accuracy and a MAE of 0.75. Performance are slightly behind for the second dataset, but this is generally the case when one increases the number of classes.

We also performed an ablation study on both datasets in order to find which frequency level contributed the most to the predictions. Results are presented in Table 4 and clearly shows that the frequency from the A1 to B1 levels are the more informative, especially the A1 level. Furthermore, one can notice that the total frequency (computed over all six levels) is also a good source of information.

4.1. FLELex vs. Lexique 3

In our experiments, we wanted to know whether the L2-specific and fine-grained frequency information provided in the CEFRLex resources would be better able to predict expert knowledge than a L1 frequency list. Table 3 shows that the models trained with FLELex slightly outperform (+5% in accuracy) the ones trained with Lexique3. However, this comparison is unfair, as the models leveraging FLELex information include more variables than the Lexique3 ones (7 vs. 1). Looking at the ablation study table, we can see performance when only the total frequency variable of FLELex is used. In such configuration, FLELex still outperforms Lexique3 by 1% accuracy, which seems to mean that L2 frequencies - even estimated on a much smaller corpus - might be used instead of L1 frequencies. This is, per se, a very interesting result, as the second language acquisition literature tends to believe the opposite and L2 intended word list created from a L1 corpus still remains the standard. In any case, those similar results can also be explained by the high correlation between the frequencies of these two lists, as was already reported in François et al. (2014). If we consider the performance of the full model (54%) compared to that of the model based only on the total frequency, the 4% improvement could be interpreted as a confirmation of the greater informational richness provided by a frequency distribution over proficiency levels compared to a unique word frequency.

	BeaccoFLELexAtoB		**BeaccoFLELexC**	
Variable	All but 1	Only 1	All but 1	Only 1
freqA1	0.54	0.53	0.43	0.43
freqA2	0.53	0.52	0.47	0.40
freqB1	0.54	0.52	0.47	0.40
freqB2	0.54	0.47	0.47	0.39
freqC1	0.54	0.45	0.47	0.36
freqC2	0.55	0.43	0.47	0.34
freqTotal	0.54	0.50	0.46	0.44

Table 4: Variable ablation study on both datasets, using the boosting model.

4.2. Problematic levels

The analysis of the precision, recall, and F1 values for each level reveals that models predictions are affected by one level in particular, level A2, which is already underrepresented in Beacco. Hence, the *BeaccoFLELexAtoB* dataset only includes 573 words at this level, whereas A1, B1 and B2 levels contain respectively 788, 1158 and 1777 words. Table 5 shows that extreme levels score much better than the middle ones, a recurrent outcome in readability classification tasks. It also reveals that, despite its lower accuracy score compare to the boosting model, the classification Tree model takes less drastic choices when assigning words to a class, which makes it a better option if we want a system that assigns words to all levels. We also noticed that, besides their under-representation in the RLD, A2 words are difficult to predict due to a high correlation between word frequencies in A1, A2 and B1 levels.

Level	Tree	SVM	Boosting
A1	0.57	0.56	0.58
A2	0.21	0.13	0.02
B1	0.26	0.23	0.32
B2	0.67	0.69	0.70

Table 5: F1 scores per level for the three models, on the *BeaccoFLELexAtoB* dataset.

Another problematic level is the C level, specially from a reading comprehension perspective. According to the CEFR descriptors, a C1 user "can understand a wide range of demanding, longer texts, and recognise implicit meaning", while a C2 user "can understand with ease virtually everything heard or read". Trying to translate these descriptors into actual words is difficult, as testified by the fact that Riba, who wrote the RLD opus for C levels, expressed some reserves concerning those descriptors, mainly because of the notion of perfection which emanate from them (Riba, 2016), and the fact that C users depicted by the CEFR are only highly educated individuals, outperforming most of the native speakers. Consequently, we had to use a simple decision to define our C words in the gold-standard: considering everything minus words from levels A1 to B2. A final issue regarding C words is the fact that textbooks for those levels are less numerous than for the lower ones, providing FLELex with fewer words to observe and count.

5. Discussion

In this section, we carried out a manual error analysis of some misclassification errors as a way to bring up to light some strengths and weaknesses of both approaches that can be used for selecting appropriate vocabulary in L2 learning: frequency vs. expert knowledge.

5.1. Lexical approach

One characteristic of the RLDs that is worth remembering is the fact that lexical chapters are organised semantically, as the authors agreed that giving a list of words ranked alphabetically is of little use when it comes to design syllabus or build a teaching sequence (Beacco et al., 2008). Hence, words evolving around the same notional scope come together, along with their synonyms, antonyms and as a matter of fact words belonging to the same family as well (e.g. "heureux/malheureux" *happy/unhappy*, "maigre, gros/ maigrir, grossir" *skinny, fat / to loose weight, to put on weight*). This conveys the idea that they should be taught together - in other words, at the same CEFR level – since building strong lexical networks is critical for vocabulary retention. Conversely, FLELex does not have such structure and is likely to estimate different frequency distributions for the various terms from a given semantic field. When we transform those distributions using either the *First occ* rule or even a machine learning algorithm, they are prone to end up at different levels (e.g. of predictions using the SVM: "gros"A2 / "grossir"B2, "heureux"A1 / "malheureux"A2). In this regard, using frequency lists to establish a vocabulary progression through several learning stages is limited because words are seen as isolated.

Beacco's semantic organisation also enables it to better capture the effect of situation frequency, usually referred to as lexical availability (Michéa, 1953). The B2 level was the first RLD written, and it consists of extensive lists of words relating to specific centers of interest. The lower levels were compiled later, gradually picking up words from the B2 RLD according to the learning stage they could be taught at. As a result of this semantically-driven procedure, Beacco includes more available words than FLELex (e.g. of missing available words are "soutien-gorge" *bra*, "cuisinière" *cooker*, "sèche-cheveux" *hair-dryer*, etc.).

5.2. Topics

The question of topics covered on the L2 learning path is very relevant for this study, because it highlights the limits of both methods. FLELex computational approach aims to report words frequencies in the CEFR levels in an objective and descriptive way, but by using L2 material, it is compelled to favour certain topics and exclude others. Compared to Beacco, we found that textbooks mainly avoid potentially polemic themes such as religion or death, or subjects in which students could have not much to say such as DIY, and topics commonly considered as complicated, for instance economics or sciences. In contrast, the topics found in FLELex are highly influenced by the choice of texts comprised in the corpus and can sometimes be overrepresented. A clear materialization of this shortcoming appeared when we looked at FLELex frequent words absent from Beacco and discovered that words related to fairytales were abundant (e.g. "château" *castle*, "reine" *queen*, "prince" *prince*, "chevalier" *knigth*, "dragon" *dragon*, "magique" *magic*, and even "épouser" *to marry* or "rêver" *dream*). This can be explained by the inclusion of a simplified reader dedicated to King Arthur legend in the corpus.

On the other hand, the RLD's semantic structure has a downside since it may lead to loose sight of the CEFR descriptors, specially in topics where finding a progression between the items in terms of language acts is arduous. The most iconic theme we came across is food and drinks, with 150 words absent from FLELex, but geography and the human body also share the same characteristics at a lesser degree. We distinguished those topics from the others because they are mostly composed of nouns with closely related meaning (e.g. in B2, "pain français", "baguette", "boule", "bâtard", "pain de campagne", "carré", "pain intégral", "pain complet", "pistolet", "petit pain", "sandwich", "petit pain au lait", all being different types of bread). The large number of words in these topics is a reflection of reality usually bypassed in textbooks, since these nouns don't offer a wide variety of communicative situations.

5.3. Reception or production

FLELex is a descriptive tool built from texts related to reading comprehension tasks in FFL materials, illustrating therefore the contents of written reception activities. The RLD also presents its contents as to be mastered in comprehension tasks, leaving the decision to teachers and curriculum designers regarding what learners should be able to produce (Beacco et al., 2008). However, we identified four POS in which the ability to produce words seems to be the selection criteria for Beacco: determiners, conjunctions (e.g. "comme" in B1), pronouns (e.g. "le" in B2), and prepositions. We detected them because the frequencies of those POS are among the highest of the corpus while their levels nevertheless vary from A1 to B2 in Beacco. Even though words belonging to these POS are probably understood at early stages due to repeated exposure, the RLD proposes a gradation in the different learning stages they should be taught at, which is likely motivated either by the CEFR descriptors regarding production and interaction or by intrinsic characteristics of the word. We therefore found that the two approaches are not compatible for those specific POS, as the prescriptive aspect of the RLD implies to take into account learners objectives and abilities in production tasks as well, while FLELex only illustrates the language used in reception tasks.

5.4. Normative and adaptable

Beacco's intent is to propose a reference calibration for CEFR levels, but not a list of words that would be mandatory and identical, in all places and at all times. In the introduction, the authors minimize the inherent normative aspect of their lists, presenting them as only a starting point to insure compatibility between syllabus and exams of different educational systems. Therefore, they display vocabulary in three possible ways:

- closed lists, e.g. "bébé, enfant, lait"
- open lists, e.g. "[...] agréable, bête, calme, content"
- list descriptors, e.g. "[...] *noms de nationalités*"

Such behavior, intended to human readers, however raises some issues for an automatic approach. Facing list descriptors, we generally ignored them in the digitizing process, which explains why words such as "anglais" *English* and "espagnol" *Spanish* – which are nationalities – were not found in our version of Beacco, although present in FLELex. For our study, open lists and list descriptors are very problematic in the sense that the absence of a word from a level cannot be considered as 100% certain. From a teacher's perspective though, those open lists and item descriptions are coherent with the authors goal to provide content adaptable to all contexts, and indications that the items are to be chosen according to the geographic, cultural and educational situation (e.g. for the nationalities, "japonais", "coréen" and "vietnamien" are likely to be taught in A1 to Asian learners, whereas they might not be needed from A1 in a South American classroom).

6. Conclusion

In this research, we aimed to infer CEFR levels from CEFRLex word frequency distribution using expert knowledge from the French RLD as a gold-standard. Such approach enabled us to apply, for the first time, machine learning algorithms to such task whereas previous work used simple mathematical rules. After standardisation of the data, we trained three machine learning models on two sets, reaching an accuracy score of 0.54 for the dataset *BeaccoFLELexA-toB* and of 0.48 for the *BeaccoFLELexC* dataset. These results clearly outperforms results reached by the *First occ* rule currently used in the CEFRLex interface. Our work has direct repercussions on this project, as our best classifier has been integrated in the interface[4], offering now the choice between *Beacco* or *First occ* to classify words.

Our experiments also yield other interesting results. First, comparing our results with those of a L1 frequency word list revealed that the distributional information contained in FLELex indeed seems richer and finer-grained than the one of a standard L1 list. Second, we carried out an analysis on the most important classification errors as a way to sharpen our understanding of the differences existing between the two approaches we compared: frequency and expert knowledge. This analysis stressed the importance of lexical networks in L2 learning to ensure a better representation of available words and of words connected to topics generally avoided in textbooks. We also noticed that although CEFRLex resources only represent receptive skills, Beacco might have sometimes classified words based on criteria relative to both receptive and productive skills. Finally, the presence of list descriptors in RLD is a serious issue for their automatic exploitation, as they contain some implicit knowledge. We believe that all these discrepancies partially explain why our statistical model is not able to better predict Beacco's level. In other words, although a better option than the *First occ* rule, using expert knowledge also has shortcomings. In the future, we plan to investigate the use of L2 learners data as an alternative source of information to transform CEFRLex distribution into levels.

7. Bibliographical References

Alfter, D., Bizzoni, Y., Agebjórn, A., Volodina, E., and Pilán, I. (2016). From distributions to labels: A lexical proficiency analysis using learner corpora. In *Proceedings of the joint workshop on NLP4CALL and NLP for Language Acquisition at SLTC*, number 130, pages 1–7. Linköping University Electronic Press.

Baayen, R., Piepenbrock, R., and van Rijn, H. (1993). *The {CELEX} lexical data base on {CD-ROM}*. Linguistic Data Consortium, Philadelphia: Univ. of Pennsylvania.

Beacco, J.-C., Lepage, S., Porquier, R., and Riba, P. (2008). *Niveau A2 pour le français: Un référentiel*. Didier.

Brysbaert, M. and New, B. (2009). Moving beyond kučera and francis: A critical evaluation of current word frequency norms and the introduction of a new and improved word frequency measure for american english. *Behavior research methods*, 41(4):977–990.

Capel, A. (2010). A1-b2 vocabulary: Insights and issues arising from the english profile wordlists project. *English Profile Journal*, 1(1):1–11.

Dürlich, L. and François, T. (2018). EFLLex: A Graded Lexical Resource for Learners of English as a Foreign Language. In *Proceedings of LREC 2018*, pages 873–879.

François, T., Gala, N., Watrin, P., and Fairon, C. (2014). FLELex: a graded lexical resource for French foreign learners. In *Proceedings of LREC 2014*, pages 3766–3773.

François, T., Volodina, E., Ildikó, P., and Tack, A. (2016). SVALex: a CEFR-graded lexical resource for Swedish foreign and second language learners. In *Proceedings of LREC 2016*, pages 213–219.

Gala, N., François, T., and Fairon, C. (2013). Towards a french lexicon with difficulty measures: Nlp helping to bridge the gap between traditional dictionaries and specialized lexicons. In *Proceedings of eLex2013*, pages 132–151.

Gougenheim, G., Michéa, R., Rivenc, P., and Sauvageot, A. (1964). *L'élaboration du français fondamental (1er degré)*. Didier, Paris.

Grabe, W. (2014). Key issues in l2 reading development. In *CELC Symposium Bridging Research and Pedagogy*, pages 8–18.

Kučera, H. and Francis, W. (1967). *Computational analysis of present-day American English*. Brown University Press, Providence.

Laufer, B. (1992). How much lexis is necessary for reading comprehension? In *Vocabulary and applied linguistics*, pages 126–132. Springer.

Leech, G., Rayson, P., and Wilson, A. (2001). Word frequencies in written and spoken english: based on the british national corpus.

Michéa, R. (1953). Mots fréquents et mots disponibles. un aspect nouveau de la statistique du langage. *Les langues modernes*, 47(4):338–344.

New, B., Brysbaert, M., Veronis, J., and Pallier, C. (2007). The use of film subtitles to estimate word frequencies. *Applied Psycholinguistics*, 28(04):661–677.

Riba, P. (2016). *Niveaux C1 / C2 pour le français: éléments pour un référentiel*. Didier.

Schmid, H. (1994). Probabilistic part-of-speech tagging using decision trees. In *Proceedings of International Conference on New Methods in Language Processing*, volume 12. Manchester, UK.

Tack, A., François, T., Ligozat, A.-L., and Fairon, C. (2016). Evaluating lexical simplification and vocabulary knowledge for learners of french: possibilities of using the flelex resource. In *Proceedings of LREC2016*, pages 230–236.

Tack, A., François, T., Desmet, P., and Fairon, C. (2018). NT2Lex: A CEFR-Graded Lexical Resource for Dutch as a Foreign Language Linked to Open Dutch WordNet. In *Proceedings of BEA 2018*.

Thorndike, E. (1921). Word knowledge in the elementary school. *The Teachers College Record*, 22(4):334–370.

Todirascu, A., Cargill, M., and François, T. (2019). Polylexfle: une base de données d'expressions polylexicales pour le fle. In *Actes de la conférence TALN 2019*, pages 143–156.

---

[4]The interface is available at `https://cental.uclouvain.be/cefrlex/analyze`.

1st Workshop on Tools and Resources to Empower People with REAding DIfficulties (READI2020), pages 93–100
Language Resources and Evaluation Conference (LREC 2020), Marseille, 11–16 May 2020
ⓒ European Language Resources Association (ELRA), licensed under CC-BY-NC

Coreference-Based Text Simplification

Rodrigo Wilkens, Bruno Oberle, Amalia Todirascu
LiLPa – University of Strasbourg
rswilkens@gmail.com, b.oberle@zoho.eu, todiras@unistra.fr

Abstract

Text simplification aims at adapting documents to make them easier to read by a given audience. Usually, simplification systems consider only lexical and syntactic levels, and, moreover, are often evaluated at the sentence level. Thus, studies on the impact of simplification in text cohesion are lacking. Some works add coreference resolution in their pipeline to address this issue. In this paper, we move forward in this direction and present a rule-based system for automatic text simplification, aiming at adapting French texts for dyslexic children. The architecture of our system takes into account not only lexical and syntactic but also discourse information, based on coreference chains. Our system has been manually evaluated in terms of grammaticality and cohesion. We have also built and used an evaluation corpus containing multiple simplification references for each sentence. It has been annotated by experts following a set of simplification guidelines, and can be used to run automatic evaluation of other simplification systems. Both the system and the evaluation corpus are freely available.

Keywords: Automatic Text Simplification (ATS), Coreference Resolution, French, Annotated and evaluation corpus

1. Introduction

Text cohesion, a crucial feature for text understanding, is reinforced by explicit cohesive devices such as coreference (expressions referring to the same discourse entity: *Dany Boon—the French actor—his* film) and anaphoric (an anaphor and its antecedent: *it—the fox*) chains. Coreference chains involves at least 3 referring expressions (such as proper names, noun phrases (NP), pronouns) indicating the same discourse entity (Schnedecker, 1997), while anaphoric chains involves a directed relation between the anaphor (the pronoun) and its antecedent. However, coreference and anaphora resolution is a difficult task for people with language disabilities, such as dyslexia (Vender, 2017; Jaffe et al., 2018; Sprenger-Charolles and Ziegler, 2019). Moreover, when concurrent referents are present in the text, the pronoun resolution task is even more difficult (Givón, 1993; McMillan et al., 2012; Li et al., 2018): the pronouns may be ambiguous and their resolution depends on user knowledge about the main topic (Le Bouëdec and Martins, 1998). This poses special issues to some NLP tasks, such as text simplification.

Automatic text simplification (ATS) adapts text for specific target audience such as L1 or L2 language learners or people with language or cognitive disabilities, as autism (Yaneva and Evans, 2015) and dyslexia (Rello et al., 2013). Existing simplification systems work at the lexical or syntactic level, or both. Lexical simplification aims to replace complex words by simpler ones (Rello et al., 2013; François et al., 2016; Billami et al., 2018), while syntactic simplification transforms complex structures (Seretan, 2012; Brouwers et al., 2014a). However, these transformations change the discourse structure and might violate some cohesion or coherence constraints.

Problems appear at discourse level because of lexical or syntactic simplifications ignoring coreference. In the following example, the substitution of *hyène 'hyena'* by *animal 'animal'* introduces an ambiguity in coreference resolution, since the animal might be *le renard 'the fox'* or *la hyène 'the hyena'*.

Original: *Le renard se trouvait au fond du puits et appellait.*

La hyène l'approcha. 'The fox was at the bottom of the well. The hyena approached it.'

Simplified: **Le renard se trouvait au fond du puits. L'animal l'approcha.** 'The fox was at the bottom of the well. The animal approached it.'

However, few existing syntactic simplification systems (e.g. Siddharthan (2006) and Canning (2002)) operate at the discourse level and replace pronouns by antecedents or fix these discourse constraints after the syntactic simplification process (Quiniou and Daille, 2018).

In this paper, we evaluate the influence of coreference in the text simplification task. In order to achieve this goal, we propose a rule-based text simplification architecture aware of coreference information, and we analyse its impact at the lexical and syntactic levels as well as for text cohesion and coherence. We also explore the use of coreference information as a simplification device in order to adapt NP accessibility and improve some coreference-related issues. For this purpose, we have developed an evaluation corpus, annotated by human experts, following discourse-based simplification guidelines.

This paper is organised as follows. We present related work on cohesion markers such as coreference chains, as well as lexical and syntactic simplification systems that take into account these elements (Section 2). Then, we present the architecture of our rule-based simplification system alongside the corpus used to build it and the corpus used to evaluate it (Section 3). The rules themselves, and the system evaluation, are presented in Section 4. Finally, Section 5 presents final remarks.

2. Related Work

Few systems explore discourse-related features (e.g. entity densities and syntactic transitions) to evaluate text readability alongside other lexical or morphosyntactic properties (Štajner et al., 2012; Todirascu et al., 2016; Pitler and Nenkova, 2008).

Linguistic theories such as Accessibility theory (Ariel, 2001) organise referring expressions and their surface forms into a hierarchy that predicts the structure of cohesion markers such as coreference chains. In this respect, a new discourse entity is introduced by a low accessibility referring expression, such as a proper noun or a full NP. On the contrary, pronouns and possessive determiners are used to recall already known entities. This theory is often used to explain coreference chain structure and properties (Todirascu et al., 2017). Other linguistic theories such as Centering theory (Grosz et al., 1995) predict discourse centres following a typology of centre shift or maintenance and explains linguistic parameters related to coherence issues. Simplification systems frequently ignore existing cohesive devices. This aspect is however taken into account by, for instance, Siddharthan (2006), Brouwers et al. (2014a) and Quiniou and Daille (2018). Canning (2002) replaces anaphor by their antecedent for a specific target audience. Siddharthan (2004) first uses anaphora detection to replace pronouns by NP. Then a set of ordered hand-made syntactic rules is applied (e.g. conjunctions are simplified before relative clauses). Rhetorical Structure Theory (Mann and Thompson, 1988) is used to reorder the output of the syntactic simplification and anaphoric relations are checked after simplification. Moreover, Siddharthan (2006) proposes a model based on Centering theory (Grosz et al., 1995) to recover broken cohesion relations, by using a specific pronoun resolution system for English. The model allows the replacement of a pronoun by its immediate antecedent. Few systems use a coreference resolution module to solve coreference issues (Barbu et al., 2013). For French, Quiniou and Daille (2018) develop a simple pronoun resolution module, inspired by (Mitkov, 2002) (e.g. searching antecedents in two sentences before the pronoun). This system previously detects expletive pronouns to exclude them from pronoun resolution. Brouwers et al. (2014a) mainly propose syntactic simplification using hand-made rules implemented with Tregex and Tsurgeon (Levy and Andrew, 2006). The only rules handling anaphora replace pronouns with NP from the previous or the current sentence. To sum up, only a few ATS approaches, mostly for English, propose discourse simplification rules or rules checking discourse constraints.[1]

3. Methodology

Taking into account our goal of analysing the impact of coreference in text simplification, we compiled two different types of corpora (one for the evaluation and other for the simplification reference), described in Section 3.1., we propose a coreference-aware architecture in Section 3.2.

3.1. Corpora

One of the most critical elements in text simplification is the target audience since it defines what types of operations should be performed. In this regard, we compiled a reference corpus composed of parallel texts manually adapted for dyslexic children in the context of the Methodolodys association[2]. This corpus consists of five manually adapted paired tales (1,143 words and 84 sentences for the dyslexic texts and 1,969 words and 151 sentences for the original texts). This corpus helps us to better understand simplifications targeting dyslexic children both for coreference chains and at the lexical and syntactic levels.

The reference corpus has been preprocessed in two steps. First, we aligned the corpus using the MEDITE tool (Fenoglio and Ganascia, 2006). This process identifies the transformations performed (phrase deletion or insertion, sentence splitting, etc.) as well as their level (i.e. lexical, syntactic or discourse). The second step consisted in the manual annotation of coreference chains (mentions and coreference relations) (Todirascu et al., 2017; Schnedecker, 1997; Todirascu et al., 2016) and referring expressions accessibility (Ariel, 1990; Ariel, 2001). Then, we compared coreference chains properties: chain size, average distance between mentions, lexical diversity (with the stability coefficient defined by Perret (2000)), annotation (mention) density, link (relation between consecutive mentions) count and density, grammatical categories of the mentions.

The reference corpus provides several meaningful descriptions of the simplification phenomenon. However, it is limited in the sense of system evaluation since it provides only one valid simplification, and it may require resources other than those currently available in NLP technology. In order to build an evaluation corpus, we manually collected simplified alternatives to the original texts (3 texts from the reference corpus and 2 new texts). We used the online PsyToolkit tool[3], and 25 annotators (master students in linguistics and computational linguistics) participated. They all provided information on age, mother tongue and education level, and replied to questionnaires to check reading time and text understanding. Additionally, we summarised the discursive observations identified in the reference corpus (presented in Section 4.1. and 4.2.) as simplification guidelines[4] provided to the annotators. The purpose of these guidelines was to drive the annotators' attention to discourse operations.

To create an evaluation corpus, the students proposed simplified alternatives to texts from the original corpus (we replaced 2 texts to broaden the text coverage). These alternatives had to follow the provided guidelines, but the students could also suggest other simplification proposals. Taking into account the task complexity and the time required to simplify a text, we ask them to simplify only some short paragraphs (894 words per person on average). We excluded from our data the responses from 6 students who did not fully understand the task. We aligned the source text and then, we identified ungrammatical transformations and typos, and replaced these answers with the original text. The evaluation corpus also offers complementary simplifications for each text. Thus, it can also be used to select the most significant simplifications required. We obtained several simplified versions for each sentence. The analysis of the simplifications performed in both reference and evaluation corpora is presented in Section 4. Furthermore, the

---

[1]For an overview of simplification studies, including systems for different needs arguing for discourse phenomena processing, see Saggion (2017).

[2]`methodolodys.ch/` is an association providing texts and exercises to improve reading and comprehension skills for dyslexic children.

[3]`psytoolkit.org`

[4]The guidelines are available on the Web site of Alector project `https://alectorsite.wordpress.com/`

system that uses the result of this analysis is introduced in Section 3.2., and its evaluation is presented in Section 4.3.

3.2. Architecture

In this paper, we propose a rule-based approach to the simplification task since, on one hand, the original and simplified parallel corpora are small, which makes applying machine learning methods difficult; and, on the other hand, this kind of approach allows us to study the impact of each type of transformation on the comprehension and reading capabilities of the target audience. In this case, it is possible to decompose the simplification rules into various levels and to evaluate them separately. In this work, we are particularly interested in discursive simplification, which aims at preserving textual cohesion markers, such as coreference chains (Schnedecker, 2017).

The proposed architecture is composed of four modules, as illustrated in Figure 1. The first module preprocesses the text in order to facilitate the application of the simplification rules. This module starts by annotating the text with a parser (Qi et al., 2019) and with coreference information, which consist of the delimitation of referring expressions (e.g. proper names or named entities, NP and pronouns) and identification of coreference relations between these expressions. It is based on the architecture proposed by Kantor and Globerson (2019) but trained on the DEMOCRAT corpus[5] (Landragin, 2016). Our trained model achieved 85,04% of CoNLL score (the standard evaluation metric for automatic coreference resolution) with predicted mentions[6]. The syntactic simplification module is inspired by the work of Siddharthan (2003) and Brouwers et al. (2014b), applying deletion and rewriting rules described in the next sections. Then the data is processed by the third module, the discursive simplification module, which modifies the structure of coreference chains detected by the first module. Finally, the last module applies lexical and morphological simplifications by replacing words. This module is based on ReSyf (Billami et al., 2018) and its API[7], which allows to query by the easiest alternative synonym to a given target word. Since ReSyf proposed different alternatives for each word sense, we selected as output only those that are the simplest in all senses and the most frequent across the senses.

To evaluate the system, taking advantage of the alternative simplification references in the evaluation corpus, we used the SARI measure that correlates to some level with human judgement of simplicity (Xu et al., 2016). Moreover, as a point of comparison, we also present the results of BLEU (Papineni et al., 2002), used in MT-based simplification methods.

A key element in our architecture is the rewriting tool (see Section 3.2.1.), that allows to search for both lexical and morphosyntactic patterns as well as to modify the syntactic parse structure.

3.2.1. Text rewriting tool

The text rewriting tool applies several text transformations and changes to the structure of the sentences: deletion of secondary information, sentence splitting and phrase changes. However, we have to transform the text without violating the grammar. We compared available rewriting tools such as Tregex and Tsurgeon (Levy and Andrew, 2006), Semgrex (Chambers et al., 2007), and Semgrex-Plus (Tamburini, 2017).

Levy and Andrew (2006) provide tree query (Tregex) and manipulation (Tsurgeon) tools that can operate on constituent trees. Tree query tools have proven invaluable to NLP research for both data exploration and corpus-based research. Complementary to Tregex queries, Tsurgeon operates at node and edge levels, to change the structure of the trees, allowing, for example, node renaming, deletion, insertion, movement and replacement.

Chambers et al. (2007) proposed Semgrex to handle dependencies instead of constituents. The tool identifies semantic patterns supporting inference in texts as an alternative to writing graph traversal coded by hand for each desired pattern. Semgrex allows inter- and extra-dependency graphs relations. For instance, queries may be used to identify direct or indirect governor associations, with or without limitation of the distance between the elements, or even the node positional relation (e.g. immediately precedes, right sibling, right immediate sibling, same nodes).

Making a step forward into graph modification alike to Tsurgeon, Tamburini (2017) developed Semgrex-Plus to convert dependency treebanks into various formats. It supports three rewriting operations: replacing the tag of a graph node, and inserting or deleting a dependency edge between two graph nodes.

Additionally to those, generic graph processing tools might be adapted for our task. For instance, Bonfante et al. (2018) present GREW, a graph rewriting tool that can perform similar queries to Semgrex, while providing graph operations close to those proposed by Tsurgeon. However, as pointed by Tamburini (2017), intricacies of the generic tools might have a significant impact on the sentence rewriting process. For querying parsed data, we selected Semgrex because it precisely fits our needs. But, regarding the sentence rewriting goal, we opted to create a new Semgrex-based sentence processing tool, given the parser restrictions and the small set of operations available on Semgrex-Plus. Concerning the operations, we developed the following: (1) *Insert* injects a node (or tree) in another node; (2) *Delete* removes a node and its subtree from the sentence graph; (3) *Split* detaches a node and its subtree; (4) *Move* detaches a node and its subtree from a tree node, attaching it to another node of the same tree; (5) *Replace tag label* replaces the node information (e.g. surface and PoS-tag); (6) *Replace node* substitutes a node by another one; and (7) *Copy subgraph* creates a deep copy of a node or a tree.

The *insert, delete, move,* and *replace node* operations are directly based on Tsurgeon while *replace label* is based both on Tsurgeon and Tsurgeon-plus. The *split* method is inspired by the Tsurgeon *excise* and *adjoin* operations. On the contrary, the *copy* operation was developed because we needed to copy parts of a sentence into different trees. In

---

[5] We trained the model on text from the 19th to the 21st century: 295,978 tokens, 81,506 relations, 43,211 chains.

[6] In NLP, a mention is a referring expressions.

[7] gitlab.com/Cental-FR/resyf-package

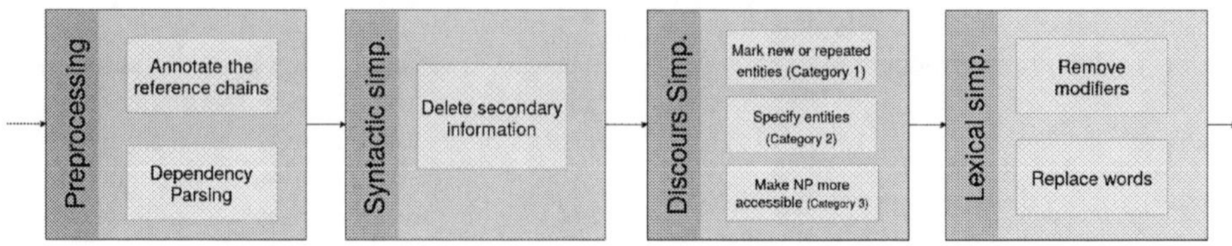

Figure 1: The architecture of the simplification system.

addition to these graph operations, we also extended Semgrex to read coreference information when available, and we simplified the morphology feature query by allowing to search by sub-elements without regular expressions.

These operations are combined into rules in order to rewrite the text. We detail the process of defining the cohesion rules necessary for our discourse simplification system in Section 4.1. and Section 4.2.

4. Results

In this section, we present and explain the reference corpus analyses of cohesion changes that have been used to design simplification rules.

4.1. Cohesion changes during the simplification

The compilation of several observations from the reference corpus is presented in this section. It supports the discourse level transformations applied in this work. For our purpose, we use Accessibility theory (Ariel, 1990; Ariel, 2001), which proposes a hierarchy of referring expressions, from those with low accessibility (such as proper nouns or definite NP; these are usually newly introduced expressions) to highly accessible ones (such as pronouns or determiners; these have usually been introduced previously). Moreover, we use Centering theory (Grosz et al., 1995), which predicts situations when the attention centre shifts to a new one, resulting in a change of the syntactic function of the centre. By exploiting these observations, we propose three categories of rules. First, we present the results from our analysis, and then we detail these rules.

As discussed in Section 3.1., we manually enriched the reference corpus with the annotation proposed in Todirascu et al. (2017), Schnedecker (1997) and Todirascu et al. (2016). This properties are presented in Section 3.1. and in Table 1. Next, we compared these annotations in both the simplified and the original texts to find discourse simplification (cohesion) rules. The comparison between the coreference chain properties in the original and simplified texts is the first step to define the cohesion rules. Next, we have to identify changes in the structure of coreference chains induced by simplifications before defining the cohesion rules. We start our study of the cohesive elements by comparing the properties and transformations of five text pairs. Each of those was manually annotated with coreference chains. Due to the lack of available data containing original and simplified texts for dyslexic people, our corpus is relatively small when compared to others simplification corpora. Moreover, manual coreference annotation is a time-consuming and challenging task, in terms of referring expression identification (delimiting expressions and finding their type) and of chain identification (linking all the referring expressions belonging to the same chain).

The adapted texts present some specific coreference property statistically differences when compared to the original ones (Table 1): link count ($p=0.01$), stability coefficient ($p=0.01$), chain density ($p=0.04$), link density ($p=0.008$), and annotation density ($p=0.02$). Additionally, the average distance between two consecutive referring expressions is higher in original than in adapted texts, as a consequence of text deletions.

We also observe interesting correlations for most of the properties (0.74 for link count, 0.81 for stability coefficient, 0.72 for chain density, and 0.74 for link density). We observe differences between original and adapted texts at the coreference level, but despite this, the correlations between the properties are still valid. Besides, a negative correlation (-0.717) is found between the length of the chains and the number of chains. In the adapted texts, longer chains are correlated with a lower number of chains (on average 10.62 against 7.0). Some referents were deleted in adapted versions, which explains this result.

Properties	Adapted	Original
Avg chain size	10.376	10.86
Avg link-to-link distance	14.550	11.920
Avg link length	1.500	1.450
Avg chain count	6.200	7.800
Avg link count	55.600	83.4
Avg chain density	0.012	0.009
Avg stability coefficient	0.607	0.471
Avg link density	0.113	0.093
Avg annotation density	0.162	0.139

Table 1: Coreference chains properties.

The composition of the chains varies with the complexity of the texts, as shown in Figure 2. In the simplified texts, the pronouns have been deleted or replaced by their referent: this explains that the percentage of personal pronouns (PRO.PER) included in coreference chains is larger in the original texts (36.5% of the mentions) than in the adapted texts (19.4%). This observation is in line with the significant difference for definite noun (NP.DEF) usage (36.0% in the simplified texts but only 18.7% in the original ones) or for proper noun (NP.NAM) usage (3.95% in simplified and 1.91% in original texts). The possessive determiners represent 10.1% in simpler texts but 12.9% in the original texts. This observation is related to our third category (see at the end of the section), concerning possessive NP replacement by a specific referent. Moreover, concerning referring expression accessibility, we observed a significant change in determinant accessibility. This may be observed in the increase of indefinite NPs (NP.INDEF) from 3.11% to 5.03%, while demonstrative NPs (NP.DEM) decrease from 0.48% to 0.36% in simpler texts. This accessibility changing is related with our second category (see end of section), and it is exemplified in cases such as:

Original: <u>le</u>$_1$ *loup*; <u>cette</u>$_2$ *hyène*. 'The$_1$ wolf; This$_2$ hyena'
Simplified: <u>un</u>$_1$ **loup**; <u>la</u>$_2$ **hyène.** 'A$_1$ wolf; The$_2$ hyena.'

Studying the stability coefficient[8] (Perret, 2000), we observed more stable chains in the dyslexic texts (0.47) than in the original texts (0.60). Thus, the coreference chains present less lexical variation (i.e. more repetitions) in the simple text versions than in the original ones. These observations support the first but also the second category of cohesion rules (see below).

To reduce coreference ambiguity, the pronoun *il 'it'* is replaced by the subject of the previous sentence (*le hérisson 'the hedgehog'*):

Original: *Le hérisson voit le loup arriver, mais <u>il</u>$_1$ n'a pas le temps de se cacher.* 'The hedgehog sees the wolf coming, but <u>it</u>$_1$ has no time to hide himself.'
Simplified: **Le hérisson voit le loup arriver, mais <u>le hérisson</u>$_1$ n'a pas le temps de se cacher.** 'The hedgehog sees that the wolf arriving, but <u>the hedgehog</u>$_1$ has no time to hide himself.'

To reduce working memory, the repeated pronoun is replaced by the referent:

Original: *Le renard$_1$ avait très soif. <u>Il</u>$_2$ aperçut un puits. Sur la poulie, il y avait une corde, et, à chaque bout de la corde, il y avait un seau. <u>Il</u>$_3$ s'assit dans un des seaux et fut entraîné au fond. Heureux, <u>il</u>$_4$ but pendant de longues minutes.* 'The fox$_1$ was very thirsty. <u>It</u>$_2$ saw a well. On the pulley, there was a rope, and at each end of the rope, there was a bucket. <u>It</u>$_3$ sat in one of the buckets and was dragged to the bottom. Happily, <u>it</u>$_4$ drank for long minutes.'
Simplified: **<u>Le renard</u>$_1$ avait très soif. <u>Le renard</u>$_2$ aperçut un puits. Sur la poulie, il y avait une corde, et, à chaque bout de la corde, il y avait un seau. <u>Le renard</u>$_3$ s'assit dans un des seaux et fut entraîné au fond. Heureux, <u>le renard</u>$_4$ but pendant de longues minutes.** 'The fox$_1$ was very thirsty. <u>The fox</u>$_2$ saw a well. On the pulley there was a rope, and at each end of the rope there was a bucket. <u>The fox</u>$_3$ sat in one of the buckets and was dragged to the bottom. Happily, <u>the fox</u>$_4$ drank for long minutes.'

Moreover, we define rules from Category 2 to reflect differences between possessive determiners (12.95% vs 10.07%) and proper noun (1.91% vs 3.95%). For instance, the possessive NP (e.g. *son mari*) should be replaced by its referent (e.g. *M. Dupont*) in the example:

Original: *Mme Dupont a préparé sa soupe. <u>Son mari</u>$_1$ dit, pour la première fois, qu'il n'aime pas sa soupe.* 'Mrs Dupont had prepared her soup. <u>Her husband</u>$_1$ says, for the first time, that he does not like her soup.'

Simplified: **Mme Dupont a fait sa soupe. <u>M. Dupont</u>$_1$ dit, pour la première fois, qu'il n'aime pas sa soupe.** 'Mrs Dupont cooked her soup. <u>Mr. Dupont</u>$_1$ said for the first time that he does not like her soup.'

The reference corpus alignment also contains pronoun deletions due to the suppression of secondary information. For example, the relative pronoun *qui 'who'* and the personal pronoun *eux 'them'* were deleted because the relative clause *qui se dirigent vers eux 'who went to them'* was deleted. We add a rule to Category 3, concerning information suppression:

Original: *En chemin, ils aperçoivent, au loin, des bandits qui se dirigent vers eux.* 'In their way, they saw, far away, bandits who went to them.'
Simplified: **En chemin, ils aperçoivent au loin des bandits.** 'In their way, they saw, far away, bandits.'

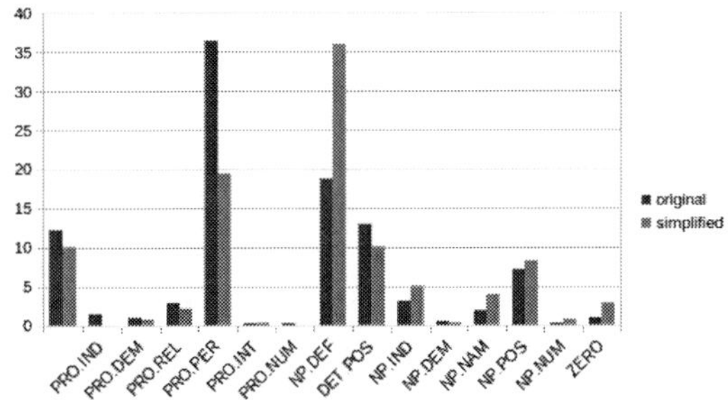

Figure 2: The distribution of referring expression types in the chains for original and simplified texts.

All the differences observed in the corpus are summarised in the three following categories, each one containing different rules.

Category 1 *mark new or repeated entities.* A referent should be found for ambiguous pronouns (i.e. several referents might be selected) or successive pronouns in the same chain. This operation decreases the number of processing inferences done by the reader to solve coreference relations.

Category 2 *specify entities.* New entities should be introduced by either an indefinite NP or a proper noun, while definite nouns phrases (formed with a definite article or a demonstrative determiner), being highly accessible, refer to known entities. The change of determiner for a more highly accessible one modifies the accessibility of the referring expression.

Category 3 *make NP more accessible.* Secondary information, such as relative or oblique clauses, should be removed. As a consequence, mentions of coreference chains are deleted (e.g. indefinite pronouns) as well as non-corefent pronouns, such as *chacun, quelqu'un*. Possessive NPs are replaced by their explicit referent (a proper noun or another NP).

The rules have been written as simplification guidelines and applied by human annotators (Master students from Linguistics and Computational Linguistics) to create an evaluation corpus for our system.

---

[8]A low stability coefficient means that there is a large variety of referring expressions in a given chain, in terms of synonyms.

4.2. Proposed simplifications

Concerning the evaluation corpus, we annotated and ranked the multiple simplification references proposed by the annotators which followed the simplification guidelines. The proposals are not unanimous, in other words, there is not a single case in which all the annotators agreed with the simplification. Moreover, we observed several parts of the texts without any simplification suggestion from the annotators. These observations are also supported by the low value of 0.189 in the Krippendorff inter-annotator agreement, which combines several annotations and annotators.

We build a typology for simplification that also includes the simplification rules. At the lexical level, one of the most applied rules concerns the deletion of modifiers (adjectives and adverbs) and the replacement of words by simpler synonyms. At the morphological level, we consistently observe a change in the tense of the verbs (usually replacing the simple past (*passé simple*) by the composed past (*passé composé*), but sometimes replacing the simple/composed past by the present). The change of the most frequent words of a morphological family by a word from the same family is observed at a lower frequency. Concerning the syntactic modifications, the suppression of secondary information, such as relative or adverbial subordinate clauses, is noticeable, followed by the sentence reduction (e.g. sentence split at conjunctions and punctuation marks). We also observed some cases of sentence rewriting in order to ensure an SVO (subject-verb-object) structure. These rewriting operations address the cleft and passive sentences.

Additionally, we also observed transformations of negative sentences into positive ones, but at a lower frequency. Furthermore, as expected, we identified several cases of discourse simplification. The most applied rules are from Category 2, followed by those from Category 1, and finally Category 3. Additionally, we also identify 10% of discourse simplifications, such as insertion of pronoun where there is a zero subject, that are not present in the guidelines.

After these observations, we coded the most recurrent rules in the rewriting tool presented in Section 3.2.1. At the syntactic level, we addressed the secondary information removal and sentence reduction. For the former, the system searches for conjunctions linking full sentences or NP, splitting them into two separated sentences. At the coreference level, the NP splits require to repeat some elements to keep reference information. Adverbial clauses are deleted when they are not required by the sentence structure.

The coded rules at the discourse level consisted of five different strategies. At first, some pronouns (e.g. *chaque* and *tout*) when non-coreferent and the subordinate pronouns with their clauses are removed. Then, determiners that are in a coreference chain are changed in order to indicate their position in the chain. Moreover, other determiners are changed following Accessibility theory. Similarly, the third rule explicits coreference relations in possessive determiners. The next rule searches for ambiguous pronouns replacing them by their referents. The last rule solves all anaphoric relations of subject pronouns.

4.3. System evaluation

The rules proposed in the last section feed the simplification system. They are coded using the operations presented in Section 3.2.1. and, as indicated in Section 3.2., the text is annotated with syntactic dependency and coreference information before the simplification pipeline starts. This pipeline stacks the syntactic, discursive and lexical simplifications shown in Figure 1.

Aiming to better understand the impact of the simplification on the coreference, we analysed the errors produced by the system. This evaluation is based on the judgement of three judges (two native speakers and one non-native, but advanced, speaker) who evaluated the grammaticality and familiarity of the system output. During this process, they first focused on text cohesion (without lexical simplifications), and then judged the choice of words (lexical simplifications). This approach was adopted to help them to concentrate on the cohesion aspects without distractions from the lexical issues. The total inter-annotator agreement was 56.59% (41.78% for the cohesion and 68.34% for the lexical judgements). Furthermore, we considered only simplification errors spotted by at least two judges.

Concerning the cohesion evaluation, we observed that most errors come from the application of rules from Category 2. It creates referential inconsistencies since it changes the determiner. These errors are caused by coreference annotation tool errors and miss-identification of idioms and collocations. The coreference tool also contributed to errors in rules from Category 1 and 2. These errors may have been caused by both coreference chain divisions (causing determination issues) or merging (mixing different entities). Errors related to Category 3 rules were less frequent, and they are mostly related to coreference chain merging.

The syntactic transformations do not generate noticeable errors. However, during preliminary evaluations, we identified that they mostly contribute to two error types: they caused cascade errors related to ambiguity if the coreference information was not kept in sentence splitting operations. The sentence deletion transformations may overdelete central elements due to parsing errors.

All these transformations generated a total of 180 errors spread into 207 sentences. Taking into account only the lexical simplifications, the systems produced a total of 96 errors (62.35% of accuracy). Considering that these errors have an undesirable impact on simplification evaluation, we changed back all incorrect transformations. Given the grammatical output and the evaluation corpus (described in Section 3), we can move to simplicity evaluation.

We evaluate the simplification using the SARI measure (Xu et al., 2016) (presented in Table 2). However, this measure, is still new, and it lacks in-depth studies. We selected random manual simplifications from the evaluation corpus and set it as a reference. The results of both the system output and the manual simplification are presented in Table 2. This table shows the SARI and BLEU scores as well as other measures related to transformations at the sentence level.

The result of the BLEU score points out a low n-gram variability in the evaluation corpus. Thus, a smaller number of operations may be a useful strategy for this corpus. The SARI score does not indicate a big difference. Moreover,

	System	Manual annotation
SARI	38.124	44.720
BLEU	74.084	91.986
Compression ratio	0.984	1.008
Sentence splits	1.026	1.056
Additions proportion	0.124	0.108
Deletions proportion	0.126	0.104

Table 2: System evaluation.

the same behaviour is observed in sentence-level measures. To better understand the results, we analysed the best and worse SARI's results by sentence, which lead us to two sources of noise: syntactic and lexical. These issues expose a contradiction in the simplification evaluation. The syntactic noise is related to the removal of secondary information. On one hand, the judges read and understand the texts without significant loss of information, on the other the candidate simplifications tend to keep the secondary information; even if this operation is one of the most performed at the syntactic level. The lexical issues are related to ReSyf. This dictionary contains lexical information graded by complexity, although most of the replacements indicated by this resource are not present in the evaluation corpus.

5. Conclusion and further work

We have presented a study of discourse-level transformations to simplify French texts.[9] This study focuses on cohesion issues related to text simplification. From the analysis of a corpus of simplified *vs* not simplified texts, we have first written guidelines for discourse-level simplifications. We have then designed a system to automatically applied these simplification guidelines. Our system has been evaluated with a corpus containing alternative simplifications proposed by 19 annotators. This corpus also supported the selection of lexical and syntactic simplification rules.

We also presented a proposal for a rule-based coreference-aware simplification system. It was evaluated in terms of text coherence and lexical substitutions by three judges. An automatic evaluation gives a SARI score of 38.13.

During the system evaluation, we identified that most of the miss-simplifications are caused by a lack of language resources. This indicates that the proposed rules seem appropriate, but that extra-linguistic resources are required or should be improved, as the graded lexicon that we used. In a purely rule-based system like ours, tuning further the rules would require a significant development time.

As future work, we intend to improve the system performance. We will explore other coreference properties, such as the negative correlation between the length and the number of chains. We will start with the inclusion of more language resources, but we also intend to explore other approaches than rule-based methods, as well as increase the number of rules through the analysis of other corpora and the use of rules tested in other works, such as Drndarevic and Saggion (2012). A comparison with baseline systems will also complete the evaluation of our system.

---

[9]The corpora and systems are available at `https://github.com/rswilkens/text-rewrite`.

We also plan to validate the simplification with a larger group of annotators, including dyslexic children. Moreover, we would like to include feedback from the simplification target-group.

6. Bibliographical References

Ariel, M. (1990). *Accessing noun-phrase antecedents.* Routledge.

Ariel, M. (2001). Accessibility theory: An overview. *Text representation: Linguistic and psycholinguistic aspects*, 8:29–87.

Barbu, E., Martín-Valdivia, M. T., and Ureña-López, L. A. (2013). Open book: a tool for helping asd users' semantic comprehension. In *Proceedings of the Workshop on Natural Language Processing for Improving Textual Accessibility*, pages 11–19.

Billami, M. B., François, T., and Gala, N. (2018). ReSyf: a French lexicon with ranked synonyms. In *Proceedings of the 27th International Conference on Computational Linguistics*, pages 2570–2581, Santa Fe, New Mexico, USA, August. Association for Computational Linguistics.

Bonfante, G., Guillaume, B., and Perrier, G. (2018). *Application of Graph Rewriting to Natural Language Processing*. Wiley Online Library.

Brouwers, L., Bernhard, D., Ligozat, A.-L., and François, T. (2014a). Syntactic sentence simplification for french. In *3rd International Workshop on Predicting and Improving Text Readability for Target Reader Populations*.

Brouwers, L., Bernhard, D., Ligozat, A., and François, T. (2014b). Syntactic sentence simplification for french. In *Proceedings of the 3rd Workshop on Predicting and Improving Text Readability for Target Reader Populations, PITR@EACL 2014, Gothenburg, Sweden, April 27, 2014*, pages 47–56.

Canning, Y. M. (2002). *Syntactic simplification of Text.* Ph.D. thesis, University of Sunderland.

Chambers, N., Cer, D., Grenager, T., Hall, D., Kiddon, C., MacCartney, B., De Marneffe, M.-C., Ramage, D., Yeh, E., and Manning, C. D. (2007). Learning alignments and leveraging natural logic. In *Proceedings of the ACL-PASCAL Workshop on Textual Entailment and Paraphrasing*, pages 165–170. Association for Computational Linguistics.

Drndarevic, B. and Saggion, H. (2012). Reducing text complexity through automatic lexical simplification: An empirical study for spanish. *Procesamiento del lenguaje natural*, 49:13–20.

Fenoglio, I. and Ganascia, J.-G. (2006). Edite, un programme pour l'approche comparative de documents de genèse. *Genesis (Manuscrits-Recherche-Invention)*, 27(1):166–168.

François, T., Billami, M., Gala, N., and Bernhard, D. (2016). Bleu, contusion, ecchymose: tri automatique de synonymes en fonction de leur difficulté de lecture et compréhension. In *JEP-TALN-RECITAL 2016*, volume 2, pages 15–28.

Givón, T. (1993). Coherence in text, coherence in mind. *Pragmatics & Cognition*, 1(2):171–227.

Grosz, B. J., Weinstein, S., and Joshi, A. K. (1995). Centering: A framework for modeling the local coherence of discourse. *Computational linguistics*, 21(2):203–225.

Jaffe, E., Shain, C., and Schuler, W. (2018). Coreference and focus in reading times. In *Proceedings of the 8th Workshop on Cognitive Modeling and Computational Linguistics (CMCL 2018)*, pages 1–9.

Kantor, B. and Globerson, A. (2019). Coreference resolution with entity equalization. In *Proceedings of the 57th Annual Meeting of the Association for Computational Linguistics*, pages 673–677.

Landragin, F. (2016). Description, modélisation et détection automatique des chaînes de référence (DEMOCRAT). *Bulletin de l'Association Française pour l'Intelligence Artificielle*, 92:11–15.

Le Bouëdec, B. and Martins, D. (1998). La production d'inférences lors de la compréhension de textes chez des adultes : une analyse de la littérature. *L'anné psychologique*, 98.

Levy, R. and Andrew, G. (2006). Tregex and tsurgeon: tools for querying and manipulating tree data structures. In *LREC*, pages 2231–2234. Citeseer.

Li, J., Fabre, M., Luh, W.-M., and Hale, J. (2018). The role of syntax during pronoun resolution: Evidence from fmri. In *Proceedings of the Eight Workshop on Cognitive Aspects of Computational Language Learning and Processing*, pages 56–64.

Mann, W. and Thompson, S. (1988). Rethorical structure theory: Toward a functional theory of text organization. *Text*, 8:243–281, 01.

McMillan, C. T., Clark, R., Gunawardena, D., Ryant, N., and Grossman, M. (2012). fmri evidence for strategic decision-making during resolution of pronoun reference. *Neuropsychologia*, 50(5):674–687.

Mitkov, R. (2002). *Anaphora Resolution*. Oxford University Press.

Papineni, K., Roukos, S., Ward, T., and Zhu, W.-J. (2002). Bleu: a method for automatic evaluation of machine translation. In *Proceedings of the 40th annual meeting on association for computational linguistics*, pages 311–318. Association for Computational Linguistics.

Perret, M. (2000). Quelques remarques sur l'anaphore nominale aux xive et xve siècles. *L'Information grammaticale*, 87(1):17–23.

Pitler, E. and Nenkova, A. (2008). Revisiting readability: A unified framework for predicting text quality. In *Proceedings of the Conference on Empirical Methods in Natural Language Processing*, pages 186–195.

Qi, P., Dozat, T., Zhang, Y., and Manning, C. D. (2019). Universal dependency parsing from scratch. *arXiv preprint arXiv:1901.10457*.

Quiniou, S. and Daille, B. (2018). Towards a diagnosis of textual difficulties for children with dyslexia. In *11th International Conference on Language Resources and Evaluation (LREC)*.

Rello, L., Baeza-Yates, R., Bott, S., and Saggion, H. (2013). Simplify or help?: text simplification strategies for people with dyslexia. In *Proceedings of the 10th International Cross-Disciplinary Conference on Web Accessibility*, page 15. ACM.

Saggion, H. (2017). Automatic text simplification: Synthesis lectures on human language technologies, vol. 10 (1). *California, Morgan & Claypool Publishers*.

Schnedecker, C. (1997). *Nom propre et chaînes de référence*. Centre d'Etudes Linguistiques des Textes et Discours de l'Université de Metz, Paris

Schnedecker, C. (2017). Les chaînes de référence: une configuration d'indices pour distinguer et identifier les genres textuels. *Langue française*, 195(3):53–72.

Seretan, V. (2012). Acquisition of syntactic simplification rules for french. In *Proceedings of the Eighth International Conference on Language Resources and Evaluation (LREC-2012)*, pages 4019–4026.

Siddharthan, A. (2003). Preserving discourse structure when simplifying text. In *Proceedings of the 9th European Workshop on Natural Language Generation (ENLG-2003) at EACL 2003*.

Siddharthan, A. (2004). *Syntactic simplification and Text Cohesion*. Number 597 in Technical Reports. University of Cambridge, 10.

Siddharthan, A. (2006). Syntactic simplification and text cohesion. *Research on Language and Computation*, 4(1):77–109.

Sprenger-Charolles, L. and Ziegler, J. C. (2019). Apprendre à lire : contrôle, automatismes et auto-apprentissage. In A. Bentollila & B. Germain, editor, *L'apprentissage de la lecture*. Nathan, September.

Štajner, S., Evans, R., Orasan, C., and Mitkov, R. (2012). What can readability measures really tell us about text complexity. In *Proceedings of workshop on natural language processing for improving textual accessibility*, pages 14–22. Citeseer.

Tamburini, F. (2017). Semgrex-plus: a tool for automatic dependency-graph rewriting. In *Proceedings of the Fourth International Conference on Dependency Linguistics (Depling 2017)*, pages 248–254.

Todirascu, A., François, T., Bernhard, D., Gala, N., and Ligozat, A.-L. (2016). Are cohesive features relevant for text readability evaluation? In *26th International Conference on Computational Linguistics (COLING 2016)*, pages 987–997.

Todirascu, A., François, T., Bernhard, D., Gala, N., Ligozat, A.-L., and Khobzi, R. (2017). Chaînes de référence et lisibilité des textes : Le projet ALLuSIF. *Langue française*, 195(3):35–52, September.

Vender, M. (2017). *Disentangling Dyslexia: Phonological and Processing Impairment in Developmental Dyslexia*. Frankfurt: Peter Lang.

Xu, W., Napoles, C., Pavlick, E., Chen, Q., and Callison-Burch, C. (2016). Optimizing statistical machine translation for text simplification. *Transactions of the Association for Computational Linguistics*, 4:401–415.

Yaneva, V. and Evans, R. (2015). Six good predictors of autistic text comprehension. In *Proceedings of the International Conference Recent Advances in Natural Language Processing*, pages 697–706.